G✡ING BACK

As they left Germany in the 1930s, it seemed like there was no going back for these Jewish women. It was a time full of humiliation and exclusion, of loss, and the threat to one's life was real. By fleeing, they escaped an uncertain destiny. Instead, their futures lay in countries with languages they never mastered speaking, and with cultures that remained foreign to them. They forged new existences, started families and came to terms with the changes life brought them. Germany couldn't possibly be their homeland anymore after the Holocaust, so why did they return?

These women have suppressed a lot of what they experienced and suffered. Yet in telling their very personal stories, memories of the past awaken. Their voices are those of witnesses to that time, and they speak for a lost generation.

GOING BACK

16 Jewish women tell their life stories, and why they returned to Germany—the country that once wanted to kill them.

Andrea von Treuenfeld

TRANSLATED BY
Cathryn Siegal-Bergman

Originally published in Germany with the title Zurück in das Land, das uns töten wollte. Jüdische Remigranten erzählen ihr Leben. by Gütersloher Verlagshaus, Gütersloh—a division of Verlagsgruppe Random House GmbH, Munich, in 2015.

Published in the United States in 2018 by Clevo Books

Clevo Books
P.O. Box 141149
Cleveland Ohio 44114
www.ClevoBooks.com

Copyright © 2015 Gütersloher Verlagshaus, Güterloh—a division of Verlagsgruppe Random House GmbH, Munich

English translation copyright © 2017 Cathryn Siegal-Bergman

All rights reserved. No part of this publication may be reproduced or transmitted in any form or by any means, electronic or mechanical, including photocopy, recording, or any information storage and retrieval system, without permission in writing from the publisher.

Library of Congress Control Number: 2017959784
Hardcover ISBN: 978-0-9973052-0-3
Paperback ISBN: 978-0-9973052-2-7
eBook ISBN: 978-0-9973052-1-0

Printed in the USA
Dust cover design by Angela Hammersmith
Interior design by Maryanne Hiti

For Antonia

Contents

8   Translator's Note

10   Introduction

12   Bela Cukierman
Berlin—Shanghai—Hadera, Jerusalem—Berlin

26   Anita Lippert
*Nordenstadt, Wiesbaden—Theresienstadt—
Wiesbaden—Philadelphia, New York City—Wiesbaden*

46   Ruth Galinski
Dresden—Warsaw, Tatra, Krakow—Berlin

62   Alisa Weil
*Stettin—Hütten—Nahalal, Givat Haim, Haifa,
Ben Shemen, Kiryat Bialik, Haifa—London—Hanover,
Heppenheim, Wuppertal, Cologne, Meckenheim*

84   Renée Brauner
*Berlin—Innsbruck—Zagreb, Ruma, Belgrade,
Split—Asti—Poschiavo, Davos, Zurich—Paris—
Frankfurt, Berlin*

98   Steffi Wittenberg
Hamburg—Montevideo—Houston, Texas—Hamburg

112   Ruth Schlesinger
Berlin—Kiryat Haim, Haifa—Berlin

122   Ruth Hacohen
*Framersheim—Heiden—Usha, Bat Galim—Ismailia—
Kiryat Haim, Kiryat Anavim, Safed, Beersheba—
Framersheim, Mainz, Frankfurt—Zurich—Frankfurt*

138   Dr. Alice Ilian-Botan
      Berlin—Bucharest—Nazareth, Kiryat Haim—
      Bad Oeynhausen, Munich

152   Ruth Stadnik Goldstein
      Berlin—Buenos Aires—Berlin

164   Ruth Wolff-Stirner
      Shanghai—Jerusalem—Munich

174   Anni Bober
      Dinslaken, Barmen—Wieringermeer—Barmen—
      Petah Tikva, Pardes Hanna, Nahariya, Pardes Hanna,
      Nahariya—Frankfurt

184   Eva Fröhlich
      Berlin—Montevideo—Rio de Janeiro,
      Cachoeiro de Itapemirim, Rio de Janeiro, Teresópolis—
      Frankfurt

196   Ruth Thorsch
      Berlin—Ramat Gan—Frankfurt

206   Margot Wisch
      Frankfurt—Santiago—Haifa—Wiesbaden

214   Gerda Rosenthal
      Remscheid—Jerusalem—Remscheid—Jerusalem,
      Tel Aviv—Wiesbaden—Portland, Chicago,
      New York City—Offenbach, Frankfurt

227   National Socialist (Nazi) measures against Jews 1933 – 1945

237   Glossary

Translator's Note

It is an honor to translate and publish this book of the personal life stories from Jewish women who survived or avoided the absolute worst time in recent human history. They add perspective to a well-documented historical era with the twist that they all go back to Germany to live, despite everything that happened there under the rule of Nazis. The current climate of antisemitism in the United States should compel us to continue sharing as many stories as possible with newer generations so that humanity may never forget what happened. Their stories also tell us something about the refugee experience: how their forced emigration inevitably shaped their personal and cultural identities, for better or worse.

The original German edition is essentially a transcription of thoughtful answers to questions posed. This testimonial style creates the effect of reading personal diary entries as each woman relates events from her childhood through late adulthood.

For any translation, but especially nonfiction, being faithful to the original is imperative. It was important to the author that she kept the syntax or usage characteristics of each storyteller unchanged. We did our best to carry that over through the style, but did occasionally have to give way to the English audience expectations of language usage and syntax. Yet, I hope the reader can imagine hearing the voices of German-speaking women in their later years, in their own accents, and give vision to their vivid depictions of unfolding events.

Changes to the glossary for this English edition include additions such as Abitur. This is a term every German would know, but needed to be defined for English speakers. The term "Lift" was removed because it was rendered as "shipping container" in English, which doesn't require explanation.

Some German terms are left in the original with a parenthetical translation or definition when needed. All foreign words (not defined by the story teller), names of organizations, many cities, events and people are listed in the glossary.

I consulted many sources, but would like to acknowledge the Blackwell Dictionary of Judaica, the Jewish Virtual Library, Yad Vashem, and even Wikipedia as providing the most frequent help on the Internet for translation support. I would also like to thank Jill Sommer (translation editor) and Marie Graf (English editor) for their help.

I dedicate my work on this translation to my husband, Robert Bergman, and son, Henry, for their generous patience and love; to my grandparents, Alvin and Laura Siegal, for their unwavering support; and to the rest of my family and circle of good friends for offering feedback at various stages.

It says in the Talmud that none are poor save him that lacks knowledge. May the reader be deeply enriched by this book!

Cathryn Siegal-Bergman

Introduction

"And then my parents went looking for relatives, friends, for anyone who had survived," says Bela Cukierman about the first days in the city where she was born, Berlin. She was ten years old and one of the few who came back with family. One of the few who even still had family.

Gerda Rosenthal didn't know anything about her family during the war and Ruth Hacohen hoped in vain for news of hers as well. It wasn't until years later in Palestine that they each heard their parents had been deported and murdered. Yet, they both live in Frankfurt today.

Anita Lippert survived Theresienstadt and Ruth Galinski survived hiding out in the Tatras. But they came back to Germany.

How could they bear to come back to this country? To the country where relatives and friends were killed, and where light-heartedness, trust and futures were destroyed. The country that also wanted to kill the 16 women who I—in search of an answer—have asked to tell me their life stories.

Their childhoods were spent in Berlin or Stettin, in Framersheim or Frankfurt. Happy and sheltered and believing that it would always be that way. Until, as Jews—something they weren't even conscious of up to this point, and even if they were, then certainly not of the stigma that came with it—they were excluded. It was insidious in the beginning, but then it became more and more brutal. First it was a girlfriend who would look away without a word. Then the schools, which remained closed to them. Finally, they descended into poverty, because their fathers lost their jobs. And then the all-pervasive threat, the fear of being arrested. In the end, only fear of the unknown remained as they were deported, forced underground or were able to emigrate just in time.

They emigrated to Shanghai and Uruguay, to Brazil and of course, to Palestine. For years, they fled from one occupied area to the next or were no longer permitted to leave communist Romania for decades. They became baptized Catholics or committed Israelis. They started families and established themselves in their new lives. They do not have German passports and fear anti-Semitism more now than back then.

And yet they count among those Jews who decided after 1945 to return—often against great opposition. They were attacked for it by survivors, who condemned remigration to the country responsible on the one hand; and were rejected from a segment of the German population, who in an effort to forget their own past and with it the associated Nazi atrocities, suddenly saw themselves confronted by them again.

So why this difficult step back to a place that could never again be home after the Holocaust? I didn't find any single, all-encompassing answer in the interviews with these women. The reasons for their remigration are just as varied as their biographies and should only be understood within the context of each story.

But I did find something unimaginable in their stories. The horror, present for just the blink of an eye in the small, almost incidental episodes that are reported. The traumas resulting from them, long buried, yet never forgotten. They often spoke of marriages, entered into far too soon, that served as a substitute for the lost home. And of bitter decisions, such as breaking off studies due to poverty and thus having to forget about a dream of earning a degree, as well as all the other changes that influenced the lives of these Jewish women. A sense of inner conflict remains in them, a search for belonging. Because although they settled here again decades ago, this country is not their country anymore.

For this reason, but also to maintain their authenticity, the word order and word choices of these contemporary witnesses, to whom I'm grateful for allowing me to share in their memories, have been largely kept as they were delivered.

Andrea von Treuenfeld

Bela Cukierman
born Bela Wolff on June 11, 1940

> “ There are no more German Jews left. German Jews with the ability to emigrate to England, to America never came back. It was people like my parents who came back, people who never adjusted to life in Palestine. ”

We left in September 1940. We went through Poland first, then continued on the Trans-Siberian Railway, then by land to Harbin. We went from there to the coast and then to Shanghai by ship. We arrived around Christmas time, but our travels were not uninterrupted—there were also stops. My mother spoke of Lake Baikal and of the infinite tediousness on the train as well. In Poland and Russia, there were Jewish groups who came to the train station and took us into their homes. This allowed my mother to bathe me or my parents could sleep.

Luckily, my mother could nurse me. She always said that if her milk had run out, then I would have starved. That's also why there are fewer people my age left. Later when I came back to Berlin, most of my youth group were born in the twenties or beginning of the thirties. And then there were those born after 1947. There are only a few from my age group from 1939/40. People had children, but they were so enfeebled that they died, or were killed.

I was born in the Jewish hospital in Berlin. My parents married in 1938 in Berlin and lived on Kantstrasse. My father came from a family that dealt in livestock, which was very common. He was a livestock dealer his whole life long. My mother grew up in Weissensee and was trained as a shop assistant before the war. People say she was very pretty. Her family and my father's family originated from West Prussia, and in 1919/20 they had to choose if they wanted to be German or Polish. They spoke no Polish, so they decided for Germany and then came to Berlin.

My parents didn't leave earlier because my father thought the German people couldn't be that stupid, Hitler wouldn't last. But as things here got worse, my mother wrote to my father's sister, who had already emigrated to Shanghai with her husband and son, that they should also send us papers. I was born in the meantime as the papers were coming. My father's parents then sold everything they had to pay for papers for me. They were also already in Shanghai. It was a free city, that's why people could go there. In the beginning, the problem wasn't getting out of Germany. The problem was where people could go.

Bela Wolff in 1954, Berlin.

Bela Wolff, first birthday, June 11, 1941.

Jews went to Shanghai originally in 1870, after the Opium Wars. The city was given to the English as a concession, and thanks to the port, business was done there. So not only soldiers went there but also business people. There were the families Sassoon, Kadoorie and Mizrahi, formerly Iraqi Jews, who built a very wealthy community. There was another group, the Russian Jews, who had fled during the revolution.

By 1941, after the Japanese attack on Pearl Harbor, the German Jews had to go into a ghetto. The Japanese were allied with the Germans, and when an SS (see page 264) delegation was sent, they told the Japanese how they were to treat the Jews. The Japanese didn't want to start a fight with all Europeans, so as a compromise, they only detained English citizens and just sent stateless people into the ghetto. Since German Jews, the ones with the "J passport," had to give up their German citizenship upon leaving, they were stateless. The established Jews were unaffected and they financed the ghetto in Hongkou. Tragically though, at some point they said,

"We cannot support more than 20,000 people."

And that was the end. Parallel to that, the development of the war proceeded. Emigration through Russia, like what our family did, was only permitted for so long until the Nazi campaign against Russia. After that, this refuge was beyond reach.

The ghetto in Hongkou, was the old port of Shanghai. The coolies and workers that lived there were released by the Japanese and they put us there. The Japanese were very brutal to the Chinese. I still remember a time when I was with my father on the Garden Bridge, which goes over the Yangtse river, and suddenly next to us Chinese people had to kneel and the Japanese shot them. Or they ordered them all to be vaccinated against typhoid. A street would be locked down and then boom, boom, boom—everyone who walked by was vaccinated.

It was hot and primitive in the ghetto and there was unimaginable poverty. The Chinese mutilated their children so they could beg. It was dirty and it stank. There were no toilets. Carriers came in every morning to pick up the buckets, which they carried on their shoulders using poles. People got sick in these unhygienic conditions. They died of TB and the dead lay wrapped in towels on the street. I got what was called Shanghai fever, I didn't even recognize my parents anymore. But I was lucky, the Americans were there already and they had penicillin.

It was just a few streets, but it was its own world. There were Japanese police, who appointed Jewish ghetto police. There were schools, but I was taught by a family with three or four other kids. My father brought them meat in exchange because we had fallen back to the barter system. Later I went to the Kadoorie School. There were doctors. There were cafés, the "Little Vienna" for example, where they made perfect *Mozartkugeln* (see page 256). They were Viennese and bought the ingredients from the Chinese. Everyone was a German-speaking Jew, even the children on the street spoke German and English in school.

We only spoke German at home. And *Oma* (English: grandmother) told me about the *Nesthäkchen* children's books and about German actresses. What surprises me today is that more than 80 years after Hitler seized power, when I see these films on television and hear the music now, I know all the words. We practically lived in a German world in Shanghai. We had a fifth column (see page 245) there and their music was played as well. When you hear it as a child, you remember a lot about it.

A lot of people lived on the money from the rich Jewish families. But we were not dependent on social help. My parents worked. My father did everything. There was this hotel on the Bund, on Prachtstrasse, it's called the Peace Hotel today, and he carried luggage there. He was very strong. He was an amateur boxer before the war. Then the whole family got started in the meat business. Anything that was available, chicken or goat. They had a stand at the market in Hongkou and my grandfather, my father and his brother sold livestock to the Chinese. My mother helped in the afternoons. At night, she worked as a barmaid or for shops where they took apart old pullovers and knit something new from the yarn—"home work" so to speak.

You sold whatever you possessed. My grandmother had embroidered beautiful table cloths when my grandfather fought in the First World War, and she sold them. They sold their bedding. Everything they brought with them. They were not allowed to bring their wedding rings, no gold. And when we left, only one piece of luggage per person was permitted. Mine was the baby stroller.

We were a large group. There was my grandmother, my grandfather from my father's side and his brother and his brother's wife. They came with their son and daughter-in-law. As well as my father's brother and his wife, who had a son there in 1947, and my father's sister and her husband and son. So, we were very strong as a family. We lived together and my grandmother cooked for everyone. We were a unit and the strain, therefore, wasn't so bad. In Europe, the war ended in May 1945—not in Shanghai. People secretly listened to the BBC, which was forbidden of course, and learned about the end of the war. They went into the streets and celebrated. Then the Japanese came and arrested people. Whoever they got their hands on, they treated them very badly. They were often also beaten or tortured to death. So, we went back home and the Japanese continued to fight until Hiroshima in August 1945, when they capitulated.

And then the ships from the Pacific fleet arrived—the American Navy! There were even Jewish soldiers with them who had no idea we were there. They brought us Hershey's chocolate and we were all in love with these American soldiers.

Then the Joint (see page 250) came too—and that was really great! They had stuff donated from America with them. You could go there and pick something out for yourself. I got a dark-red velvet

The Wolff family in Shanghai, 1941: Father, Hans and mother, Herta (left), Clara (grandmother, right) and Salomon (grandfather, seated) with Bela.

dress, stood in front of the mirror and was smitten with it. My mother was always so practical. I was Papa's girl. And when my brother was born and *Mutti* (English: mommy) was still in the hospital, my father bought me red patent leather shoes. That was so crazy!

We were doing well then, relatively. My father had his meat stand, the whole family worked there. We moved into the French Concession area. There was a café next to our apartment and I used to sit on our terrace and watch as the Chinese danced the Tango. That was so western. At the same time, there were cinemas, too, with American films. And when my brother was born on August 1, 1948, my parents named him Gary, after Gary Cooper, who my mother thought was great.

Everyone wanted to go to America, that was the Promised Land after the war, but most of them never got there. There were quotas according to year of birth, and my parents both fell outside the Polish quota. Although my father came from the Posen province and my mother from Thorn. But the Polish quota was pretty well exhausted already and aside from that, you needed two sponsors in America and we didn't have that. We didn't have any reference points anywhere.

My mother did not want to go back to Germany, of course. Her mother died before the war. Her father and all her siblings were all deported and killed. She had two sisters and two brothers;

they were married and already had their own children. Her younger brother was deported from a *Hachsharah* (see page 246) camp, her other siblings were forced laborers in Berlin and were taken from their work places. After the war, letters came from the camps which the Red Cross brought to Shanghai. And then there were lists, people stood in front of them and searched for family member's names. My mother received documents later, on which—Germany is honest, after all—the reason for death was given, "shot during flee attempt" or some such thing. But we didn't live solitary lives. Everyone in our circle had to live with the loss of loved ones. I didn't know anything else as a child. So where should we go? Israel, said the Joint. It had just been founded in May. We were not a religious family; my father couldn't speak Hebrew very well. But it was the land of hope. A country that would take you. If Israel had existed in 1938 and if the English hadn't sent back the people who went to Palestine, then everyone would have been saved.

The Joint hired Italian freight ships that were stranded in Shanghai. And the more people the Italians took, the more they were paid. So, the ships were packed full. There were no cabins, only large cargo holds. Bunk beds were built in them.

We weren't allowed in any port, because we were "displaced persons." The stateless who always had to remain outside the three-mile zone. As we were off the coast of Cape Town, the Jewish immigrants living there rented boats and came to us to throw things to us. There were even people among them that my father still knew from Berlin. We had two or three funerals on the ship. There was a small ceremony and then the body was thrown into the ocean. We also had students on board who taught the children. But I didn't participate in that, I was too seasick, because the boat rocked dreadfully.

In Naples, the *Carabinieri* (see page 241) were waiting for us with machine guns with bayonets attached to them. We were taken from the Italian ship to the Israeli one, which was even smaller. Our luggage was just stuffed in and everything broke.

When we arrived in Haifa, it was *Shabbat* (see page 263). So we were not unloaded and had to spend another full day on board. And then the musicians on our ship played *Hatikva*, the national anthem. That is still very strong in my memory. And the women who stood there handing out sandwiches as we were permitted off the ship in the evening. They were from WIZO (Women's International Zionist Organization). That impressed me so much that later, in Berlin, I joined the board of the WIZO.

We were loaded onto a truck with my grandparents and taken to Beth Olim, the refugee camp in Hadera. Today it's a pretty small town, back then it was just sand. A sort of hangar stood there, gigantic and inside were rows and rows of cots close together. Men, women, packed close together—people shoved the luggage under the cots. There were canteens where we lined up to get something to eat. And there were lessons under a tree. But I didn't go to those because I already knew them. I studied the multiplication table up to five again and again. And every time I went to a new school, they were on the same material. I even learned about Moses' Exodus from Egypt a few times.

We stayed a few months, and conditions were worse than in Shanghai. I'm not blaming Israel. That was right after the war against the Arabs, the country was overwhelmed, with the immigrants, too. They came from all over the world and some had totally foreign cultures. We started avoiding the toilets pretty soon and went in the little wood instead. At night the jackals howled.

My father's brother and his wife and son also came with us from Shanghai. My aunt had located a relative in Jerusalem, who was in the *Histadrut*, the worker's union. He organized jobs for my father and uncle in construction. That was our springboard out of Beth Olim. We drove a truck from Hadera to Jerusalem. Back then, this street had just been liberated, today the tanks are still there as a reminder of the battle of Latrun. My mother could ride in the cabin with my brother because he was the smallest baby, but the rest of the family, even my grandparents (they were around 70 at the time), sat on top of the luggage.

We found a house in the Katamon quarter without windows, doors or floors—and we all lived together again. At night, my father and my uncle would set off and take doors that were hanging in empty houses and hang them in ours. Water came from a fountain, we had no water pipes. But we had rabbits and chickens, and Oma would always wait for the chickens to lay eggs, so she could make us some noodles. This was during the *Tzena* (English: austerity) part of Israel's history, when food was heavily rationed.

Then I started school. It was one of the religious girl's schools sponsored by the Mizrahi family. But I was the only immigrant child in the quarter. And the only one who couldn't speak *Ivrit* (see page 249). They thought I was mentally retarded. I had tutoring help, but I couldn't get into gear.

Everyone tried to earn money. My grandfather found a job as a night watchman. He was taken to a construction site at night, put in a chair and picked up again in the morning. He had cataracts and was already blind in one eye. My father and my uncle started in construction. My uncle learned iron bending, and my father stood in the ditches and had to catch buckets full of wet cement. Papa was born in 1904, he had survived Shanghai and at some point, he said he just couldn't do it anymore.

My mother then drove to her cousin's in Haifa who rented to officers in the Israeli navy. Everything worked through sponsorship and so she got my father work. He (who couldn't cook) became a cook on the ships that went to Tripoli and picked up refugees. He was always seasick. And when he arrived in Haifa, my mother would drive there from Jerusalem, sometimes with us kids. My father would have three or four hours of leave and then he'd get back on the ship. That was no life, and he could barely feed the family. In the end, he told my mother he wasn't going to do it anymore. He couldn't speak the language and couldn't adjust. And he wanted to go back to Germany. My mother didn't want that. And he said he'd go alone. He would go when he got to Naples on the boat and go back to Germany. What was my mother supposed to do? So, we went back to Germany.

We took a ship to Naples, and from there took a train to Frankfurt. Berlin was occupied by the Russians. Soviet soldiers stood on the border. We had these *Nansen* passports (see page 256), we were expatriated Germans, stateless. It was 1950 and September again—exactly ten years that we were gone.

This time we were alone. Papa, Mama, my brother and me. My grandfather sat on the terrace in Jerusalem at night and dreamed of Germany. I think he wanted to go back. But he never made it—he died. It is difficult to say what he loved about Germany. He was raised in this culture. He was a soldier in the First World War. He and my grandmother were German and Israel was in the East. Yes, it was Jewish, but it was foreign.

We were in Frankfurt, but my father wanted to go back to Berlin. We didn't know that we needed some kind of visa for Berlin. We came to the zone border and the Russian soldiers checked our papers and said,

"No, Comrades!"

They took us off the train and brought us to a guard room. We sat there the whole night. They sent us back to Frankfurt the next day. We had no money. It was September, *Sukkot* (see page 265), and my parents went to the synagogue. My mother sat there with a two-year-old and a ten-year-old child and cried. And then we were taken down to the Jewish old people's home, to the attic at the top. My mother just had a few marks (German money).

My brother wanted this and that. And Mama said,

"No, we have to think hard about what we spend this money on."

She wanted to buy something to eat and then she lost these two or three marks. That stayed with me, deep in my memories.

My father finally ran into people he knew from Shanghai and borrowed money from them. We used it to fly to West Berlin, to Tempelhof airport. We didn't have to go through East Germany. After Frankfurt, my parents were smarter. We went straight to the Jewish old people's home on Iranische Strasse and said,

"Here we are, help us."

They gave us a room. And then my parents went in search of relatives, friends and of anyone at all who survived. They found little Aunt Marie in East Berlin. She was married to a Christian man and they took us in. My father made inquiries at the slaughter houses and immediately found more people he knew again. They were the same business people as before. He went again to the livestock markets in West Germany and bought cattle, which were then brought back to Berlin on trains, slaughtered in Spandau and sold to retailers. We were repatriated—we got German passports. The first apartment that we had was in Moabit, on Pritzwalcker Strasse. My family lived alone for the first time. I went to elementary school and had the best teacher ever. I adored him. I could speak German, but I couldn't write a word and I also couldn't speak as well as the others. That's why my mother told him,

"She's ten now, but she can't do a thing. Put her in first grade."

"We can't do that! Fourth grade!" he said.

He could handle it. He had faith in me. And when we had dictation on the first day, he let me copy. I think I had 90 mistakes in half a page. But he passed me. I never sat back a year. Ever. I was very good in religion, of course, because I had always learned the same thing, the Old Testament. I was allowed to go in the schoolyard during those classes. But it was fun for me because I knew more than the others.

My *Opa* (English: grandfather) died in Jerusalem in 1952. A year later, my father brought his mother and his brother, along with his family (they'd had a daughter in the meantime), back from Israel. They took over our apartment in Moabit and we moved to Charlottenburg with my *Oma*, to Giesebrechtstrasse.

I went to the girl's school on Leibnizstrasse. I had always liked to draw and I studied fashion illustration at the Lette Verein (see page 254). The course lasted three years and I loved it—art history, fashion history and drawing. In the end, I worked in clothing production, in haute couture on Meineckestrasse. I quit after a year, because my parents made it possible for me to travel around America for a year. That was revolutionary back then. It was 1960.

I turned 20 in America. It was an incredibly formative time in my life. It was a totally different world and I had to pay attention. I had an interview at Bloomingdale's and they took me on as a fashion designer. But I went back home and met my husband.

I met Renée (Brauner, see page 83) in the Jewish youth group on Joachimsthalerstrasse in Berlin when she came back with her family in 1954. She also had a younger brother who was born in 1947—we were like sisters. Even when she got married, we went out with the gang, and sometimes her husband came with her and sometimes it was just her. And later my husband too. He was 15 years older than I was, in his mid-30s. He called again and again, and then I went out with him. That was in the summer. In November we were engaged. We married in June 1962. I had my first son in 1963 and the next two in 1966 and 1974.

My husband was from Poland, from a small city near Lodz. His family was forced into a ghetto. His parents were killed. He was in Mauthausen (see page 255), and one of his brothers went to Auschwitz (see page 238). One brother was shot in Lodz (see page 254) with his wife and child. The other four siblings survived. After the war, they all went back to Lodz and found each other again. His oldest sister was 18 years older and like a mother to him and, later, like a mother-in-law to me.

He had to go into the Polish military, but of course he didn't want to at all. Poland was still very anti-Semitic after the war. That's why so many Jews went to America or Palestine—through Stettin and Berlin. They had a transit camp near the Schlachtensee. He was there with his older brother, who then went to Munich with his wife. Their daughter survived Auschwitz because she was very cute and a woman overseer probably saw her as a toy. Their son died. And my husband's sister's son also died when the Russians moved in and the Nazis relocated the camp. The prisoners were transported in railcars. The door was closed, and his arm was caught in it. He died in 1945.

My husband stayed in Berlin. His father had a weaving mill and he took over a few knitting machines on Wilmersdorferstrasse and started production again. He built the company up, which we still have today, Suprema Strick-and Wirkwarenfabrik (warp and weft knitted fabrics mill). We produce mostly women's knits and are suppliers for companies under whose label we work. When my husband died during bypass surgery in 1985, I couldn't just let the people go. I had a choice, either close the business and pay a fortune in severance pay or try to keep it going. I hadn't worked for years because of the children. But I knew about clothing production, not independently, but I had always drawn the collections. And I knew the buyers and they were really very nice to me—they didn't take me for a ride and even showed me how to make the presentations. And it worked. Well, it had to keep going, I had to pay the salaries. There were 50 people back then, who worked in three shifts. Then my oldest son came back from America and joined the company. All three boys studied economics at Brandeis, a Jewish university in Boston. The second one built a real estate company, which is in the same building. The third one stayed in America, he works for a big bank in New York.

Bela Cukierman in Berlin.

I never had problems as a Jewish woman. But we were always a little bit exotic. We drove to Wyk auf Föhr (town on second largest Frisian Island) when things got better for my parents. People would come up to us—my mother and brother had much darker hair than I had—and say,

"Oh, you look so exotic. Where are you from?"

It's always been that way for me. My six grandchildren are all blond and have blue eyes. One of my sons married a woman who converted to Judaism, and even though I'm not very religious, it is nice that they'll all be raised Jewish.

"Oh," a woman in the Lions Club said to me, "I thought your grandchildren were Jewish!"

Or it's,

"See, if they were all like you, nothing would ever have happened." Is that anti-Semitism? No, but it's still exclusion. It's not hatred. I don't think most people hated Jews back then either. They were indifferent to them, "sure, the Jews were deported into forced labor, but it wasn't that bad." Not that bad? The people saw what was going on. Grunewald train station, 70,000 Jews! And they never screamed? Never cried? They just went quietly from truck to train? And train after train went by...

"Don't you know Esther? She lived here and there," someone will ask.

"No, I don't know her."

"I wonder what happened to her?"

"Well," I say, "probably gassed?"

This disinterest. Today and back then. And envy, too. Jews were doctors, lawyers, high earning salespeople. A lot of envy. When we came back to Germany, we went everywhere my parents had lived. On Kantstrasse, a chandelier hung in the doorman's apartment in the basement. It was the chandelier from my grandparents' apartment. Great, he can just take it for himself.

No, I never heard any direct anti-Semitic speech, but I did experience exclusion. Even today still, when people say,

"Oh, well, hey. Of course, you see it that way."

Or,

"We have a Jew in our group, too."

It always gets mentioned where there's a Jew involved. Even if a Jew converts, it sticks with him. Total assimilation? I don't believe it! Anyway, it is different today. The Jewish union in Berlin is up to three quarters Russian. There are no more German Jews left. German Jews with the ability to emigrate to England or America never came back. It was people like my parents who came back, people who never adjusted to life in Palestine.

Anita Lippert
born Anita Rosel Fried on May 5, 1931

" Do I feel German? The country didn't want me. I'm more American than German. The decision back then to come back to Germany was mostly because of my parents. I'm the sole survivor of Wiesbaden today. And I'll never stop asking, "Why did you do that to us?" "

Our transport to Theresienstadt was the last one from Wiesbaden. The Americans had already reached the Rhine river on February 14, 1945, but that didn't stop the Nazis from carrying out their plan to wipe us out to the last Jew. They wanted to be sure that not one was left.

Until the beginning of February 1945, we were still protected, because, per the Nazi racial ideology, my mother was considered an "Aryan" who lived in a "mixed marriage." She married 39-year-old Ludwig Fried in 1929 and converted to Judaism. Her relatives disapproved of the union and completely renounced her. But my mother totally immersed herself in the Jewish faith, she became 200% a Jewish woman and kept a strictly kosher house.

When I was born on May 5, 1931, the Jewish world in Germany was still more or less intact. Still, they didn't give me a Jewish middle name like Rebecca or Rachel after my great and great-great grandmothers. Because that would have been dubious even at that time. Just don't attract attention. And that's why they named me Rosel. It sounded non-Jewish. And Anita is also not a Jewish name.

My first years of life were spent near Wiesbaden, in Nordenstadt, a town with barely 1,000 inhabitants. My father was a grocer with a lucrative grocery store in our building, which had been owned by the family since the 1700s. My parents were very religious and I accompanied them to synagogue in Wallau, about 1.5 kilometers away from Nordenstadt, every Friday evening and Saturday and on all the Jewish holidays. It goes without saying that we went by foot to the services because we were not permitted to use a car on that day. We were in close contact with our non-Jewish neighbors. I played with their children, in their houses as well as in ours, so I never had the feeling that I was different.

That changed suddenly when I was supposed to go to school. A sign on the school in Nordenstadt said "Jews are not welcome here." Because the Jewish children were excluded from the schools in town, there was a Jewish elementary school that started in the mid-30s in Wiesbaden. I started there in 1937. During my first school year, I lived at my Aunt Martha's in Wiesbaden during the

Anita Fried on the passage to the United States, 1947.

Elisabeth (mother), Ludwig (father) and Anita (right), Fanny (grandmother), Martha and Josef Schiffer with their son, Herbert (middle), Selma (left) in Nordenstadt, 1935.

week, because my parents thought it would be too much of a strain to go back and forth from Nordenstadt to Wiesbaden. Plus, I didn't do well on the bus. I was always so nauseated that my mother was armed with a bucket and cleaning rag when she came to pick me up at the bus stop. As unpleasant as that was, at least I was still allowed to ride the bus. One morning, however, the head teacher, Mr. Metzler, a definite Nazi, stood in the bus and told the driver to drive on without me—with the added note that,

"Jewish pigs do not ride the bus."

This teacher, Mr. Metzler, incited his students with words and scornful letters against us Jews so much that I could barely get together with my Christian playmates anymore. They were afraid that their families would be reported by him. My carefree childhood was over. And I was constantly warned by my worried parents to behave quietly and modestly and not to attract attention. This caution shaped my entire life.

For a long time, my father was under the false impression that, first, it's not as bad as it seems and, second, no one would do anything to him because as a soldier on the Front from 1914–1918, he had earned the Iron Cross and a Wound Badge. But in 1937 or 1938, my parents applied to travel to America where a friend of my mother would sponsor us. The immigrant quota in the United States was very low and our application number was very high, which seemed to make leaving soon hopeless. Pretty soon after that, the Nazis decided that American sponsors had to be relatives, which more or less shattered our emigration plans.

Then came November 9th, 1938. I lay with fever in bed when sometime in the afternoon my mother suddenly picked me up. She ran with me to the window, held me out of it and implored the gawking neighbors,

"Please take my child from me!"

But no one listened to her. A few men came up the steps, grabbed the sewing machine that stood there and threw it with a high arch over the railings into the yard. My *Oma* and my aunt Selma had locked themselves in their rooms. My father was nowhere to be seen either, so my mother stood there with me alone, in terror and helpless in that dreadful moment. These men made a terrible racket, smashing everything in our store on the ground floor to pieces. The whole thing only lasted ten minutes at the most, but the chaos left behind by these vandals was horrific. All the shelves full of groceries, glasses and plates were overturned, the sacks of salt, sugar, raisins cut open, the taps on the wall-mounted containers with vinegar, oil and petroleum were opened, and the barrel with herring in it was tipped over. Everything was mixed together on the floor into a slippery, horrible smelling puddle. My father's life, like all Jews in Germany on that day, was ruined. He didn't surface again for another few hours. He had hidden in a corn field out of fear that these men would beat him to death.

On November 11th, Nazi agents came and took my father away, along with all the other Jewish men from Nordenstadt. When we got a sign of my Papa's life, it was a pre-printed postcard from

Buchenwald. He was freed on December 6th, 1938, but his condition was devastating. He was covered in scabs and dirt on his head and body, his hair shaved off completely. And his hemorrhoid problem had got worse from being malnourished and from lacking hygiene. It was horribly painful; he had had them operated on twice already. And he didn't even have paper to wipe himself with. There were enough doctors among the prisoners that could've helped him of course, but they had no water and no soap. Under those horrid circumstances, doctors wouldn't even risk looking at an open wound. That must have been like being in limbo. Do you know what a *Donnerbox* is? (English: thunder box, a Donnerbox was an improvised toilet consisting of a sturdy log positioned above a pit.) The men were too weak; they couldn't hold on tight enough. They would fall backwards and drown in the pit.

My *Oma* died a few months later, in March 1939, in her own bed, thank Heaven. My Aunt Martha, and her husband, Josef, left Wiesbaden with their son, Herbert, and went to Belgium illegally to escape the Jewish persecution. But in 1942, they were deported "to the east" from Brussels, probably to *Treblinka* (see page 266). We never heard from them again.

We moved into their apartment in Wiesbaden in July 1939. We were forced to sell our building. Papa got a ridiculously low price for it. They took his motorcycle with side car and forced him to do different jobs. He was put to work doing road construction, then building bunkers and firefighting water basins and then in a tannery. The pay was well below normal wages.

In September 1941, we were forced to wear the yellow Star of David sewn on the chest of our clothes. We weren't allowed to cover it or we could be arrested immediately. We also always had to carry our ID card, marked with a big "J," and had to know the number and issue date by heart. They also decreed that we had to use the names Sara and Israel, which we were to be called at every questioning.

We were practicing Jews and belonged to the Jewish community right at the time when the Nuremberg race laws were issued. From that point on, my parents' marriage was considered a "Jewish mixed marriage," although my mother converted from Christianity to Judaism. Denomination didn't count to the Nazis, only their ideology of race, and so my mother was considered "Aryan." My father and I had to wear the "Jewish star," but even my mother was discriminated against because we had to stick a white Star of David on the apartment door. It was forbidden under punishment, which usually meant immediate arrest, for non-Jews and Jews to socialize or even just to talk to each other on the street. As a result, my mother always had to walk five steps ahead or behind my father and me.

Among the many laws that were imposed on us, we were also not allowed to use public transportation and we were only permitted to travel within a seven-kilometer radius around Wiesbaden. We could only cross Wilhelmstrasse, Wiesbaden's grand boulevard at Rheinstrasse and at Friedrichstrasse, but we couldn't walk along it. Entry into parks and other green spaces for us was prohibited. Bicycles, scooters, ice skates and roller skates had already been taken away from us long before that. The Nazis even stole all our jewelry and everything made of precious metals. My *Oma* on my father's side had given me a little gold Star of David when I was born. *Mutti* sewed that into a piece of clothing, which saved it. I still wear it today.

The deportation of most Jews from Wiesbaden followed in June 1942. My Aunt Selma, my father's older sister, was among them. The last time I saw her was when she got into the boxcar. Only the very elderly were allowed to stay behind, and five children and their fathers, who were in so-called "privileged mixed marriages" married to "Aryans."

Shortly after that, the Gestapo appeared and ordered us to leave our apartment. We were put with an older Jewish widow and I set myself up in one of the empty rooms (her furniture had already been confiscated by the Gestapo) so that I could play with my dolls and study my school books. Private lessons, even by the remaining Jews, was forbidden.

A *Standartenführer* (English: standard leader, equivalent rank to colonel) in the SA (see page 262) lived in the building too. He knew that his son and I played with each other in the backyard. He never said a word to us, of course, but he closed his eyes to his child often coming to our apartment. Once in a while, a newspaper lay in front of our door, as if by accident. It was prohibited for us to have newspapers and magazines.

One day in December 1943, I found a letter to my father in the mailbox from the Wiesbaden *Gestapo* (see page 245). I wanted to know really badly what was in it, but naturally was not allowed to open it. It also wouldn't have mattered much because the *Gestapo* never gave the real reason for them. People were just summoned. Should I give the letter to my father immediately upon his coming home from work? Would he react spontaneously and take his own life instead of delivering himself to the *Gestapo*? Or should I just hold it back to avoid the worst? I gave him the letter that night during an air attack which we waited out in our coal cellar, we weren't allowed to go to the shelters built for air raids. I will never forget the pain I saw in my parents' eyes when I described my thoughts. I was twelve years old then and it was a very hard decision for me. Because it was as I'd thought, a summons for the next day, seven in the morning at the *Gestapo* on Paulinenstrasse.

Papa said I should go with him that morning. In front of the *Gestapo* he instructed me to wait 15 minutes and then, should he not be back by then, to go home. We said goodbye. It could have been the last time I ever saw my Papa. But luckily, he came back out very soon. They only wanted to tell him that we had to move again. Men from the Gestapo came into our apartment again and looked around. Then they announced that the chandelier would remain where it hung on the ceiling, the down comforters would be left behind and the coal was to be left in the cellar.

We didn't know the next family but assumed they were also Jewish since the *Gestapo* put as many Jews as possible in buildings they called "Jewish houses" to ease their eventual transport out. As it turned out, the man, a Jew, who was also living in a "mixed marriage," had received another summons from the Gestapo. Since he had already been in the police station jail for months, he believed that this time the Gestapo wouldn't let him out so soon again. In fact, he left his apartment, went to the woods, slit open his veins and bled to death. And so, as we arrived in December with our remaining household items, a hearse stood before the door to pick him up after someone had found him in the woods and brought him home. A very macabre meeting. The mood on that day carried over to the mood in general and made living together, with a communal kitchen and bath, awkward. But over time, a strong friendship developed between the two families. We occupied two rooms, the one was my parents' bedroom and our living and dining room as well, the other was my room.

Apart from my "mixed marriage" family, there were still three others who stayed in Wiesbaden. The five children met, alternating between apartments, to play or study together. We would arrive separately to avoid a "star crowd" and so attract any unnecessary attention.

I was sent to a somewhat sickly woman, also in a "mixed marriage," to clean for her. It was a 45-minute walk and she paid me with a glass of milk and buttered bread. When she offered me a second slice of bread on my first day, I declined out of politeness. But I could have put away three slices, I was so hungry. Because only *Mutti* had a grocery card for a full ration. Papa's and my cards had the word "Jew" printed all over them—and most of our allotments were reduced by more than half. For Christmas, the people were given an additional portion of butter, sugar, flour and eggs—with the instruction that "Jews, Eastern workers, and Gypsies are excluded from distribution." We also couldn't get clothes or shoes. *Mutti* was able to arrange something with a cobbler through bartering. That's how Papa got our shoes repaired. *Mutti* cut his hair, since it was also forbidden for us to go to a beauty parlor.

There were a lot of air raid alarms during that time. Even though we were always in danger, we welcomed every bomb that fell on Germany. In the hope that it would hasten the end of the war and, with it, the end of Nazi rule.

But in January 1945, we got the news we feared, that Papa and I were to be evacuated. Although she requested it, *Mutti* was not permitted to come with us. We were advised to pack sturdy shoes and warm clothes; our destination was a work camp. The transport was supposed to leave at the beginning of February, but the air raid on the night of 2nd or 3rd of February delayed our trip until the 14th of February. And on that morning when we had to report to the train station, no one thought of hiding anymore. It wasn't possible, Wiesbaden was too small. And *Gestapo* Chief Bodewisch knew all of us. Moral courage was gone. But it was a hard time and helping someone was really difficult and possibly punishable by death. What I do not believe, however, is that people knew nothing. The Nazis put out so much propaganda against the Jews —everyone knew what was going on.

We had to pay for the tickets to Frankfurt out of our own pockets. Under the strict eye of Bodewisch, *"Bösewicht"* (English: evil goblin) we called him, we climbed into the train compartment. Everyone who remained cried. We didn't know if we would see each other again. Had we known what lay before us, that separation would have been even more heart wrenching. But up to this point, we still knew nothing about the death camps. No one ever came back to tell anyone about it. We were still ignorant—work camp, or so we thought.

In Frankfurt we had to walk through the city to Markthalle.

Bystanders stood still and stared at us, but I didn't notice any of them stir. At four in the afternoon, we were loaded into livestock carriages. Just at that moment, there was an alarm and a sudden attack from low flying airplanes that shot at the train station. We sought cover under the carriages, a few bombs exploded near us. In the end, they crammed us into the carriage, 40 to 50 people in one compartment. We left sometime during the night. The doors were opened every six to eight hours so people could relieve themselves. Out in the open, men and women together. I will never forget that. It was shocking.

ANITA LIPPERT

Our route went through Weimar, Leipzig, Chemnitz, Eger, Aussig and Leitmeritz. The train stopped often and for a while in open spaces. We arrived in Theresienstadt on the 18th of February. We sat in a hall until morning. We didn't know what would happen to us. Our odyssey began at around 8:30 in the morning. The first thing was that every person was registered. My number was X11/10-530. Then all valuable items had to be handed over, followed by a doctor's exam. Many were sent immediately for a "disinfestation bath"—for vermin that we didn't bring with us, but that we would have a lot of later. Then they said,

"Cut off the hair!"

Theresienstadt had become a garrison city during the First World War. The headquarters were at the front, with barbed wire around it so that we couldn't get in, though we didn't want to. Then came the large barracks. The Nazis named them after German cities: the Hamburg, the Dresden, the Magdeburg barracks. And the men and women were housed separately in them. My father did not live in a barracks but in a run-down house with five other men in one room.

We children were escorted by an attendant to the children's home, L414. There were multiple stories: the girls were upstairs; the boys were downstairs. The rooms were large, but every centimeter was used up: 24 spaces to sleep, with tall bedsteads, each with three bunks on top of each other. We became acquainted with bugs, fleas and pubic lice. I spent most of my free time with my father and only slept in the children's home. We were looked after by older women there who also gave us lessons when possible. Sometimes they even had us do schoolwork. But that was forbidden, so there was always a girl guarding at the door because we were checked often.

Every prisoner above a certain age had to work. I wasn't 14 years old yet when I was placed to work in the Hohen Elbe hospital. I was a nurse in the morning and a few hours in the afternoon, outfitted with bonnet and a white apron, first with an ear, nose and throat doctor and then with a general practitioner, where I filled syringes and sterilized medical instruments. I probably got infected with measles at the ENT's office and later contracted scarlet fever.

We children also played and sometimes laughed, although there wasn't much to laugh about. We were in an atmosphere where laughing was a crime. There was misery everywhere, with the people there who were crammed in a living space together, and the little food that we were given. We were constantly hungry. Our ration was a quarter loaf of bread, which had to last for three days. We practically shaved the bread, sliced really thin, but when you're hungry I didn't always have the discipline to hold off to the last day—that's when you had almost nothing left. In addition to that, there was a cup of "coffee" or a brown brew in the morning, a warm, meager and fat free meal in the afternoon. There was hardly anything in the evening. Papa and I would always put our food together, that way it looked like more.

However, we got *matzo* for Passover. It probably came from the Red Cross, as well as Ovaltine for the children. And there was a little margarine or butter. It was rancid, but that didn't matter. And we got pasteurized milk. You couldn't hide it and when you went to bed at night it would be gone. The word for stolen was *geschleusst*, (English: smuggled) and a rumor was *Bonkes*. They had their own language in Theresienstadt. And not one woman menstruated. The men were impotent. It wasn't due to lack of nutrition; it was because they put something in the food. The moment I returned home, I got my period again immediately. We wore our private clothes, with the Jewish star. There were only Jews, but we also had to wear the star in Theresienstadt.

The winter of 1944/1945 was hard and long and we were dreadfully freezing. The days went by with the same empty rhythm. But every day that we survived was a gift. We didn't know what the next day would bring.

Theresienstadt was overpopulated. The people lay on top of each other more than next to each other. It was catastrophic. Then people left, no one knew where they went. And we didn't know that they were sent to extermination camps either. However, we did know that Theresienstadt didn't have an incinerator. But then a rumor started that the Nazis were building one. My father knew that I knew about it. I knew that he knew about it. We never talked about it. Thank God it never came to that. Theresienstadt was a stopover for many people not an extermination camp. But still, it was the stop before.

The propaganda film "The Führer Gives a City to the Jews" was made after the International Red Cross first came to visit in June of 1944. At the beginning of April 1945, representatives of the Red Cross were supposed to come a second time. Before they got there, we had to scrub the little yellow stones in the walk with scrubbing brushes. We got blankets and chocolate, which was taken from us again later. When the people from the Red Cross were taken around, there was cheering, fussing and cheerfulness. We could not give them a clue. How were we supposed to do that? We were watched, of course. Then they left again—it's wasn't so bad in Theresienstadt after all! Everything was alright. The children have blankets, they don't have to freeze. And they have chocolate, too. And they performed a song, it was called *Glühwürmchen* (glowworm). The musicians still had their instruments and played secretly in the beginning. Then the SS passed a law and forced them to play. Concerts were even held there as well. Many of the musicians knew that they would be deported the next day and yet they still had to play in the evenings. So crazy and so unreal.

On the 5th of May, my 14th birthday, my Papa gave me a slice of bread and a small piece of sausage. He scrimped and saved for them. This gift was the most valuable that I had ever received in my life. And I got a piece of gingerbread as a gift. From Rolf. He was the son of one of the families with whom we were friends. All five of us Wiesbaden children were all the same age. Marianne and Erich were born in 1929; Günther, Erich's brother, was born in my year, 1931, and then Rolf was two years younger. He was just eleven and alone in Theresienstadt. His "Aryan" mother wasn't allowed to come with him. His father had already been taken by the Nazis in 1943 and transported to Auschwitz.

One day, a big white bus stood there. They said the Danes were going back home now. We were skeptical. Where are they really going? It was the Swedish Red Cross, they really had come to pick up the Danes and Norwegians from Theresienstadt in their famous white buses. But at the time we thought they were being taken to be killed. You always had to assume the worst. I still dream about those days, I can't process it. Did I feel hatred, I would later be asked. I don't know if a 13- or 14-year-old is capable of hatred. I held a grudge and I've worked through it over the course of time. When you think about it, it is so unreal. And you ask, how could this happen? Why? Why did this have to happen to us? What did we do? It's still incomprehensible. I can't understand it. I wouldn't treat an animal the way we were treated. The hatred these people had must have been so great to do something so cruel to other people.

One very cold day in May, I sat in front of the children's home to catch a few warming rays of sun. Suddenly I heard unfamiliar noises. Someone yelled that I should go in the building right away, there was shooting. Since we had no contact to the outside world, we didn't know that Russian troops had advanced. I missed the troop march into Theresienstadt that was cheered on as our liberation on the 8th of May because I lay in hospital with scarlet fever, and that required a quarantine of 35 days.

When I was released, our passports were already filled in and prepared by the Russian commanding officer. Most of the Wiesbaden Jews who were brought with us to Theresienstadt wanted to leave the camp together. We were about 20 people, even the five children from the four so-called "mixed marriages" were there.

We left on a truck on June 12, 1945. It was an adventurous trip back; it took us ten days to get from Theresienstadt to Wiesbaden. At some point, they said our guards weren't inclined to allow us to go any farther, and so we had to wait until relief came. Then we went on again with a horse drawn carriage. Then came a train that was supposed to take us home. We came to the station just before ours and they said, "everyone off!" It was chaotic. It was so disorganized. The trains were not running according to schedule and often stopped for hours at a time where there was only one track, and so we had a lot of stops in between. We had to stay overnight in different accommodations, sometimes on chairs, sometimes straw sacks with fleas. Everyone pressed on, we wanted to get home as quickly as possible. But sometimes we couldn't go any farther and our mood was just as subdued. We received refreshment along the way because of our passports, which were in German, English and Russian, so we had free passage with them. We went past Chemnitz, Aue, Nuremberg, Würzburg and saw nothing but ruins.

We finally arrived on June 22, 1945, in Mainz-Bischofsheim. That was the end of the line. Papa went with a man from our group into the city and they organized a car with a driver. We loaded our luggage and drove to the Main River, ferried across it and drove to the train station. We were finally in Wiesbaden by eleven o' clock at night. But we still weren't home yet.

Papa was so exhausted, and not just physically, that he just couldn't go any farther. He sent me to the apartment on Heiligenbornstrasse, the last place we lived, to get a little cart. I was stopped by an armed guard in front of an American night club. There was a curfew. We were not allowed on the street, which we couldn't have known. I showed him my trilingual ID and, using my tiny bit of school English, also showed him the white armband with "Theresienstadt" on it. He ordered a soldier to go with me and carry my luggage. When we turned onto the street, I saw immediately that our building had been destroyed. The exact corner where we lived was as if it had been razed to the ground.

We had been able to write my mother from Theresienstadt, but we never received anything from her. And so we didn't know what had happened in March. *Mutti* had come home from work, lay in bed and fell asleep. Suddenly she woke up, she told us later, and looked at the bucket for coal ashes, which was usually emptied by the woman she lived with. This time she wanted to do it herself, so she went to the cellar and got the bucket. At that moment, there was an air raid alarm. My mother closed the cellar door quickly—and a bomb fell. It hit that room and the bed in which *Mutti* was lying only a few moments before. She would have been dead instantly.

When I saw that the building was destroyed, I started crying and called for *Mutti*. The soldier stood helpless next to me, put the luggage down and doubled back. When the neighbors, who weren't permitted to open their windows or doors during the curfew, saw the American was gone, a woman came to the gate.

"Are you Anita?"

"Yes! Where is my *Mutti*?"

"She's alive! She's living with a friend, but I don't know where."

She gave me a bicycle trailer for our luggage and I made my way back to the train station, where Papa was waiting.

Rolf had also come back in our transport. He went to his grandparents, because he believed his mother might be there. And when the window opened, it wasn't his mother, but my *Mutti* that looked out. She stayed there overnight because our apartment in the building next door wasn't ready yet. My mother had arranged it because she knew that we had survived. A few men from Wiesbaden had already returned from Theresienstadt before us and had naturally told all of their relatives,

"They're alive! They're coming!"

After Rolf told her where we were, my mother put on a sleeveless overall over her nightgown and ran. Who cared about curfew?! She made it to the station before I did.

Sadness was suddenly replaced with happiness and cheer as we lay in each other's arms. You stand there and just can't believe it. All three of us survived! It was a miracle. We were home again, and we were a family again. My mother had been pressured by the *Gestapo* many times to get a divorce even before our transport. Had she done that, Papa and I would have been completely helpless. We would have been murdered too. But we knew that *Mutti* would never abandon us. We have her to thank for our lives.

After the bombing, *Mutti* rummaged through the building rubble and only found our *Shabbat* lamp, which has been in our family for generations. We didn't have any furniture anymore, nothing was left of my books or toys and the clothes were riddled with bomb fragments.

We set up in the new apartment and rebuilt our lives. And reestablished contact with people that we knew and who were good to us. These were people who had taken care of us. We were given bread cards anonymously, but we always knew where they came from. There were also people who placed food at our door under the cover of darkness. When my father was in Buchenwald, there was a woman in Nordenstadt who dressed up as a man and would come at night to put food on the doorstep for us. These are things one should never forget and these are people one can never forget. We knew who was and who was not a Nazi.

Anita Fried in New York, 1948.

Much later, I was 24 or 25 years old, I made myself up to look very nice, went to my old school and knocked on the door of a classroom. When the door opened, I recognized him immediately, but still asked

"Are you Herr Metzler?

"Yes."

"You don't know who I am," I said. "I'm the Jewish pig that

wasn't allowed to ride on the bus anymore."

He was flabbergasted.

"You'll be hearing from me again," I said.

I hoped that maybe he might not sleep for a night or two and wonder what was going to happen, what could yet happen to him. Of course, I didn't do anything else. What would I do? It was so many years later, the middle of the 50s, he was de-Nazified and was a teacher again. Something I still can't understand.

We wanted to emigrate to America, we had our papers already, but were waiting to be investigated. And then we found out that my father had TB. Our furniture, clothing, dinnerware, everything was already in America. But he wasn't allowed to go.

Then came the reparations. Everyone thinks the Jews got rich from them. That's a misconception. The reparations were based on the amount last earned in 1938—and my father's store had already gone downhill by then because people didn't buy from Jews anymore. But then my father received a pension because during the war he was forced to work on the roads, dig trenches and build bunkers. He was born in 1890 and was still young when the war ended.

On April 30th, 1947, I went to America alone from Bremen. The passage on the ship was paid for by the Joint, they were transporting emigrants. When we parted, we thought we would see each other in America again, Papa will be okay, but that didn't happen.

I arrived in New York on June 7th. Relatives picked me up and we drove to Philadelphia. I had different jobs as a maid—and I became an American citizen. At some point, I went back to New York and stayed there. For seven years, I had a permanent job at Macy's, a good job. In 1950, I married an American. I was 19 years old and it was an escape into marriage. It lasted five years. We divorced in 1955.

A year before that, I went back to Wiesbaden. But it was hard to find a job. I had become an American citizen in the meantime and had to give up my German citizenship to do that. I learned typing then and got my first job using that with the Americans in Wiesbaden. I stayed there with the Air Force for 16 years, with interruptions, then worked for one year at an Israeli company in

Frankfurt, and then from 1977, I worked for another 16 years as an executive secretary at an English company.

In between all that, I married a second time. He was the love of my life, but it was over after five years. My son came out of that marriage, he was born in 1962. Today he lives in Nordenstadt with his wife and son. So the circle is now complete.

I married two non-Jews, but that didn't bother my mother at all. And when I asked him if I should raise my son as a Jew or a Christian, even my father said,

"Enough is enough."

He didn't want the child to be Jewish. I don't know if he envisioned that things would never end. There is never an end to it, anti-Semitism is as old as humanity. So my son was baptized and confirmed. I regretted it though. When my father died in 1966 my son was too old to sit with me in the synagogue—the women sit upstairs and the men downstairs—and he would have sat down there all alone. But I go to the Jewish community center, and the older I get, the more religious I become. It's about unity, there is another community here now.

After 1945, there was neither open opposition to us nor open rejection. No one cared about it, and most of them also didn't even want to know more. And we didn't want to talk to everyone either. My philosophy is: I was born in 1931. I was 14 when the war ended. People born the same time as me or later, I have no problem with. Everyone born before 1928, I have doubts about. My son once said to me,

"There won't be peace until that generation is dead."

He isn't wrong. But anti-Semitism is growing again. When they put up a memorial for the murdered Jews in Wiesbaden, a journalist asked me,

"What do you think of the memorial?"

"The memorial is nice," I said at the time. "But how long before it gets vandalized for the first time?"

It took less than three months.

The names of the dead are on the memorial. That is important.

Do you know why? When the Messiah comes, he'll call them all by name. I know a lot of the names on the memorial. Children who sat next to me in school, my teacher, many Jewish families with whom we were friends. When I look at it, I say to myself, I knew her, her, and her—22 people in my family were killed.

They erected steles in Nordenstadt for people who were still deported up to the very end. The people of Nordenstadt had a very hard time with that. And neither the Mayor nor the local representative have given me much thought. They have totally ignored me up

to now. I had two *stolpersteins* (see page 264) laid in front of our building in Nordenstadt for my aunts. And behind it are five more *stolpersteins* where relatives lived as well.

Emigrating to Israel never occurred to me. Do I feel German? The country didn't want me. I'm more American than German. The decision to come back to Germany was mostly because of my parents. I'm the sole survivor of Wiesbaden today. And I'll never stop asking,

"Why did you do that to us?"

ANITA LIPPERT

Ruth Galinski

born Ruth Weinberg on July 19, 1921

" Did the Germans feel guilty about what they did to us? I don't believe they ever had much of a conscience. The Germans didn't like Jews, not even after the war. Years ago, they found that 15 percent admitted being anti-Semitic. Today it's much more. But no one talks about it. Sometimes I ask myself, why did we stay? "

Back then there were travelers who would go into the province with suitcases and sell table clothes or similar things. My father was one of them and he earned quite a lot of money. Once the Nazis came to power, he was immediately forbidden from doing that. Then my mother worked. She could paint well; she wanted to study painting and had received permission to copy paintings from the Dresden Art Gallery. I always sat next to her, I knew that gallery inside and out. But that didn't last long either because we couldn't sell the paintings. Then my mother worked in the community center. They served inexpensive food for Jews there, they called it "Middle Class Cuisine." My father also helped at the community center. I don't know if he earned much for it.

We had it bad, we had it really bad. We had to leave our apartment—we had to do that a few times, because we couldn't pay the rent. We had lived really well at one point, then we just kept going downhill. In the end, we lived at the Wettiner train station five minutes from the Zwinger Palace. A fifth-floor walkup. The toilets were up half a flight of stairs. I thought it was terrible when I sometimes really had to go at night in the dark and I couldn't always wake my mother. The first time I returned to Dresden after the war, Wettiner Strasse didn't exist anymore. It was completely destroyed and was never rebuilt.

We weren't religious, but we went to synagogue on the holidays anyway. I went to a Jewish daycare, but went to a public elementary school around Easter 1928 because there was no Jewish school. They didn't have one until we were thrown out of the public schools. That was in 1934 or 1935. The school year was coming to a close and there was a celebration in the auditorium. We (there was one other Jewish girl in my class and one in the next class) were nicely dressed, as nicely as we could be, given our clothes. We got our report cards. And then we were called up to the principal. While we were in his office, he said,

"So, you have your leaving certificates and they're good, unfortunately. But thank goodness the last Jews are out of the school now."

Ruth Weinberg in Dresden, 1925.

I'll never forget these words. And that is how we left the Wettin school. In such a mean way. That was an abrupt ending. The others had a party. And what did we have?

I kept playing more sports. At four years old, I had already joined the Jewish sports union, *Bar Kochba*. I was always an athlete. I loved it. If I hadn't had that, I would have been an unhappy child. Being active always gave me joy and filled me with ambition. I was the German junior champion in track and field. When I was younger, I received a certificate from Hindenburg. I lost that and everything else after I was arrested later.

The Jewish community center had opened a provisional school and we continued to study there. Religion, for example. The others had lessons in religion at the public school, too. We had to go to the center on Sundays to study Hebrew. That was frustrating, Sundays were my only free days. My girlfriends withdrew from me, but I also didn't really have very close girlfriends. It was the Nazi era. And Dresden was a big Nazi town. Everything happened earlier there than in Berlin, because Berlin was an international city, where the 1936 Olympics took place, during which they could show that everything was fine in Germany. In Dresden, that wasn't necessary, and the *Gauleiter* (English: district leader)—he was hanged in Poland afterward, thank God—was one of the worst. We couldn't ride the street cars or buses, we couldn't walk through parks and we couldn't go to the sports fields. I never saw the inside of the Semper Opera House because I wasn't allowed in. I was never in a theater there, because at ten you didn't go to the theater yet, and afterward, when my father was forbidden to work, we didn't have any money for it. And as a Jew, I wouldn't have been allowed in anyhow.

My father emigrated to Argentina in June of 1938. But first he had to spend a year at Hachscharah in Berlin, and then he was supposed to get the visa. But then the Argentinian authorities said that entire families couldn't come together anymore, only the man of the house. And he couldn't work in a city. He had to go to a farm for one year, and then he can send for his family. Our visa arrived earlier than that—and was in Berlin. In October 1938. And at the end of the month, we were arrested in Dresden during the *Polenaktion* (see page 260).

I had secretly kept playing table tennis at night in the Jewish sport center. It had already been forbidden but I wanted to become a trainer one day. I also wanted to go to *Bar Kochba* that evening, but looked out the window and saw a policeman come into the building. And shortly after, our doorbell rang.

"What's the matter?" I asked.

"You must all come to the station."

He was very nice, we knew him from our constantly having to show our papers. To extend the date on our passports we had to go send them to Leipzig because there was no Polish consulate in Dresden. Only my father, Abraham, born in 1897, came from Poland, or back then it was Russia—Bialystok was sometimes in Russia, sometimes Poland. He had fought on the Polish-Russian side in the First World War and came to Dresden as a prisoner where he met my mother, who was three years younger than he was. She was from Dresden and she became Jewish when she got married against her parents' wishes. And I know that when she was called to the police, my father was already gone. She was told,

"You are a German woman, get a divorce."

"A German woman stands by her family," my mother said. "I am a German woman. And now I am a Polish woman and stand just as firmly by my family."

She got the Polish passport through marriage and we children were whatever our father was. So I had a Polish passport, although I didn't speak a word of Polish. And because my mother converted to Judaism I was considered a "full Jew." That's what they called it, it was even in my papers.

Some women did get divorced, which I can understand. Maybe that saved their children. But if they hadn't gotten the divorces, their husbands might not have been murdered. But that's easy to say after the fact. Today I'm wiser, I ask myself, if it had happened to you what would you have done?

"Get dressed and come with me," said the policeman. "And bring your passport with you."

"Is something wrong?" I asked.

"No. Just checking passports."

Okay, since we knew him, we trusted him. He had also believed it himself, by the way. We went to the station, my mother and I, my brother Gerson was still climbing in Saxon Switzerland (National Park). That's why the police waited for him in the apartment, until he came back at 11 at night—then brought him in. We had to go into a large room. Every Jew in the Dresden area was brought here throughout the night. Collected. We were a big group. We waited until morning and then we became restless.

"March!" someone suddenly shouted.

We went over the Elbe to Neustadt to the train station. It was a long way over the bridge. Other people saw what was happening, of course. No one said anything against it. There were SS men standing at the station. Into the carriages we went. The SS stood on the boards outside and locked us in. Then a whistle sounded and I saw the policeman who brought us here.

"They don't have anything with them!" he shouted.

"You said we didn't need anything."

"If only I had known!"

We rode for many hours, stopping now and then. They were old carriages, "wood class." And in each one sat an SS man. They took our money; we could only keep ten marks. I didn't even have ten marks, that was a lot of money back then. Someone else gave me ten marks, someone who rode with us and who I knew.

"Take it. I have so much money. They'll take it away from me anyway."

We stopped in Zbąszyń (see page 271) on the green border to Poland. It was dark and we had to get out. It was raining, horrible weather, it was the end of October after all. We had nothing with us, we had gone as we were. Then we stood there all night, outside in the open. Poland wouldn't let us in and the Germans told us,

"We will shoot you if you come back."

There were, in fact, a few who had been shot, so we stood there like a herd of sheep. The next day a few people from the Red Cross and the Jewish centers in Poland came and sought out certain people who could go in. Us, for example, because we could say we had received a visa. We were transported further to a refugee camp in Warsaw. It was a health spa for lung disease patients and the buildings weren't used during the winter. We went to a villa that was abandoned by a Jewish owner. It was simple, but it had furniture.

We lived there. I had to stay in bed if I washed my clothes. I had nothing else there. Then a clothing store was set up, they brought used clothing from the Jewish community centers. They were the only people who helped. Polish Jews, especially students, took care of us. More than we might have done, because the Polish had more heart. They also cooked for us. My mother was allowed to help cook, that way she could get in the kitchen and do something as well. We didn't starve. And we had no idea what would happen. At first it tasted a little of freedom because there were no Nazis. The war didn't start until the next year.

But then it started and the bombs fell. Right on the first day, you could see the airplanes in the sky, it was a blue sky, and no one knew what to do. It was horrible. We could hear on the radio that there was war. I had learned Polish in the meantime. Which was good because later I had to live illegally. If I hadn't spoken Polish, I would have immediately been exposed.

We got fake IDs, the Catholic church sold them. Nevertheless, my mother, brother and I were brought to Warsaw. To the ghetto. It was still open at first. Then the wall was built and you could only get out if you worked outside. There were six of us living in one and half rooms.

I got married while in the ghetto. I was 18 and in love, the first man in my life! Leon Davidson came from Lviv and had studied law in Warsaw. During his studies, even before Hitler, Jews were only allowed to sit on the left in the rooms at the universities. Oh, anti-Semitism! I didn't want to believe it, but he showed me. I don't know if that was only in Warsaw. But it was definitely like that there, others confirmed that to me as well.

Then we all got out of the ghetto illegally. My mother wanted to go to a friend in Czechoslovakia. I didn't know if she got there, until I saw my brother, who told me she did. In the meantime, he had become a resistance fighter and had heard through other resistance fighters that I was alive and where I was hidden. He came to where I was, during the Warsaw revolt and in a Polish uniform. We saw each other and separated again. But we also thought we were winning. In the first four weeks, the Germans were rooted out by the Poles. We could even see the Russians on the other side of the Vistula from Warsaw. We were happy! We danced in the streets, because we were free again! Then the Germans brought in more soldiers from who knows where and destroyed Warsaw. They bombed everything to pieces. I lived with my husband illegally. His parents were in the ghetto in Lviv, they didn't want to be illegal. Too old. They did promise though that if the ghetto were to close, then they would send a telegram for us to come get them with the fake papers that we had acquired for them. We were always together, my husband and I, but on the day that it came, I lay in bed sick. And he went alone and never came back. I don't know what happened. If he was discovered on the train first. The tragedy is that even if he had gotten there to save his parents, the ghetto was already cleared out. I wasn't there. I was usually always with him, but not on that day.

A friend of my husbands from college, a non-Jew, who was a professor in Krakow came to get me out of Warsaw. I had to get away! The house I lived in wasn't destroyed by bombs. But why should I have stayed? I knew many Jewish friends who had been killed. Where should I flee to?

"You're coming with me," he said. "We're going to the mountains. I have a small resistance group, six or eight students. Do not tell them you are Jewish. They don't need to know."

They also had to leave, but for political reasons. And so, we made our way into the Tatras. I didn't know how to ski, but without skis you couldn't move if you wanted to go to the mountains. There was a lot of snow. They gave me a pair of ski boots, they were size 44. I'm a 37. They stuffed them with paper. And I got skis for jumping, which are very long. I put them on and they quickly slipped out from under me and I fell on my tail bone. It hurt, I felt the pain from it for over a year. But I had to run. And we ran and ran and ran. And it worked. My life depended on it, too.

The men were armed, but they weren't active. We lived totally alone in a protective hut. We had wood, it just had to be dried, but there were enough trees. We even had a small oven. We had brought flour with us in large sacks. But I was still half starved. Once in a while, one of them went down to Zakopane and stole a few potatoes. Sometimes they caught a dog and slaughtered it. I always had to cook, but they cooked the dog themselves because they sensed I couldn't do it. I was the only woman, but there were no assaults against me. On the contrary, they were well-raised and affluent people once upon a time. But I was never sure if they wouldn't indeed betray me, or say, what is she doing with us?

I didn't feel well, but I wanted to survive. I still believed I would find my family. I already knew my mother had arrived in Czechoslovakia from my brother, but I didn't know whether she was still alive after that. I didn't hear from him again either. I assumed that my husband was dead. He was probably shot. If they found Jews, they were usually just killed. Or put in concentration camps. Even later I never found out anything, not through *Yad Vashem* (see page 270), the Red Cross, or through the Joint.

In January of 1945, two Russians came and reported that the war had ended there. But even then, I still never said I was Jewish. We drove down to Zakopane and then I told them who I was. And they all said,

"Yeah, we knew that."

I don't know if that was true. But they didn't give much more thought to me after that and I went to Krakow to the Jewish community center. I was registered there; they gave me an ID and rented a room for me with an older gentleman who had returned from Auschwitz. He treated me like a daughter and I worked the cash register in his store, a very nice, big store for sewing materials, and made good money. Almost one year. I was also part of the Krakow sports club. I joined a swim team again right away. But I couldn't do track and field anymore. If you haven't trained for more than six years and are already over 20, competitive sports are done. But I needed to be athletic, it was my life.

I didn't want to go back to Germany. Why should I? I only hated it. And then the Joint and the Red Cross found me. They had sent the names of all survivors around the world right after the war. And my father had read in Buenos Aires, "Ruth Weinberg is living in Krakow." He wrote me a letter that said, "Go to Berlin right away. Your mother, brother and his wife"—he had gotten married to a very religious woman from the ghetto—"are in Berlin. They already have visas and you'll get one too." The consulate was in Berlin. So, I told the old man who wanted to keep me as his family because he'd lost his wife in Auschwitz, "I have to go! I want to go to Argentina!"

I think I didn't hear until later that there were more pogroms in Poland even after the war. Surviving Jews went back to their hometowns there and were slaughtered. At least I was done with Poland anyway.

During Pentecost 1946, I left with a girlfriend. She was Polish, but her husband was already in Berlin. But we could only get there illegally on the train. I didn't have a passport any more, it was taken away from me by the Germans. I only had the Polish identity card from the Jewish community center. The Poles allowed us to leave, but they checked us on the German side. We had to get out of the train. I only had a small suitcase, but my friend had a really big one. We had cigarettes in it, that was our fortune. And then she was caught. She didn't speak German, had no visa and then she took them out. I stood there and thought, "what are you doing?" I was scared at first, but then I went to them. They took everything out of my suitcase of course. After they stole everything—the Germans, after the war!—we could cross.

I first went to the displaced persons camp at Schlachtensee.

That was really good. They registered me, I got something to eat and drink. My brother sent me there. He even had an apartment there and a position with the police where he verified whether there were any SS people among the police. They had a symbol—their blood type—tattooed on the underside of their forearm.

I stayed with him and with a woman I had met and who had become a very good friend. She had a large old apartment on the Kaiserdamm and she offered to let me move in. The Joint gave us packages and I only had to sell one pack of cigarettes and we had money for rent.

I co-founded the *Hakoah* sports club. As captain of the handball team I got flowers when we won and Heinz Galinski was the one who handed them to me. That was in June 1947. On July 19th, 1947, my birthday, we were engaged and we married in October. The marriage worked, it lasted 46 years.

He was ten years older than me. He had also lost his first wife. In Auschwitz. And his mother. The family came from Marienburg, West Prussia, and the final years were spent in Berlin, on Schönhauser Allee. Because Heinz was the only son he didn't want to leave his parents, and then they were all rounded up during the *Fabrikaktion* (see page 244) in February 1943. Heinz, his wife, his mother and father. He fought on the front during the First World War and so he always thought nothing would happen to him. They went to the Jewish hospital. That was the camp they were deported from. Heinz is the one who later made sure that it is a Jewish hospital again today. And the street that it is on is called Heinz-Galinski-Strasse. He was in Auschwitz, in Dora-Mittlebau and Bergen-Belsen.

"Auschwitz was hell," he said. "But if anywhere was more hellish, then it was Dora. There were only men there, and also, many non-Jews. There were only men in Dora because that's where the V2 rockets were built. They bore tunnels in the rock and the prisoners built the V2-missiles inside them. You can still see the tunnels today as well as a barracks, a train car in which the people were transported, and you can see the gas chambers. It's

Engagement of Ruth Weinberg to Heinz Galinski in Berlin on July 19, 1947.

all unbelievable. Also, because there was a concentration camp in every town around Dora. You only have to go 100 meters and there is a barracks and over there is a hole in the ground. That's where the prisoners lived. When the concentration camp was closed down, they sent the men on a death march to Bergen-Belsen. Heinz was freed from there by the English in April 1945.

In 1949, he was the first head of the Jewish community center in Berlin and we moved from our two-room apartment in Charlottenburg into a three-room apartment in Schmargendorf. It had central heat. Later we had three and a half rooms on Südwestkorso Strasse. And until his death, we lived in a dream penthouse apartment with windows made of bulletproof glass.

As the president of the Central Council of Jews, from 1954–63 and 1988–92, he had—we had, bodyguards. And that was terrible.

There were four people with us: the driver and a man next to him and two more men in the car behind us. At some point, he forbade that. Because when we went shopping, and he loved shopping, there were always six of us in the store. My husband often got angry with them, they weren't supposed to get so close. He then managed to get it so there were only ever two. But that was also all that was needed! The police picked him up early in the morning and brought him home at night. They were out in front of the building every night. I was always worried for our lives. But it was a fear accompanied by the police at the front door, I had a certain amount of protection. It was different than in the Nazi days. I was really scared.

Heinz was attacked often. Even six years after his death, someone tried to blow up his grave with an explosive in September 1998. Only one piece of his grave stone was broken. But a few months later, in December, the entire grave plate was broken by an attack. The pieces were preserved, one of them says, "Explosive attack by an unknown evildoer." They never found the people who did it. Years before, a cleaning woman found a bomb in the center on Fasanenstrasse – directly under the hall where a celebration was supposed to start where he would speak. They were able to disarm it. And then, in 1975, someone sent him a letter bomb to his office. His secretary noticed that the letter was so thick and gave it to the police. In the beginning, it was all done anonymously. Later, a threatening letter would sporadically come signed. That's how things in Germany developed again. But he always said, "I didn't survive to keep quiet. I promised myself in the concentration camp that Hitler would not be right. That the Jews will not be stamped out."

He wanted to fight for that. That was his purpose in life. His father died just after being arrested and his first wife and mother were also killed. They rode in the same train car with him to Auschwitz. The women went straight into the gas chambers and he was put to work, because he was still young and strong. We talked about the past one time, then never again. But we didn't

GOING BACK

From left to right: Dr. Andreas Nachama, Dr. Michel Friedman, Ruth Galinski in Berlin, February 1992, at the twice destroyed grave of Heinz Galinski.

make it a secret either. I imagined that we had completely come to terms with it. That was not the case.

In 2000, when I had heart surgery, which lasted nine hours, the anesthesia was too strong or they gave me too much, so I spoke incoherently for over 14 days. And only about those days. And I hit everything around me, not allowing anyone near my bed. Only the professor and later the chief doctor from the Jewish hospital, because I knew them well. But whenever anyone else in a white coat came in, I screamed,

"Don't come closer! You want to take me away! They couldn't do it before, and now you're trying!"

I was scared to death. It was worse than the worst times. Worse because I was panic-stricken. I was deathly afraid of people who had done nothing to me. In the first few days, I was in the Virchow Clinic, where my husband died. He had the same operation, bypass surgery. He did very well afterward, three days and then there was a complete collapse. He lay in a medically-induced coma for four weeks, but fought to the end. He died in 1992 on my birthday, which was also the day we were engaged. The feeling of finality didn't come for another year. My life changed a lot after his death. I didn't just lose my husband. We had been invited to receptions, knew politicians and queens, and that went away at some point. They sent me invitations for a short while still, because Heinz Ehrenbürger (honorary citizen) was from Berlin.

When I came back, I didn't want to stay in Berlin or Germany. But my husband wanted to rebuild. He was right too, and he did a very good job rebuilding the Jewish community center in Berlin. Only in recent years has it changed so much.

I would have been happy to emigrate to America, not Argentina anymore. Although my family lived there. My father found work in a spinning mill, he worked hard and earned very little. But my parents didn't want to come back to Germany at all. They even learned Spanish. When I was a child, they always thought it was good that I didn't speak the Saxon dialect. My father had spoken more Yiddish at home. Of course, I didn't know it was Yiddish. I

Ruth Galinski in the 90s in Berlin.

always thought, he's a foreigner and doesn't speak very good German. When I heard it later in Warsaw, then I realized it was Yiddish. And that it was similar to German, that I could understand it too.

In the first few years I couldn't visit them because we didn't have the money for the flight. My husband worked as a representative voice for the victims of fascism. Then he was elected to head the community center. It was a volunteer position. Finally, someone said he should get paid for it. We weren't rich though. Who was, among those who came back?

I didn't work. My husband didn't want me to, and I hadn't studied very much either. But in 1953, I helped found the League of Jewish Women in Germany again, with Jeanette Wolff. She was an influential woman, an SPD politician who was also in German Parliament. She was sent to a concentration camp as a political prisoner, was set free and then deported with her family as a Jew. All of them were killed, only she and one daughter survived.

We had 500 members in our Berlin women's group at the best of times. We met every week and visited the sick. But the most important thing was to make connections. It was after the war. We had survived.

Did the Germans feel guilty about what they did to us? I don't believe they ever had much of a conscience. The Germans didn't like Jews, not even after the war. Years ago, they found that 15 percent admitted being anti-Semitic. Today it's much more. But no one talks about it. Sometimes I ask myself, why did we stay?

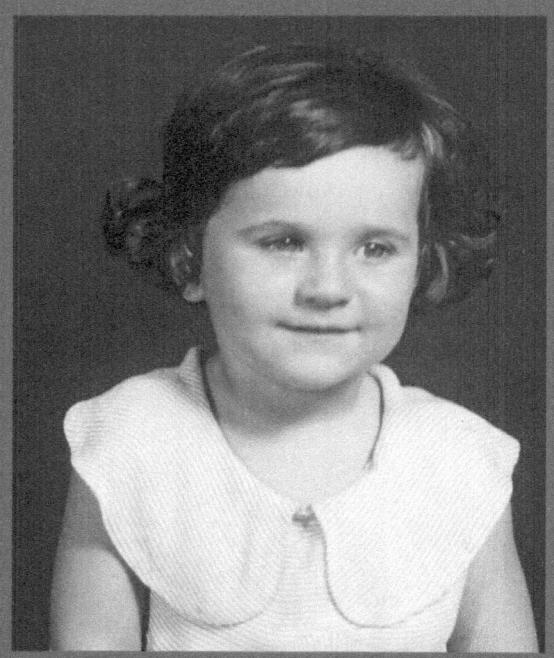

Alisa Weil

born Angelika Levin on February 4, 1931

" My parents said the whole time we were in Palestine, which was for at least eleven years, "When the nightmare in Germany is over, then we must all go back. There will be Nazis or whoever there, who were born into National Socialism and don't know anything else. We must go back to build the country up again as a democratic country." They weren't alone in their thinking. "

It wasn't a problem that my mother married a Jewish man. Her parents loved their son-in-law, they knew him for a long time, because they, like him, were also social democrats. My grandparents were generally incredibly liberal. My grandmother taught comparative religion. She wasn't a teacher, she was a housewife and raised her four children. But even back then she wanted her children to know that there isn't just one religion, but many. And then she had a seat in the Weimar National Assembly. There were only three women overall, two of them for the SPD. One of them was Else Höfs, my grandmother, who founded the Worker's Welfare Association (*Arbeiterwohlfahrt*) with Marie Juchacz. And my grandfather was on the town council and a social democrat from Stettin, where we were all born.

My father was something else entirely. He came from a rich, very respected business family. His father was in the textile business. The family was Jewish, so of course they went to synagogue on the high holidays, but they weren't orthodox. After four daughters, my father was finally born—a son to be prince. Then they had another son, so there were six children.

My father wanted to sell books and studied to do it as well. But his father had a heart attack, couldn't feed the family anymore, and thought the boy learned the business of books, and business is business, now he'll be in the business of textiles. My father really tried, but there was high inflation at that time so it didn't come to anything. Then my grandmother died of diabetes and my grandfather died as a result of the heart attack.

My father's two older sisters rented out part of their seven-room apartment and that's how they survived. The two younger sisters and the younger brother, a cabinet maker, were communists. One worked as a secretary for a well-known communist party member. The other was a florist first and then worked for my mother's father as a housekeeper. The families had known each other for a long time.

My mother was a trained kindergarten teacher and hired by the state to be a social worker. Until she was let go because she had

Angelika Levin around Stettin, 1935.

Margarete (mother) and Werner (father) Levin with Angelika in Stettin, March 1932.

a "husband of Jewish origin." My parents wedding was in 1927 and four years later I was the first born. They named me Angelika and later named my sister Renate. My mother was very proud of our beautiful German names. She had no idea we would end up in Palestine.

I have some memories of how things were after 1933. When I was three or four years old, my parents moved out of my grandparent's house into a settlement. One time my mother was in the laundry room in the basement. I looked for her down there, when a voice said,

"What are you doing here?!"

It was the block warden. He came from behind me in the dark and scared me. I still carried around the fear that experience instilled in me when I was back in Germany. Whenever I was in a restaurant, I always sat against the wall so that no one could come up behind me. That block warden also spoke to me at a party in the community garden, saying,

"Aren't you the little Levin girl?

And I was naturally beaming,

"Yes, I'm the little Levin girl!"

"You're not allowed to be here! You're a half-breed!"

I went crying to my mother.

"I'm a half-breed and am not allowed to go to the party!"

My mother took me on her lap—everything was explained to me later, of course—and she said,

"Look, you know how I bake a cake. I take flour and milk and butter and sugar. And if I didn't use so many things and mix them up, then I wouldn't have such a nice cake in the end. And that's how it is with you, too. You are a wonderful cake, because you're a mixture of things.

That's a very nice story and that was the way she consoled me.

My sister was born in June of 1936 and we traveled to Switzerland. But before we went, my parents took me to the school and asked the rector,

"When we come back, Angelika will be six years old. What are her prospects? Will she be able to be enrolled?"

He just laughed and said,

"Of course! We've known each other for years! Of course, we'll take Angelika in our school, she can stay here until her *Abitur* (see page 237)."

Or so he thought.

We went to the Quakers near Zurich. The man was a pastor and his family invited us to stay for six weeks. When the time was up, and we had no money left (we were only permitted to take four gold marks per person), it became clear to my parents that going back would no longer be easy. But they hadn't yet reached the point where they thought they couldn't go back at all.

My father's brother had looked after our apartment in the

meantime. Shortly before we were going to return he found a letter under the door. He opened it—it was a summons from the *Gestapo*. That was now the second summons, my parents had already been summoned to the *Gestapo* once. They didn't get anything out of them, because they both agreed beforehand that if anyone says, "your husband or your wife already told us what we want to know, you can tell us everything," then it meant the opposite. They planned it exactly. There was someone from the *Gestapo* at that interrogation, of course, but the other was a policeman from our neighborhood who my parents knew. Maybe that's why it went well. But they were sure that they wouldn't get out of a second summons. My uncle sent the letter to us in Switzerland, which was strictly forbidden. No one was permitted to send statements from the *Gestapo* outside the country, especially not a summons. He could have been nabbed for that. He had his own family and after that, he immediately fled with them to Czechoslovakia.

When the summons date came (it was because they were social democrats and not because my father was Jewish), they went to the authorities in Zurich, explained everything and were told they had "six months of asylum."

After that they would have handed us over and we wouldn't have survived. None of us. During that time, my father was naturally always preoccupied with the question of where we would go. Four people without money basically had no chance.

"Go to South America. They're looking for teachers, German teachers," someone said.

"Go to southern France and pick plums," the Quakers suggested.

My parents would have done it. They would have done anything. Then a friend of my parents, who was already in Palestine, wrote to my father, "And you probably haven't given any thought to going to Palestine, have you?" He really hadn't. They weren't Zionists and weren't very religious Jews that they wanted to go to the Holy Land. But then he went to the Zionists in Zurich and they told him,

"If we put your name on the schedule list now, you might get

Angelika Levin with her sister, Renate in Hütten, Switzerland, winter 1936.

there in about two or three years. But if you have capital, the British will let you in now."

My father went back to the Quakers, who were still feeding us, and told them. And then a miracle happened. The Quaker wife had a sister who had heard about us, but had never met us, and she said,

"I have a little capital. It would be just enough for that. I have to have it back though, because I live off of it. But I'll sign it over to Mr. Levin so that the family can emigrate and he can send it back to me after that."

My parents went back to the Zionists to tell them they had the money.

"That is good," they said, "we'll write that on your certificate. But the English aren't that stupid either. If you show up in July with two children in winter clothing, they won't believe you. And so, we have to add a nanny to your certificate. Not an additional person, of course, but a young girl, who is already on the list. And second, you'll receive money to tide you over," which was supposed to help with a new start there, "that you'll have to spend now for clothes. Because you're so rich that naturally you can't go there wearing winter clothes."

My father bought a pith helmet and a white suit, and my mother bought a hat with a blue veil. My mother! And long kid gloves, a white outfit with a blue blouse. And the girl was entered on our certificate. We never saw her before and we didn't see her after either.

And so, we went in July 1937 on a French troop transporter with soldiers on their way to Africa. And this I can remember exactly: the ship going into the harbor at Haifa and the gangway being let down; my father leaving my mother with baby and me, standing there on the ship, and him running down that gangway like crazy. I'm thinking, we're standing here and he's leaving us. He was running to the first bank he could find to transfer that money back to the woman in Switzerland. My father was an exceptional man.

But the money we had to tide us over was finally spent with that, and so we had nothing left. Not one penny. And as we were still standing there at the harbor, someone from the *Hitachdut Olej Germania*, an association advising European immigrants in Palestine, came to us and said,

"We have a building over there and the bus is right here."

We went up to Carmel and it was the grandest thing anyone could ever have offered us, a building where everyone got their own living unit. But then my parents made a crazy mistake. Instead of staying on Mt. Carmel and saying, "we are teachers and caregivers, find us work, even if we can't speak the language yet, we'll learn as we go," they wanted to go to a kibbutz. They were social democrats, after all. But the kibbutz said that it would be out of the question without a *hachscharah*. So, they went to *Moshav Nahalal* (see page 256) in the Jezreel Valley for half a year. It was hot there, and my father developed pappataci fever, a less serious variety of malaria. On the way, they bought a bed—I have no idea where the money came from. The bus drove up, the bed was fastened to the roof, and we got on. The bed let everyone in the bus know that we were new here.

"What are the children's names?" a man wanted to know.

My mother answered full of pride,

"Angelika and Renate."

He looked at us skeptically, went to the front, had a proper little conference with the others in the bus, came back and said,

"The children can't go around with those names. But we thought about it, and they should keep their initials."

It was really very thoughtful, they were all farmers from Nahalal, don't forget.

"We can call one Alisa and the other Rinah."

Alisa means "the happy one," and Rinah is "rejoicing song." It couldn't have been nicer. Right away my parents agreed. Somehow, they accepted it. And so, we both got our new names on the bus to Nahalal. I loved the name Alisa so much that I could hardly stand it later, when we left Palestine for London and I suddenly had to write Angelika in my passport, because it was on my birth certificate, in Hebrew letters.

We were given a wooden shipping container in Nahalal. It had been placed on stone and a door was sawed into it, and it also had a window with a screen. One day my mother came home with a towel that had been hanging outside and wanted to wrap my sister in it – and then I suddenly saw a yellow scorpion in it. I screamed and screamed. My mother didn't know why, but she let the towel fall. The yellow ones are deadly, for a baby anyway.

Everything was pretty different in Palestine, especially the climate. It was murder for my parents. They didn't speak any Hebrew, and most of the people in Nahalal were Russians. The family that took us in were very kind and could speak a little Yiddish. My father had to do his *hachscharah* training with a farmer two fields over. He didn't get any money for it, but he did get milk, tomatoes and other groceries. If it wasn't enough, the people we lived with gave us a little more.

At that time, my mother came down with typhus and went to the hospital. She was gone, my father was getting *hachscharah* training, and I wasn't old enough to care for a baby. I was taken care of, my father made me a sandwich in the mornings. And he could take my sister down to the small *Kibbutz Hefzibah*. When Rinah came home, she only spoke Hebrew and my mother only spoke German. That was very amusing, I would constantly hear,

"Alisa, what did she just say?" Or, "tell her this or that!"

My mother never really did learn Hebrew. And yet everywhere it was,

"*Rak Ivrit! Rak Ivrit!*"

We were supposed to speak *Ivrit*, Hebrew. But we were never picked on if we spoke German. My parents always spoke German with each other and my sister eventually learned it. They sent me to a children's home in Bialik during our time in Nahalal to learn Hebrew before I started school. I must have been able to do it in those six weeks. But not without tears, I cried every night. I wasn't even six and there was no one there who spoke German. My parents were not aware of just how hard that was for me.

Then my father finished his *hachscharah*, and we went to the *Kibbutz Givat Haim*. Back then, the *kibbutzim* were still selective with people, so they had a probationary half year. After that they decided whether or not they would take you. My mother worked in the laundry room and was so capable that they soon gave her the night shift, because they knew it was okay if Grete did it. Grete? Now you are Margalit! They weren't overly sensitive in the *kibbutz*. Only my father, Werner, didn't get a Hebrew name. *Kibbutz* life was exactly the right thing for my mother. She'd get up in the morning, work eight hours, shower and eat in the dining hall. Then she would go to the children's house and take her two daughters and play with them. We would put my little sister to bed together and then she would put me to bed. I was delighted in the children's house. There were no individual living units yet, my parents lived in a loft again and with a *primus*. In the *kibbutz*, a *primus* was a third person living in a loft. It was a night guard who slept during the day and my parents slept at night. They only had these big boxes in which to live. They didn't need wardrobes, dirty clothes went to the laundry room and people had shelves. No table either, people ate in the dining hall. They had shower rooms and shared bathrooms. Provisions were made for my mother.

It was never a problem that she wasn't Jewish. After time on the *kibbutz*, we lived in Haifa, where there were *Yekkes* everywhere. Many of them were Jewish men with non-Jewish wives, we were hardly an exception. And no one frowned on us. On the contrary, if it ever came up, then it was, "you came with your Jewish husbands. And now you're working here like mad and we give you credit for that." No one ever said, "Oh, you're a German." Instead it was, "You're *Yekkes*, that's good, that's what we all are."

But I didn't want to be a *Yekke*, because I had the feeling that as long as I was a *Yekke*, I would never quite feel at home. That's why I only made friends with people who were born there, *Sabres*. They were rare! But you were something if you hung around with a *Sabre*. I tried to speak a very clear Hebrew. No one ever heard that I was a *Yekke* when I spoke! I was very good in school, and I was also part of the youth movement, *Hamahanot ha-Olim*.

I started school in the *kibbutz*. There were only five of us in our first school year, four boys and one girl. They didn't have any more children. The boys were all born on the *kibbutz*, I was the only outsider, so to speak. And then the President of the World Zionist Organization, Chaim Weizman, came to the *kibbutz* to see it. But of course, they showed him their own productions—four boys! Stubborn like an I don't know what, they said nothing at all when he asked them questions. So, he came to me and I said,

"I'll show you the *kibbutz*."

He took my hand and walked with me through the entire *kibbutz*. That news spread like wildfire and the mothers of the four other children, one was a teacher, one a secretary—in other words important *kibbutzniks*—were so angry. They couldn't understand that at all, we had only been there a couple of weeks.

My father worked with a *turiah*, a heavy tool, in an orange grove, and he passed out in the sun. That also went around the entire *kibbutz*,

"Margalit can work, but Werner, he passes out."

After six months, the *kibbutzniks* said at their meeting, that

"The Levin family is too much of a burden. They have two children already."

Up to that point, everyone only had one and weren't supposed to have any more either. But my parents came with two already, they could hardly kill one. The father of one of the boys in my class stood up and said,

"There may come a time when we're thankful anyone wants to join us at all. Think about that when voting."

They voted against us anyway and they arranged a job for my father in Haifa as a librarian in the labor union. My parents took it very badly. Of course, they really wanted to be on a *kibbutz* and they wouldn't take them. And my father had done his *hachscharah* for six months for that.

We came to Haifa and because my parents didn't want their daughters to live in the lower half of the town where the Arabs and English soldiers were, they looked for an apartment in the upper section, in Hadar. They found a one-room apartment. There were two buildings, each with six apartments, with stairs outside, along Mt. Carmel. My father cleaned them twice a week to pay for the apartment because no one could live with two children on what he earned as a librarian. There were months when he didn't get any money from the labor union. The people put up with it for one month, but then after another went by, they went in and asked,

"Where is our money?"

"You just have to go to the store and tell them you're an employee of the labor union and you'll get everything on credit. But our unemployed must have cash."

Ha, simple as that. Three months with no money and then nothing retroactive either, so my mother had to do more cleaning. She really wanted to learn Hebrew, a friend of my father even offered to give her private lessons, mornings at eight. After a half hour, she laid her head on the table and fell asleep. She then went to the employment agency and said,

"Put me in a factory so that I can hear and then also learn *Ivrit* there."

They laughed in her face.

"What? You'll hear *Ivrit* in a factory? You'll hear Romanian, Polish, and Russian. But not *Ivrit*."

And that was the end of her dream of learning *Ivrit*. And then

Alisa Levin (back row, fourth child from the left) in the 2nd grade, Haifa, May 1938.

she cleaned more and more. Even in a building two streets below us. It was a day care and school for kids just starting school. Today it's the famous Leo Baeck School. It was founded by a young rabbi from Stettin who had also buried both of my grandparents. My sister went to the day care and I went to the labor union school. But only for one year.

Because we were still four people living in one room, I was put directly in school and took my schoolwork seriously. If I sat there brooding over my work, my sister would come over with a red pencil wanting to write also and she went through my notebook with it. I felt desperate to get away from her. But Haifa has steps that go all the way from the lower city up to the top of Mt. Carmel. So, I sat down on them and did my homework on my knees. I didn't make it home that day. My mother went out of her mind. She took me to a psychologist and he sealed my fate, or that's how it felt to me anyway.

"Alisa needs a regular routine, but she can't get that with you," he said. "So, a home."

And that's how I ended up at *Ben Shemen* (sepage 240) at eight years old. Our last president, Shimon Peres, also grew up there. The founders and heads of the home were two German brothers, and it was certainly a great home. Later it developed into something completely different too, as I feared it would. But in the beginning, I just cried. In the meantime, I could speak *Ivrit*, but now I had a Russian and a Polish woman as caregivers and they were completely different. One time I got myself a thick book during lunchtime, lay myself under an olive tree and didn't come back until dinnertime. But I was supposed to be working in the afternoons, feeding chickens or in the garden.

"I was reading and lost track of time."

"That's totally unbelievable," they said, looking at me as if I'd done something else, and punished me with night duty with the chickens. We only saw our parents three times a year. They came during the long break, when there was a big festival, and they took their kids home. Then they came to visit briefly for Passover and Hanukkah. We took the bus home and the driver had a machine gun and so did one of the caregivers, and the children had to lie between the seats. The bus was armored with our backpacks and suitcases, so that any bullets would hit the luggage and not the children. We were really scared to drive through the Arab cities of Lod and Ramla. It was 1939, there was still unrest and everyone knew that those were the places where one could lose their life. And I had to go farther than those places to reach Haifa. From *Ben Shemen*, that was at the end of the world on the other side of Tel Aviv. And that's how it felt to me, too. I really suffered during that first year. But then my mother spoke to a social worker, she knew that a Strauss family lived nearby. I was allowed to go there for the monthly weekends that children went home. It was far. They lived at the very edge of *Ben Shemen*. I marched in and an old man sat on the veranda, who said,

"Come here, Alisa, and I'll tell you a story before lunch."

It was Martin Buber, but I had no idea who he was. To me he was *Saba*, grandfather to both young sons in the family. And he always caught me, sat me on his lap, and told me a story. It wasn't until much later that I realized Buber lectured in Jerusalem and visited his daughter and son-in-law (author Ludwig Strauss) on the weekends—and what it meant to have sat on Buber's lap! From the moment that I could go there once a month, everything was better.

When I had been there four years, which is a long time to a child, my father came and said that he found me a place in a home that was close to Haifa. If I had been able to go there from the start, it would have been so much easier for me. But by then, it was a critical time for me. First, I felt settled in *Ben Shemen,* and second, this other home was more religious. *Ahava* was practically all German. Most of the children there came from Berlin because that's where it was founded.

"Then Rinah can maybe come to the home too," I said.

But my mother shouted immediately,

"No, no! She is too young!"

But she was the same age I was when I went to *Ben Shemen*, and that was so much farther away. It stung, of course, to hear *Ima* say that Rinah was still too young. She told me later that she would have been glad to go somewhere.

Anyway, I lived in *Ahava* for three years and went from there to another school in Kiryat Bialik. When I was supposed to leave, the teachers begged my parents to let me stay at *Ahava* and in the school, they even offered to waive the fee so that only the cost of my food needed to be paid.

But my father said,

Alisa Levin (center) with her sister, Rinah (right, next to Alisa), Haifa, October 1943.

"We can't, she has to work."

I had the feeling for a long time, now that I was grown up, my parents couldn't do anything about it. It was because of the Nazis. If we had been able to stay in Stettin, I would have done my *Abitur* and would have gone to Berlin to study. Then all these interruptions never would have happened. But my poor parents never really came to terms with the situation. They both studied and had professions. If they had been allowed to practice them, then money would never have been an issue.

I had just turned 14 when I had to leave school. Then once I was home, however, my parents had a bad feeling and enrolled me in a women's technical college in Haifa run by the WIZO (Women's International Zionist Organization.) It was horrible. Cooking and sewing—and I would have really preferred studying the *Tanakh* (see page 266), or Bible texts, and more *Ivrit*. After three quarters of a year, they took me out again and arranged for me to work in the *ganon*. That's a care center for little ones, before they start in a regular pre-school. One day, the dancer Yardena Cohen came to my parents and asked if I could watch her two-year-old son in the afternoons. They understood that to be a full eight-hour work day. They had a bit of a hard time with that, I have to say in their defense. But Papa was so eager to relieve Mama, at least with one less cleaning job a day, that they agreed. And then I did both jobs. The little boy depended on me - and I on him, and then I had to leave the child, the dancer and the country. It was terrible. But I was convinced I would be back within two years at the latest. I never would have thought that I was never going to leave Germany again.

At the time, I was in the WIZO school, I was recruited from the *Haganah* (see page 247). That was normal at age 14 and it would have been horrible not to have been accepted. I had to swear on the *Tanach* to stick to my agreement. But I pushed to be the only one permitted to tell my parents when I was traveling for *Haganah*. My mother's heart was weak and I had to be able to tell her why I wasn't there. Not where, not how long, and sometimes it was for days, I couldn't tell her any of that. You weren't allowed to talk about it with anyone. Only in your own three-person team could you talk about anything, but then you also only knew these three girls and the commander. I told him,

"My parents are going to London and want to take me with them to learn a profession there. I need to be relieved to do that."

I never would have been able to leave the country without that approval.

"You are relieved," he told me after a couple of days. "You can go train for a job in London for two years, and then, of course, come back again."

I was happy about that. That would have been a terrible fight between the *Haganah* and my parents.

My mother and father were very different people. He was an intellectual and she had repeatedly saved his life. His younger brother went with his wife to Czechoslovakia first and then to Italy. And when the Germans reached Italy, he had had enough. He took his own life. His wife was not Jewish, and she tried to take her two daughters back to Stettin. She gave the younger one up to a pastor on the way.

"It is dangerous to bring the child back to Stettin. This or that person might recognize whose child it is."

"I can adopt her," he said. "But then I also have to baptize her."

But my aunt said that didn't matter to her. She went a little farther with the older daughter, who wasn't from my uncle. Somewhere they bumped into Russians and the communist comrades put them in a Jeep and took them to Berlin. There was a children's home there, and she was a teacher. She worked there the rest of her life, later as the director and, of course, she went back to get her daughter.

My father's family all died. The entire family. Except him, he survived in Palestine. But only thanks to my mother, who never left him. He would probably also have killed himself. He knew that his four sisters and one brother were all dead. His two oldest sisters were put into forced labor by the magistrate in Stettin. They were already pretty old though and became sick and died. The third sister was deported. My father started the process to bring her to Palestine. She didn't want to though; she didn't believe that anything bad would happen to her. She went to Lublin first, then to Auschwitz. And the fourth sister killed herself when my maternal grandfather died. She had apparently loved him. He was divorced of course, my grandmother had left him and married a colleague in Berlin. He was a bastard, an anti-Semite. Before we had left Germany, he said to my mother,

"You and the child (my sister wasn't born yet) can come over sometime. But you have to leave your husband at home."

This grandmother went with her husband to Stralsund and he was arrested there. She made a trek all the way back to Stettin and then was raped by the Russians. She never recovered from that. My *Oma* had a seat in the Weimar National Assembly. So, my father was the only one left from the entire family. I had the feeling even as a child that we are safe and sound here, while over there one after the other dies. Really horrible! I still remember when the letter to my aunt came back, "Moved, whereabouts unknown." That was a phrase everyone around us had gotten. And everyone knew what it meant: dead. But of course, no one quite knew how or where.

When we left Palestine at the beginning of 1948, it was still a British Mandate and that's why people there could only travel to England. The first thing my parents did in London was to find the exiled party executive office of the SPD (Social Democratic Party of Germany). There was a group of people who wanted to go back to Germany, to the cities from where they came. But we couldn't go back, because Stettin had become Polish in the meantime. So, that meant,

"The best thing is to go back to Hanover; the party is gathering there."

But the fact that the party was gathering there meant we still wouldn't have a home. We climbed out of the occupying forces train – warmth, food!—and stood in a devastated Hanover. My parents wanted to go there in particular, and they didn't feel this way, but for us children it was horrible. We were given a lot in a bunker, and then people we knew took us in to their apartments. And my mother went to the central committee office for the Worker's Welfare Association. A woman sat behind the front desk and slowly stood and said,

"Else!"

"I'm not Else, I'm her daughter."

She still remembered my grandmother, who had co-founded the Worker's Welfare Association. My mother was hired immediately as an advisor. Later, after the Federal Republic was founded, the Worker's Welfare Association moved to Bonn. My parents moved with it and grew old there. My mother lived to age 88 and my father 84, after having studied psychology and worked until he was 72 as a certified therapist.

My sister and I went to the Odenwald school. My parents had to pay something, and that was fine because my mother found work right away. My father was supposed to work as a teacher. But he had only taken classes, he had never worked as a teacher. In Israel, he couldn't because he didn't know the language, and before that, in Germany, he was no longer permitted. He stood there in front of a class of 52 children and just couldn't handle it. Some people said later that it was,

"Because they were German children!"

Nonsense! They came back here specifically so they could work here. My parents had told us the whole time we were in Palestine, which was for at least eleven years,

"When the nightmare in Germany is over, then we must all go back to Germany. There will just be Nazis or whoever there, who were born into National Socialism and don't know anything else. We must go back to rebuild the country into a democracy."

They weren't alone in their thinking. A lot of people came back again for this reason. They were all a) idealists, b) dreamers, and c) very German. German to the core. When my parents were in Palestine, they had to go to a *kibbutz*, of course, because they were social democrats. But they never identified with the place in any other way. Staying there wasn't an option for them. They always felt like Germans, even in Palestine. There was no such thing as Israel yet and only ardent Zionists believed it would ever come into being. It might have turned out differently if we had stayed until Israel was founded. But my mother went on about the green trees and rivers in Germany and my father was convinced that all the volunteers had to go back again, because otherwise it could come to naught. He had the right idea from the start. But whether it was a necessity for him, or more to the point, us children, that was another question.

I made the attempt to go back to Palestine once. In the spring of 1948. The Odenwald school took a day trip to Heidelberg. We were in the castle courtyard and suddenly a girl says to me,

"Look! There are your people."

Who are my people, I asked myself?

"They all look like the people in your pictures."

She noticed a group of young people, all with white shirts and all with shorts, even the girls. I wouldn't have even noticed, it was such a normal look to me. But here, certainly at the end of the 1940s, it wasn't normal at all. They were children from concentration camps who had been gathered by a Jewish-American officer and dressed in stuff from Palestine. They were brought down to Lindenfels, not far from the Odenwald school, with the purpose of being smuggled to Italy and from there they would go to Palestine by ship.

And then came my attempt and it failed! I wrote a letter to my parents, to the school principal, to my house mother and to my sister. Then I packed my few clothes, we didn't have much, and went barefoot through the Odenwald. We always went barefoot, because we didn't get any soles for shoes, it was directly after the war. I got to Lindenfels, but no one was there anymore. But the farmers there told me that Aharon, the commander, had left something behind for me. A Bible, and on the first page it said, "For Alisa, as pledge." Decades later, I met him again in Israel and he explained to me why he deliberately gave me the wrong date of departure.

"Those children," he told me, "who we had collected from the concentration camps, no one cared about them or if they went to

Munich and from there to Italy. If I had taken Alisa with me, however, her parents in Germany would have gone to the Odenwald school and they could have sent the police after me. Then the whole thing would have come to light."

And then Israel was founded. That took care of my oath to return to the *Haganah*. It was dissolved. But the country always remained my country. I was five when we went there and started school at six. I grew up there. But then a doctor told my father,

"If your wife stays another year in this climate and under these work conditions," she only ever cleaned, sometimes three different places a day, "then she'll die."

And that was the last push he needed to tell himself, I have to get her out of here. He came to me and said,

"We're leaving."

"Ok, you can go. I'm staying here."

"No, that is out of the question," my mother said then. "We came here together and we'll also leave here together. And if not, then I'll also stay here."

Then I felt like I would be murdering my mother if I didn't agree to go. I thought about coming back to Palestine. I have always felt Israeli and I'm still not a German today. And won't become one, that is over and done with. I'm an Israeli with a mission here in Germany: to make clear to every person, whether they want to hear it or not, what Israel is. I worked for a long time as a lecturer in the trade union where I covered Israel and Judaism. But one must not forget, I have never had an Israeli passport. I've always regretted that. Sometimes my husband says,

"That was such a long time ago! Can't you get that out of your head? You are so fixated on it!"

But I am fixated! It's just in me to be that way. I was in the underground movement from the age of 14. I was definitely too patriotic as a child and young woman for someone to just change my mind at some point. No one can. Palestine was the most beautiful thing in the world to me. And Haifa was my hometown. Years later, when I was 30, I was running down the stairs, when a woman called to me,

"Aren't you the little Levin girl? You move just like she did. She was always running from Arlozorov down the Hechaluz to her father."

I was at home in Haifa and Palestine. I had to seize the country for myself. And once I did seize it, it was my home. I didn't want to leave.

At the end of 1948, I went to Essen to study to become a gymnastics teacher. My mother took me there and told the two Jewish women who headed the school again,

"Alisa can't live alone, because she says "*du*" (personal form of "you") to everyone. And if she sees a poor person, she tells them "come with me, I'll give you something to eat.""

"I have a daughter who is also starting her studies at this school," responded the one teacher. "And if you would like, Alisa can live with us."

And so, every day we drove as a threesome from Wuppertal to Essen. Three years, from 1949 to 1952. We were a three-woman house and there were only girls at the school too and only female teachers. But I was always mixed in with boys in Palestine. Even the Odenwald school was co-ed. After half a year, the teacher once asked me if I was enjoying myself there.

"Yeah, it's okay. But I miss a man."

She nearly fainted. Then she drew in a deep breath and asked me,

"How do you mean that?"

"We have no male teachers at the school, no male schoolmates, and it's just us girls here. There were always men wherever I went. And I just miss that."

She understood what I meant by that and calmed down. Then she recommended taking a class at the mixed adult education center. The lecturer came in—and he later became my husband. It was as if lightning struck him at this first meeting. I know now that it wasn't because I was so beautiful or smart, but because I was just a different sort than the other people who lived there. They were oppressed or submissive, and I was just different. And when we married in 1951, he said,

"If you want to move to Israel, I'll come with you."

That wasn't very realistic though because he was a civil servant. And he could only speak German, no Hebrew, and not very good English. But also, he was German, he wasn't Jewish—there was no foundation. But I still wanted a child. And then I had the child in 1953 and was sick from that moment on. Actually, I was overjoyed. My son Wolfgang was healthy and I was healthy. But three days after the birth, the nurses found me under the bed. Of course, it's not quite right for a woman who just gave birth to spend a night on the tile under the bed. They wanted to bring me out, but I said,

"Leave me alone! Alisa has to repent!"

I have no idea why I said repent. That is definitely not Jewish. There were experts then who said that was the persecution coming out right after childbirth and the puerperium.

I left Hans in 1966 and went to Bonn, where I met Manfred. Our daughter, Shulamit, was born in 1968, and we got married three years later. We were the first couple to be married in the Bonn synagogue after the war.

Manfred is from Cologne, he fled to Antwerp in 1939 and escaped from the French internment camp, Gurs, in 1940. He and his brother both hid out in France, Belgium and even in Germany. They had both been interned in Switzerland in 1943.

Manfred is a painter. My uncle Julo Levin was also a painter. He was killed in a concentration camp. He would have been 100 in 2001, and they had a large exhibit of his works in the city of his birth, Stettin, and they tried to contact relatives who still remembered him. I was the only one.

Renée Brauner
born Renate Rebecca Nessel on July 12, 1939

" When my parents decided that we would return to Germany, I said, "then I'll kill myself!" I really hated the Germans. I came to France when I was seven years old, and we French—even without a passport we felt French—hated the Germans to death. "

My father wanted to emigrate to Palestine, he even had the papers already. But he wanted to emigrate with a wife, so he was introduced to my mother. They met in Berlin and it was love at first sight for them both. My mother's parents were beside themselves, they were German Jews and my father's family were from Krakow. That's why he was deported to Zbąszyń during the *Polenaktion* at the end of October 1938.

My mother stayed behind (she had just been married in August and I was on the way) and tried to reach my father. In the end, she went after him. She was blond and had blue eyes and if a Jew wanted to go to Poland, no one gave them a hard time. She met a nice SS man there who told her she could turn to him if she had any difficulties. She came back to the border because they couldn't find my father. And the Germans didn't want to let her back in. The SS man put her up in a hotel. With his help, she traveled back into Germany and went back to Berlin. At some point, my father came back too, because he was supposed to settle his affairs. Same with my grandfather. They arrested him too. He was in the Sachsenhausen (see page 262) concentration camp, and they let him out to get his things in order, to sell his land and his sawdust mill in Niedergebra in Thuringia (see page 257). But that was later, in 1940, and we were gone by then. I only mention it to show that some things were possible.

Even before he was deported, my father wasn't allowed to work anymore. He was a miller, born in 1912 and raised in Leipzig. My mother was born in 1915 and became a fashion designer, but never worked. She couldn't anymore, that was a time when there was no more work for Jews.

So, my father came back from Poland and lived in Berlin, illegally, of course. He tried to emigrate through France to Palestine with my mother and me in September 1939, at the start of the war. The French had given him a stamp the day before that said he could pass through, and the Belgians had too. Then there was a checkpoint in Aachen and my father was taken off the train because he was a Pole and the fighting with Poland had begun in the previous

Renate Nessel, Poschiavo, Switzerland, 1943.

few hours. They took him to jail and advised my mother to continue on with me. I was a six-week-old newborn. She didn't know what she should do. Keep going to her mother who was already in Paris? She got off and stayed. He was locked up in Cologne, and she went back to Berlin because her father still lived there. Her sister had already been sent to England with the *Kindertransport* (see page 252), her one brother was in France in the Foreign Legion and the other was still young and, therefore, still in Berlin.

And because she was still in Germany, my father was set free. They would likely have deported him before. He lived with mama and me illegally again in whichever apartments Jews were permitted to live in. But he went to the Palestinian office on Meinekestrasse every day to find a way to emigrate. At some point he heard about a travel agent next to the Palestinian office that belonged to a Herr Schleich. He helped bring people to Yugoslavia, and apparently the *Gestapo* knew. He helped us, too. They gave me sleep medicine so that I wouldn't scream. We arrived in Yugoslavia and I was sick. Mama told me later, I was one year old, she had no diapers and I had diarrhea.

Before that, we hid in the mountains for a few weeks near Innsbruck. And when this Josef Schleich had gathered enough people, he brought them over the border. He saved a lot of people. They say even more than Oskar Schindler. But he is nowhere to be found in *Yad Vashem* under the people who were honored as one of the righteous for having saved people. Probably because he took money for it.

In April of 1941, the war started against Yugoslavia and the Germans cut off that connection. My maternal grandfather had stayed in Berlin and had a heart attack that same year and died. But my paternal grandfather also came along this route, after they let him out of the Sachsenhausen concentration camp.

We were in Zagreb, we were in Ruma, we were in Belgrade, and we were in Split. I was two and my father sometimes took me begging with him on Fridays to the rich Jews. I stood on a table for them and sang, *"Bel Ami, du hast Glück bei den Frauen, Bel Ami"* (Bel

Ami, you have luck with the ladies, Bel Ami). We got something for that. It was degrading for my parents.

My mother was often sent from Zagreb to Belgrade to do something for the Jewish community center. In the meantime, she got "Aryan" papers. My father made them himself. One day they both went out on the street and someone called out from a surge going by (that's what they called them, when people were being deported),

"Say hello to my wife!"

At which point my father and my grandfather were arrested. Because if someone called something to them in German, then it was clear that they were also German. They were sent to a camp and my mother got my father out again. She had heard that an electrician was sought in their area and she told the head electrician about my father. He went to the camp then and said he needed an electrician and wanted Nessel. My father and grandfather appeared. And then my grandfather said,

"You go. You have a wife and child."

He died of starvation in the camp in Yugoslavia, in Gospic. I think that tortured my father for the rest of his life. He never talked about it. Ever. Not even about the others in his family. But he didn't find out about it until after the war. We already knew a lot during the war. It's a lie to say that no one knew anything. Otherwise, Jews wouldn't have kept running away the whole time. And where were these large numbers of people? They did write to relatives for a while still.

My mother's grandmother ended up in Theresienstadt. She was 80. She died there two months later. And her daughter was killed in Auschwitz. But they didn't transport everyone in the family together. Instead, they took my great-grandmother, and three or four months later, her daughter. Why didn't they at least take them together? So they could have stayed together.

How many people in my family were killed? I don't know. On my father's side, he and two sisters survived. The family had seven children. One sister was married, she'd had two little children.

They were all killed. Children! It was difficult for me later, during school celebrations and similar circumstances to see a lot of children. I would always think, "the millions of children who never even had this chance..."

One sister was in Romania with her child, she managed to survive. And the other sister survived in Palestine, she had already gone there in 1935. Later when I was in nursery school in Italy, the only address I knew exactly was Arlozorov 70a, this aunt's address in Haifa. That was drummed into my head so that I could say where I belonged if anything happened.

As the Germans marched into Split and the Italians withdrew, they were decent and humane and told us,

"It would be better for you to come with us, because terrible things will happen."

We were taken to Triest on a ship with others. On our arrival, the men were bound and the Italians became enraged in the street. They wanted to know why the men were bound while wives and children were with them. But the soldiers had to then explain why they even brought us. They pretended we were their prisoners being sent to Asti in Piedmont as civilian war internees. Every province took so many people on. My mother said those people had been so great. We were assigned a room and there was milk and bread out front every morning. We never found out who brought it. My parents listened to the radio secretly at night. And the next morning I would say,

"bum, bum, bum..."

It was the English broadcaster's station identification signal. And in the evenings, the Italians would stand in front of our building, throw rocks at my parents' windows and call out,

"Turn it up a little! We want to hear it, too!"

There were deserters in Asti as well. They told everyone what they had seen. People in Italy knew for sure what was going on no later than 1942. They knew that the people in the camps were being killed. They just didn't know the extent to which it was happening.

Because my father worked as an electrician and as a miller, we were in pretty good shape. I actually have hardly any of this anxiety that people my age still carry around. I was always secure and led a totally normal life in Italy. I spoke Italian and played with the children and eventually even went to nursery school. There was a party one day and the mayor was there with his sash. I went up to him and told him he was a mean person because everyone in the nursery school was allowed to go but me. The race laws were there also and Jewish children were not allowed to attend nursery school. So, he said to my mother, "Just send her there, too!"

Where we lived, there was a large courtyard and the rooms were off of a gallery. And there was a toilet somewhere that was a board with a hole. One day my Papa came home from work and asked where I was, and Mama said I was on the toilet. My father ran down. I was hanging inside it and he pulled me right out with one arm. I would have died if he hadn't come.

Then we fled again in 1943. Because once the Germans occupied Italy, they deported Jews. The nuns in the nursery school wanted to keep me there. They made a big impression on me. I could pray and make the sign of the cross. I was particularly fond of the veneration of the Virgin Mary.

"It's dangerous for such a small child," the nuns said. "When it is all over, then you can come back to us and pick her up."

But my father said,

"No, my destiny and that of my child are the same!"

We wanted to go to Switzerland. Once everything was arranged, my mother went to the church where a priest from the Vatican was supposed to pick her up. But two SS men came in. My mother of course fled and hid herself. The SS men went away again and my mother asked one of the priests what they were thinking in betraying her. The priest explained to her that those were monks dressed as SS men. They wouldn't stop an SS man, certainly not two of them. It worked out in the end, they took us and others over the border at night.

We arrived. The Swiss didn't want to let us in, of course, because they didn't take refugees. But a farmer's wife there took me in and gave me a glass of milk. I was four and had light blue

Renate Nessel with her mother, Ruth, Davos, Switzerland, 1944.

eyes and really blond hair. My mother always said I was an extraordinarily cute kid. So much so that everyone always felt compelled to protect me. Like this woman did in Switzerland, or the nuns before her in Italy, or before that even the landlord we lived with in Zagreb. She took me to the church and had me blessed so that I would survive everything.

The border guards phoned someone in Bern to find out what they should do because children under six years old were not sent back. We were allowed in, in fact, and with us came the entire group of 13 people. The men went into one camp and the women into another. My father was in Le Prese (see page 263) and worked as a shoemaker, and we were in Poschiavo (see page 260). Every weekend, or every other weekend, the camp commander was supposed to let the people out to visit with family. But he dealt with that however he wanted. Yes, when his mood was good; no, when his mood was bad. But otherwise, the Swiss were okay. Even in Davos in 1944 when we saw that Jews walked on one side of the street, while the Germans vacationing there walked on the other side. And there were cafés with "Jews not welcome" signs. But at least we were free.

My mother was released quickly because I became sick and they didn't want a child to die there. It became clear in Davos that I had TB. We went there because my grandmother was there. She went to Paris first, then was deported to Gurs. My uncle too; they both survived it.

The air in Davos cured my TB. And at some point, my father

also came. He worked in a hotel supported by refugee help, Haus Rose Hotel, in which we also lived. And then my brother came into the world in April 1946. People started having children pretty quickly to compensate for the losses. 1946, 1947, and 1948 were the years with the highest birth rates for European Jews. From Davos, we went to Zurich. The Italian government offered financial assistance to the Jewish refugees who had come from Italy. My parents considered it, of course, but my mother wanted to go to Paris because her mother and both of her brothers had gone back there. They all went there because no one wanted to go back to Germany. Especially not my father.

My name was Renate Rebecca Nessel. But when we got to France, the French said,

"Renate? Not anymore!"

Sure, it was 1946! So since I was seven, I was no longer Renate Rebecca, but Renée.

I had been in school since we were in Zurich. But then we moved to Paris, and that was a tragedy. I had to go back to nursery school to learn French. I couldn't speak a word. Then I went to a private school with nuns. I didn't like it at all, we had to pray constantly. Finally, I was sent to a normal elementary school and in one year I caught up on three years of school. I wasn't stupid, you know, I just didn't know the language. But missing these three years of school stayed with me my whole life, I always lagged behind. I can speak French without mistakes, but can I write it? Or write German? I don't even want to talk about English. I can actually write in Italian well, because it's so backward.

From that school, I went to a lyceum (in Germany: girl's secondary school). I had to pass a test and Mama made me a beautiful blue floral dress with straps on it. I only stayed there a year because I never adjusted. Other girls couldn't visit me because of the area we lived in. We were like pariahs. First we lived in the 17th *arrondissement* (municipal subdivision) and that worked out. But then my father was offered this apartment in the 20th *arrondissement*. It was a worker district, an area my mother didn't want to live in. The apartment was tiny and when you looked out, you could shake hands with the people across the way. But it had a toilet, its very own toilet! We had a large pot. Water was boiled in it. Then we were bathed in it. Once a week we went to the family baths at the public bathhouse. That was how life was for refugees or poor folks.

It was tough for my parents. My father worked as a traveling salesman for the Americans. Then he opened a buttonhole factory with my uncle as the owner. He was already a Frenchman because he was in the Foreign Legion and the proprietor had to be French. There was another partner, but that didn't work out. And my mother really wanted to be with her mother, who was living in Germany again. On top of it all, I was not an easy child, I was pretty nervous. Well, Yugoslavia, Italy, Switzerland, France, and no friends. We lacked stability. When my parents decided that we would return to Germany, I said,

"Then I'll kill myself."

I really hated the Germans. I came to France when I was seven years old, and we French – even without a passport we felt French—hated the Germans to death. That's why I was called Renée and not Renate. But then I thought, what do I have to do with the Nazis? And the younger people also had nothing to do with it.

My mother always said that she received help in 1939 and 1940, the year when my father was living illegally in Berlin. Sometimes there would be a piece of butter or a liter of milk in my stroller. People had an idea, or they knew, that someone there was living illegally, thus without food rations. When they found the first piece of butter or milk in the stroller, they moved. They were afraid that one of these people would betray them.

In Yugoslavia, when my mother wanted to get my father out of the camp, she was at the *Gestapo* office. Because she was so blond, she was roundly attacked, asked why she was in Yugoslavia with a Jew, she should go back to her father in Germany. But nothing happened to her. Even that SS man in Poland who helped her get back into Germany called her a few weeks later. He wanted to meet with her. He was traveling through Berlin on his way to going underground.

He didn't want to keep participating in what he had seen in Poland. My mother never had a negative experience, in spite of everything. She was lucky. Just as all survival was a thing of luck back then. After she died, I discovered in her papers that she also had to carry the name Sara. I went into a fit of tears.

My father was always going into Germany after the war to smuggle sewing machines into France. We had to live on something. Sometimes I went with him. We all traveled together in the summer of 1954. First we went to Bad Homburg, then we spent three months in Frankfurt and finally moved to Berlin. We were in Germany and never went back to France. In the beginning, we sublet two rooms in the back of a house on Meinekestrasse. Then we got a permit to move to Tempelhof. People weren't really allowed to live wherever they wanted. My grandparents and my mother lived in Mariendorf before the war and, therefore, we got a permit for that area. That is the part of town my father opened a PVC business, a company called Nessel, in which my brother and I would later both work.

We were still stateless. But then we were naturalized. We even had to pay a naturalization fee. It wasn't a repatriation, which would have been normal, since I was actually born here.

I had only been used to girls' schools and suddenly, at the French Gymnasium in Berlin, I was mixed in with boys. The director was constantly calling my mother to come to his office. He was pretty unhappy with me. I wasn't supposed to wear tight sweaters and I wasn't supposed to wear trousers—he had to look out for his boys. I loved that, so many boys. I always had a crush. Then I had a boyfriend, and at some point, a fight with another girl.

"It's a shame they didn't gas you like all the others," she said to me suddenly.

I just looked at her, I didn't react at all. But my boyfriend went crazy. It was all reported to the director, of course. The girl was suspended from classes at first. She had to apologize to me and was then expected to leave the school completely. Her parents called mine, they had no idea where she got that idea. My father said to my mother,

"What good will it do to send her away from the school? She should just stay."

My father was very pragmatic. Later at the *Lette House* (see page 254), where I did my training, I experienced a similar story. Some girl started talking to me and said,

"A bunch of disgusting old Jews sit around and bother me at that Café Old-Vienna."

"Why do you go there then?" was my response.

I didn't go further into it at all. But my girlfriend, Bela (Cukierman, see p. 11) heard that exchange and flew into a rage. I never react like that. Why should I? It does no good. You cannot get such thoughts out of the minds of people who have had them drummed into their heads for years. They didn't really think it was all that bad back then. On the contrary, everyone had a job, of course, and the people built the highways. Of course, there was no poverty, the people went into the Jews' apartments which were taken away or stolen or they simply moved in. My mother put together a package of personal effects. They took it and auctioned the contents in Hamburg. There was a Bernstein piano with it. We also never got any of my father's things back. The building in Leipzig doesn't exist anymore. I saw it again when I was there with my father in the early sixties.

"Look," he said, "that's the stove my mother cooked on."

His sister had lived on the floor above. The woman who had lived there since then knew that my aunt was taken away with her two small children. That was on Reclamstrasse. When the Wall fell the building was torn down. There's a school and a housing development on the land in Niedergebra. There was compensation for it, but that was also not given back.

The Jewish youth met in Berlin as a youth group on Thursday evenings at Joachimsthalerstrasse 13. We got together, we spent the holidays together, we celebrated *Purim*. It wasn't about religion. People also brought Christian friends with them. But I never would have married someone who wasn't Jewish. I never would have

Renée and Wolf Brauner on their honeymoon, Venice, Italy, 1960.

married a German. I would never have done that to my father whose family was murdered. I couldn't have. I also could not have been intimate with a German. I never even thought about it.

My husband Wolf, he fled from Poland to Russia and came to Germany after the war. I met him at the Hannukah Ball in 1955. I was sixteen and a half and thought he was great. He was really good looking. He was sixteen years older than I was and he asked me to dance. I was thrilled. But once I heard he was still married, I was as interested in him as a piece of furniture. The next time I saw him he was divorced. Then I ran into him a third time at a party on March 16, 1959. We talked on the phone and made a date. He gave me a French screenplay and I was supposed to translate it into German in ten days. I was finished after a few days and, of course, that impressed him. One year later, on March 17, 1960, we were married, because my *Oma* said,

"Either people get married within a year or they don't marry each other at all."

It was the first wedding in the reconstructed Jewish community center on Fasanenstrasse in Berlin. Then came three daughters—Gigi in 1961, Jessica in 1964 and Sharon in 1969 and in 1976, I threw my husband out of the house. I packed his suitcases and carried them to the street.

My daughters all married men who weren't Jewish. The husband of my second daughter, who was first to marry, turned back to Judaism. His grandmother was Jewish. The other two left the church, one was Protestant, the other Catholic. They don't count to us Jews. For us Jews, my daughters have illegitimate children. But my daughters know full well that they are Jews and that their children are Jews. And if my grandson marries a Christian woman, she will become a Jew. It's that simple. There's no discussion. And if the women don't want to, my grandson won't marry them.

I only have Jewish friends, and I was on the board of the WIZO for a while. We used to have a group, we went out together, the children were in the same nursery school, the Jewish one. Having other friends just never happened. And today, I don't make new friends. Because then I always think, I don't have to have these senseless conversations, where every one of the 65 million Germans helped at least one Jew, thus saving 65 million Jews. But there were only 500,000 Jews in Germany in 1933.

RENÉE BRAUNER

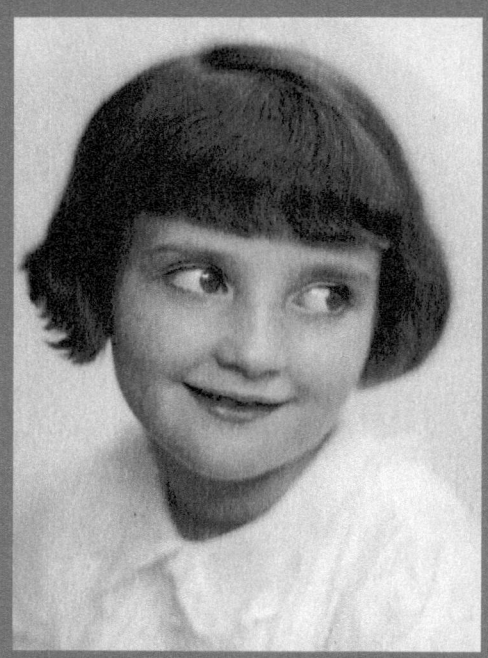

Steffi Wittenberg
born Steffi Hammerschlag on February 15, 1926

" They name streets after the victims today. They lay memorial plaques. They remember. People know what sorts of crimes were committed. Why shouldn't I live here? There is no reason. I can say anything. I don't have to be afraid that someone will report me and that I'll go to jail. "

"We have to leave Germany. We Jews will all be killed."
My mother said that on January 30, 1933, when Hindenburg named Hitler as Chancellor of the Reich. She wasn't necessarily a woman of great foresight, but she was a very anxious one. But in the end, even *Die Stürmer* (newspaper) displayed signs. Hitler made no secret about the fact that they would kill the Jews. "Worthless life" they said. Then people in the neighborhood, the shopkeeper, the hairdresser, stopped greeting us. One woman told my mother,

"Oh, Frau Hammerschlag, if only all Jews were like you! But, the good ones will just have to suffer along with the bad ones."

For me, that is a typical sign of brain washing. That's certainly how a lot of people thought—most the population. But there were also people who were decent and thought it was dreadful. And then there were people who accepted it saying "well, that's just the way it is." Then there were the tacit supporters and there were a lot of them who were informants as well. They went to the police and made reports. So many people were arrested because someone reported them.

I was afraid when I saw the Hitler youth and especially the SA marching in their brown uniforms. I always found that terrifying. And they always sang songs, too, like, *"Wenn das Judenblut vom Messer spritzt"* (see page 268). At home, my father traded leather goods and, of course, noticed that business got worse, that clients didn't buy from him anymore. We never talked about Jews. Instead, we talked about *Enosh* (Book of Genesis of Hebrew Bible). Out of fear perhaps, so no one noticed what we were talking about.

I grew up in Hamburg at Mittelweg 30, and first went to school in the Grindelviertel at the Jahn school. Today it's the Ida Ehre school. It was a Nazi school, also called *Turnvater Jahn*, because his nationalistic ideas of *frisch, fromm, fröhlich, frei* (fresh, devout, cheerful, free) or the four 'fs' were used in the gymnast's cross (*Turnerkreuz*), a type of swastika with round corners. All of the students had these crosses sewn on their clothes, except the Jews. The local NSDAP (Nazi Party) office that oversaw the area for this

Steffi Hammerschlag, Hamburg, 1937.

Steffi Hammerschlag (second from left) and her brother, Gerd (right) with friends in June 1930.

school made a decision with the school leadership in 1935:

"It is no longer permitted that Jews go to school with us. We do not want these alien children here."

So, that is how I went to the Jewish school that year. I transferred at Easter and after the fall break I attended the fourth grade at Johnsallee. Naturally, I felt comfortable with Jewish children and teachers. I only had Jewish girlfriends and so I found it totally normal that I was going to a Jewish school now. After half a year, I was sent to the Israelite school for girls on Karolinenstrasse. I felt comfortable there too.

My parents were liberal, not politically, but when it came to religion. They only went to the temple on *Oberstrasse* on *Rosh Hashanah* and *Yom Kippur*. The Rolf Lieberman studio of the NDR (*Norddeutscher Rundfunk*, a public radio and TV broadcaster in Hamburg) is in that building today, but the outside looks just as it did then. It had an organ, which isn't allowed in orthodox synagogues, and the prayers were in German, not Hebrew. We always celebrated Christmas until 1933, then we only celebrated *Hannukah*. It was the Nazi era, we wanted to differentiate ourselves. Christmas was no longer our holiday. Jesus' birth was no longer our concern.

I became religious during that time and went to synagogue on Joseph Carlebach Platz, called Bornplatz then. A beautiful synagogue. I also heard the Chief Rabbi, Joseph Carlebach, there. Even at eleven or twelve years old, his sermons made an impression on me. Of course, he always said we must believe in God, that he'll help us and that this time might be a test that we must pass. He was very comforting. I now have a book about him in which his sermons are printed. It also mentions how he went to families and encouraged them to be brave before his deportation in 1941. These were families, who had already received orders to report to the Transport. And that he also still preached in the Jungfernhof (see page 251) concentration camp, until he was then taken out and shot.

How long did my faith hold out? Just until geography classes came along and the Earth's development was described. That is not at all in agreement with the religious history of the planet, I thought, and so I stopped believing and was no longer religious. I don't remember if I also stopped going to synagogue. It was over by November 9, 1938, anyway. There was another house of God, the *Neue Dammtorsynagoge*, which had worship services until about 1942. It was destroyed by bombs in 1943.

First came the *Polenaktion* at the end of October 1938. We were very quiet that morning and our teacher asked us what was wrong.

"Miriam Friedfertig's father was picked up today and is supposed to be sent to Poland."

And on the next day Miriam Friedfertig wasn't there. The entire family had been deported. The father had a Polish passport and, usually, the whole family carried the father's nationality. Miriam survived. There is a pamphlet called *Letters of What Became of Children* that features letters that we exchanged with her. In them we told her, even if very carefully and in a roundabout way, about the events of November 9, 1938. One student wrote, "I'm glad you're not here, it's terrible here. We had four deaths in our family. And God cannot actually permit this, we are the chosen people, after all!" And Miriam wrote her back, "Be brave!"

My mother had already been to the Uruguayan consulate. There was a rumor going around that they were issuing visas for a fee. It wasn't that high and we could raise it. She came home with the visas and said,

"First the men!"

For Jews that was the right thing at the time, because the men were the first to be locked up. So, my father and brother, Gerd, who is two and half years older, took a ship from Hamburg to Montevideo on the 12th of October 1938. My mother and I were supposed to close up the apartment and follow them two months later. Because we increasingly had the feeling that we were being persecuted, when the doorbell rang, we were afraid it was the *Gestapo*. We had heard about people being arrested even before the 9th of November. On top of that was a fear of the SA running around. That was always a shock, even if I was still a happy girl otherwise. We were all still happy. And you can still see that in the letters from Rabbi Carlebach's children. They still wrote with such a joy for life in 1939. They might have mentioned events that made life harder, but they were totally optimistic. They had no idea that two years later they would be murdered.

And then there was the night of November 9th. That morning, on my way to school, children were coming in the opposite direction and said,

"There is no school today. The synagogue is burning."

I turned back to go home. My mother was there and there was a lot of excitement. Two Jewish families asked if their men could stay overnight in our apartment, because after my father and brother left, there were no men with us who were registered with the police. If they stayed with us, they would be safe. They did stay with us and nothing happened to them. The one family was able to emigrate to the United States, the other one wasn't. They had a nine-year-old son and, in 1941, they were all deported to Lodz and killed.

But I stayed at home on the 10th of November. So I didn't see the destroyed shops and burning synagogues. Later I heard that in the Talmud Tora, that was the boy's school, the teachers and students in their final year were arrested and deported to the Fuhlsbüttel and Sachsenhausen concentration camps, just like the fathers of many of my schoolmates.

Then the *Kindertransports* to England started. That was very hard because it often meant goodbye forever. Some parents followed their children afterward or went somewhere else and met up again after the war. Other parents, however, never came out and were killed.

The restrictions became much, much greater. We were no longer allowed to go to the movies or to the theater. The benches said "only for Aryans." We also couldn't go to the seaside resorts, not even to Timmendorf. It said, "Jews not welcome." There were actually "not welcome" signs everywhere. Then the shops were "aryanized," employees were let go. Children whose father or mother was Jewish, "half-Jewish" children, as they were called, they were still permitted to go to the public schools a little longer. And then they too were restricted to Jewish schools.

My mother and I were supposed to go to Uruguay in December 1938, but we received a telegram from my father. Our visas were not valid. It came out that the consulate was taking bribes. We couldn't go anymore. I'd already said my goodbyes to the class and then I had to go back to school again. That's also why I made the move to the Talmud Tora school at Easter of 1939. Classes thinned out with the Kindertransports and so the Hamburg authorities decided that we girls should also go to Talmud Tora. The main building was cleared out and we were taught in the adjacent building along with the boys. The teachers were released again ten days after they were arrested. They were shaved bald, limping, with wounds on their faces and terror in their eyes.

Then came September 1st, 1939.

"Now it's war! Now we'll never get out!," my mother said. "Now all of us Jews will be murdered!"

I comforted her. But in my diary I wrote an entry, "The Führer called the military to arms today. Right on Aunt Grete's birthday." That's how I thought, I still wanted to celebrate, too. You can see how divided my world was in that.

By then we were living on Rothenbaumchaussee. Another telegram came there from my father, "You can come, I have a new visa for you." On the 20th of December, 1939, we took the train from Hamburg to Antwerp. Nothing happened to us at the border.

I had dark brown hair with a reddish shimmer and I don't know whether I looked Jewish. There are people who you can immediately recognize as Jewish. Often, just as Arabs do, they look a little Semitic. But there are also a lot of people today who look Jewish, but they aren't Jews at all. Or I meet people and they surprise me suddenly when they say they are of Jewish descent. Back then there were German Jews though—today there are no more. People who had the same German culture, who were equally as interested in German literature and theater, but also still had a Jewish background. They are gone. They were wiped out. It might be a little better still in Berlin than in Hamburg. There were 22,000 Jews here. Berlin had 145,000 members in the community center. That's why so much more went on there. But here too, there was a substantial Jewish cultural life. After *Kristallnacht* (see page 253), you could still go to the chamber theater until 1940 or 1941. It was reserved for Jewish theater or charity events. After that, it became one of the deportation offices. The theater troupe went to Auschwitz.

I first learned about it when I came back to Germany. We knew about the fall of France and Belgium in Montevideo. And that people were tortured and killed in concentration camps. You heard that, too.

We arrived in Montevideo on the 28th of January, 1940. I had just turned 14, so I went to school briefly and learned Spanish there, more or less. I later took private lessons and went to a trade school where I learned stenography and typing, along with English and Spanish. With that training, I worked as a foreign language secretary until retirement.

My husband, Kurt, was born in 1920. I met him in the anti-fascist committee, where he was very active. His family had lived in Osterode, East Prussia. The Germans persecuted the Jews there, too. They led his father around the city with a sign that said, "I, Jew, may not hit any German boys," after the boys stuck posters up in his leather shop with "Jew slave" on them. Then they locked him up. He was freed again, but had to report to the police station three times a day. After that, the family decided to emigrate. Kurt had

Steffi Hammerschlag (seated, far right) with friends in the Jewish sports association, Maccabi, in Montevideo around 1943.

to interrupt his studies to train as a mason in Breslau because he thought you could lay bricks everywhere.

He also experienced Kristallnacht in Breslau. He lived with a widow there and the *Gestapo* came and arrested her older son on the 9th of November. They could have taken Kurt as well, he was actually 18 then. But he slept in the maid's room and they didn't look there. The son was released and went to Uruguay with his brother. They never got their mother out. She was murdered.

My husband arrived in Montevideo with his parents at the end of 1938. His sister had already been sent with a *Kindertransport* to Atlanta, Georgia in 1937. After the war, her parents wanted to see her again. All three of them went to Houston, Texas, because a relative had a meat processing factory there. My husband and his father worked there as security guards at night.

For the first several days, Kurt was excited by all the modernity. But he quickly picked up on the fact that there was great discrimination against the black population. That everything was separate, the neighborhoods, the schools, the movie theaters. For someone who came from Nazi Germany and remembered how the Jews were alienated, of course it came as a great shock to him. In Uruguay, Kurt was embedded in the union of the emigrated youth. In America he felt lonely and unhappy. He wrote, asking if I would like to come. After discussing it with my parents and friends, I went to Houston in January 1948. A month later, we were married.

I got a job and supported my husband, who was politically engaged with the Civil Rights Congress and the NAACP (the National Association for the Advancement of Colored People), and also, in the Communist Party. It was tiny, but it existed. He was especially dedicated to fighting racism there. I jumped into that fight as well, I was as much an advocate as he was. Of course, we also talked about our German pasts.

When the workers in the meat processing factory where my husband worked wanted to start a worker's union, the boss was against it, so they went on strike. My husband had a choice, stand with his cousin, the boss, or go on strike with his work colleagues. He chose the latter.

As a result, the cousin reported us to the immigration authorities as communists. The Communist Party was not illegal, in fact, but they were accused of campaigning to overthrow the government. We were ordered to appear before the authorities and make a statement about ourselves and what our political activity looked like. We refused. The questioning stopped, but then there was a file with our names on it, "Kurt and Steffi Wittenberg." And it was publicized in the press that there was a lawsuit against us in which they accused us of participating in taking down the government.

It became increasingly harder for us. Kurt had lost his job and worked for a demolition company. I was also let go and worked in the office at a shoe store. The Korean war started in 1950 and one day a colleague slapped me and yelled,

"You damned communist! Our boys are fighting against the communists—and you are a communist!"

It was the McCarthy Era, a time when anti-Communist hysteria broke out. There was the House Committee on Un-American Activities, in which there was always only one important question at those terrible hearings:

"Are you [now or] have you ever been a member of the communist party?"

Because we made less money (I had lost my job again), we had to sublet. None of our friends or neighbors harassed us, but the majority of the German Jews, who themselves had experienced racial discrimination, didn't understand our fight. Second generation East European Jews, however, supported us and collected money so that we could go to Europe. Because more and more, we were ready to leave the country. We tried to get permits to travel to East Germany. In 1950 or 1951 we wrote the government there, "We would very much like to participate in building a socialist Germany." The answer was, "very nice," but if we wanted to participate in building a peaceful Germany, then we should go to West Germany. From their point of view within East Germany, they were afraid that someone was a spy from the West, and rightly so if they came from America. But we really did want to build a different Germany.

After we had signed away our right to return to the USA in May 1951, we drove from Houston to New Orleans, accompanied by an immigration officer. He escorted us onto the ship and gave the captain our passports. Getting them was not easy. All emigrants, whether politically persecuted or Jewish refugees, were stripped of citizenship from Nazi-Germany. It was now the Federal Republic of Germany. Our citizenship was not automatically reinstated. Instead, we had to put a request in for naturalization documents. We sent them to the German consulate in New York and then received our passports.

In Hamburg, we were met by a man from German immigration with the words,

"Hello, Herr and Frau Wittenberg. Welcome to Germany!"

That was our greeting, very proper. We were picked up by Aunt Gertrud, one of my mother's sisters. My mother had nine siblings, of which two sisters and a brother-in-law were deported to Lodz and killed either there or in Chełmno (see page 242). We had already heard that through correspondence from Aunt Gertrud. That took a long time because Uruguay, although it was one of the Allies, didn't declare war against Germany until very late. Then naturally, we had no more contact. But since my aunts were deported with the first transport from Hamburg to Lodz on October 25, 1941, we knew.

The second and third transports went on the 8th and 18th of November 1941, to Minsk. One of my school friends was transported on one. The fourth took place on December 6, 1941, and that's the one in which Chief Rabbi Joseph Carlebach, his wife Lotte, his three youngest daughters and a son were deported to the Jungfernhof concentration camp. The son survived, because on that exact day in March 1942, when they were all taken into the forest near Riga to be shot, he had been assigned to forced labor. He went from one terrible place to the next, but he survived and later became a rabbi.

My school friend, Rita Kaplan, and her mother were also at Jungfernhof. And she was also taken away on that day in March 1942. They all knew what would happen. But there was a new driver who didn't have exact instructions and brought them to the ghetto in Riga, instead of the forest. That allowed them to escape that death sentence. When the Germans neared Riga, they were deported to the Stutthof (see page 265) concentration camp. Rita was separated out as labor, the mother was in line with those people for whom death had been ordered. But somehow, she managed to get back over to her daughter's side. Even later they were able to save themselves. They got typhoid, first the mother, then Rita. Then the Russians came and freed them.

I found her again—even Esther Bauer, the daughter of the principal, Dr. Alberto Jonas, at the Israelite girl's school. He was warned on November 9, 1938, and he hid. "Unfortunately," said his daughter in her witness account. Because then he would have been in the concentration camp where most had survived. Even if a few died in the six or eight weeks at the camp, he would have known how bad everything is and he might not have refused to emigrate.

She, Esther Bauer, was in Theresienstadt with her parents, where her father died after six weeks. She married a Czech, who was then transported away to Dresden. That's what she thought anyway, when they told the wives,

"If you want to follow your husbands, then you may."

She registered to do that, but then didn't go to Dresden but Auschwitz instead. She never found him there. He had already been killed. Later, her mother, Dr. Marie Anna Jonas, was also deported to Auschwitz and killed there. Esther was transported again to Freiberg near Dresden, then to Mauthausen, where she was freed by the Americans.

My aunt Gertrud survived because her husband wasn't a Jew. But the other aunts, who had also married non-Jews, they were deported anyway and were murdered. And even Gertrud had received a deportation order for February 14th, 1945, but she hid. That was easier to do then because there were so many bombed out places. All her papers were gone, she said, and that's how she survived.

So, she picked us up in Hamburg and brought us down to the Jewish old people's home, where we stayed for a month. We made contact with the Union of Persecutees of the Nazi Regime (VVN: Vereinigung der Verfolgten des Naziregimes) and got two rooms with a family. The VVN was an organization that was sympathetic to us, because they were the people who had stood in opposition to fascism. My husband became active there and we participated in the fight against rearmament.

I worked in offices again, the longest time was for an international shipping company. Kurt worked in a leather goods shop on Jungfernstieg. He later went into exports for the last 17 years before he retired in Berlin. When he stopped, I also retired. Our two sons were born in 1955 and 1960. The oldest one is a judge on the social security tribunal in Hamburg. He has a girl and a boy. The younger son is a theater director in Berlin.

My parents stayed in Uruguay, but came back to Germany a lot to visit us. That was possible when the so-called reparations were paid. They were always sad when they left again and considered for years whether to stay here or there. They were sensible enough to stay there with their circle of friends. They would have been lonely here.

In the beginning, my brother was in exports in Montevideo and it was going well for him economically. But after he joined a Zionist movement, he wanted to go to Israel. He's been on a kibbutz since 1961. He married there and had one daughter.

I never considered going to Israel. I had no ties to it. I couldn't speak Hebrew anymore and wasn't anchored in Hebrew culture. Why should I go there? Being Jewish was a part of my story and I never denied that, I even thought it was important. But I don't have to live in Israel because of it.

I had more connections to the German culture, to the German language. Yes, I was expelled from this country, or it was like an expulsion. Many of my relatives were killed. But I know a lot of people who fought against that. And I really respect them. They name streets after the victims today. They lay memorial plaques. They remember. People know what sorts of crimes were committed. Why shouldn't I live here? There is no reason. I can say anything. I don't have to be afraid that someone will report me and that I'll go to jail. I don't want to say this is the ideal country. Especially not when we're in new wars. I wish for peace. And for no more neo-Nazis. They aren't only in Germany, but here I find it especially bad that people just let them be.

STEFFI WITTENBERG

Ruth Schlesinger

born Ruth Caro on July 6, 1928

" My childhood and youth were spent here, as a young woman I was there and had my most wonderful years there, and then I was here again. So where is my home? I have no home. Okay fine, I'm at an age now where I'll say here, of course. But I yearn for Israel and I would say I'm Israeli. "

My mother, Frieda, had already converted to Judaism by the time I was born. Yet they told her later, either she divorces my father, Kurt, or I would have to leave the school. But we said, she will absolutely not divorce my father, and they stayed together.

I started school in 1935. It was a public school on Elbestrasse, because there were no Jews in our neighborhood in Neukölln. I only stayed there for three years and then I went to a Jewish school on Auguststrasse. That was after we moved to my *Oma's* at Schönhauser Allee 62, because we had to leave our apartment in 1938. I can remember how I stood at the window and my mother said,

"Get away from the window, get away from the window! The synagogues are burning!"

And that's when it began. I didn't really understand as a child. For me, it was like an adventure. But then we weren't allowed to do anything anymore. We couldn't go to certain places or parks any longer. We couldn't drive. My father had to sell his car because Jews had their driver's licenses revoked. At the end of 1938, he also lost his job. He worked in sales at a clothing manufacturer. Then he was a forced laborer.

I had to wear the Star from September, 1941. I had a houndstooth coat and hid the star in a pleat. But that was a risk to my life.

We continued to live with my grandmother, Else, until the Nazis came to collect everyone. She was my father's mother. At first my father's two younger brothers, Walter and Werner, also still lived with her. In the spring of 1939, Werner moved in with a Christian woman on Trautenausstrasse, who had previously been married to a Jew. Her daughter, Charlotte, also lived there, and Walter was engaged to her. In January 1940, both uncles were also fired and were forced into labor. But they had been warned before the *Fabrikaktion* at the end of February, 1943, and had already gone underground. From that point onward they lived illegally. Walter was living with Charlotte for a while, but someone informed on him and, in September of 1943, he was arrested. Charlotte was too, for hiding him. They went to the Ravensbrück (see page 261) concentration camp and survived.

Walter was locked up in the assembly camp in the former Jewish hospital. The entrance was on Schulstrasse and only separated from the orphanage on Iranische Strasse by a barbed wire fence. A friend of mine lived there because her mother had already been taken away. I visited her there and we always threw packages of bread over the fence on Schulstrasse. When I think about it now! I would have made my parents unhappy with that, they would have left immediately. But I was never caught, thank God. Naturally my friend knew that her mother and her older sister had been taken to a concentration camp. Yes, people knew. Everyone saw that we were being picked up. The cars would pull up out front and people were loaded into them. It's nonsense that no one knew anything!

My uncle fled from Schulstrasse after a bomb attack and was caught in a telephone booth by Herr Isaaksohn and turned in. Rolf Isaaksohn was a Jew here in Berlin who would first sell false identification and then would report the people afterward. That's the story I know. But there is another version, too, that in April of 1944, my uncle had been deported directly to Auschwitz from the assembly camp. Much later a memorial stone was laid for him in front of the building where he last lived.

From the time he was released, my father was forced into labor. My mother was forced into labor. I was forced into labor. Papa was at the Anhalter train station working on the tracks, *Mutti* was in a vacuum factory and I was in a military uniform factory. I was 13 years old when the Jewish employment office placed me there. The bloody uniforms would come in already washed, but you knew that they had been bloody. They had to be repaired, then taken up to the fourth floor. The clothes, mountains and mountains of trousers, were unloaded for us and then a man with a gold party badge said,

"Go, run and take it up!"

But I must say, he was not bad to us. Okay, we earned next to nothing. That's also why I don't have a pension today, because nothing was paid into it for us. And my spine is totally kaput. I've suffered since I was 18 years old, and naturally it's gotten worse with age.

There was a place where Jews had to pick up food ration books. My mother and her sister were with me there. My mother would have never let me to go anywhere alone out of fear that I wouldn't come back. But it was from there that they took me away. I wanted to say goodbye to my mother, but they put a rifle butt between us and said,

"There will be no more hugs here! Go now! Out!"

I was taken to the former Jewish old-age home on Grosse Hamburger Strasse. It had become an assembly camp. It was forbidden for us to say anything if we weren't asked anything. I was afraid, so I didn't say anything. And one day I heard a voice down below, "I want my daughter back!" It was my mother, and she screamed, "I want my daughter back!"

My name was already on the list for transport to Theresienstadt. But she looked everywhere for me and did, in fact, get me out. And the man from the *Gestapo* said,

"Why didn't you tell us your mother is Aryan?"

"You didn't ask me about it. We weren't allowed to say anything."

Strangely, I had the courage to say that. But I left my bag there, I didn't go back up. I couldn't say goodbye. I couldn't manage to say,

"I'm free and you're staying here."

Papa had already been taken away and brought to the assembly camp on Grosse Hamburger Strasse during the *Fabrikaktion* at the end of February 1943. He was later taken to one on Rosenstrasse, where men and children from "mixed marriages" were locked up. My mother was one of the women who stood outside the building for days trying to save their loved ones. She was shot at, but she got him out. A courageous woman. I didn't understand everything at the time. I was just happy to be home again.

My father was not taken away until the end of the war, because he lived in a "mixed marriage." Until that one time, when they took him from the tracks he was working on. Sometimes people from the military would throw food ration cards at the forced laborers where he was working on the tracks. Papa brought them back and I ran to my aunt's on Lilienthalstrasse in Kreuzberg and went shopping because no one knew me there. My father and I never got cards for milk or anything like that. Only my mother received food rations. We had help from relatives. If it hadn't been for them, we would have only had bread and potatoes. Meat was rare, if we had it at all.

After 1945, I didn't do anything at all at first. My parents wanted me to study fashion design. But I was so young, so "ha, it's not that pressing, I would like to live a little first." So, I didn't do it. Then I joined the Jewish youth group, the one that didn't want to take me at first because I had left the community center two or three years prior to that. My mother had believed that if I weren't a member there I could continue going to school. The rector had convinced her of that. But it wasn't the case. And so, after that I had to resume my membership in the community center. And because we still lived on Schönhauser Allee after the war, it was the center on Oranienburger Strasse. I wanted to join, I wanted to be Jewish. My parents gave me the choice.

I wanted to emigrate with this Jewish youth group to Palestine. We knew that we would go right into the military there, so we were trained for the military while still here, on weekends, at Brüningslinden castle.

At the end of July 1948, we went from Berlin to Heidenheim. From there, we went to Italy and then we went on a ship, which was small like a fishing trawler. But we were young. One guy played the accordion, we felt good, we fell in love. I was twenty. When we arrived in Haifa, it wasn't Palestine anymore, it was now Israel.

We went to a *kibbutz* first and were divided up into groups. My girlfriends and I tried to stay together, of course. My best friend still lives in Israel today. We ended up in tents somewhere, but I was set back four weeks because I was so weak. I was so thin! Until I went to Qiryat Haim too, which from Tel Aviv is right before Haifa.

One day I got a letter from my parents in which they wrote that they also wanted to come at the end of the year. My father just couldn't live without me. I was a complete daddy's girl, although I have my mother to thank for my life. My parents went back into clothing manufacturing after the war. My grandmother was no longer alive, but my parents lived in her massive old apartment in Schönhauser Allee. They set up shop in the walk-through room, what used to be called the *Berliner Zimmer*. But then my father was under so much pressure, because he was afraid he wouldn't be able to produce what the Russians ordered. The orders came from the Russians. And so, he decided to go to Israel. He wasn't a Zionist, not at all. I found an apartment for my parents on top of Mt. Carmel in Haifa. A sublet, which was really common. At the time, I was still in a military camp and was employed in an auto parts warehouse, I managed the files. I even wore a uniform. And I was proud of that, of the uniform and the country. I love that country. Even today. If I had family in Israel, or if I had money or was healthy, then I would be there. But over there I could never pay for something like a Jewish old-age home, like the one I live in here. But if you had asked me then, or even today, where my home is, I would not be able to answer. My childhood and youth were spent here, as a young woman I was there and had my most wonderful years there, and then I was here again. So where is my home? I have no home. Okay fine, I'm at an age now where I'll say here, of course. But I yearn for Israel, and I would say I'm Israeli.

I met my husband while still in the military. We married quickly in 1950, and lived in Haifa. Two years later, when I was 24, I had my first son. I was working in the tailor shop. Since my father and both uncles made clothes, I learned it too, while still in Germany. And after the war, when my Papa had his own production going, I had to work there too, on a sewing machine. Then in Haifa, I worked in a very large men's and women's clothing store where I made all the skirts there.

My husband was five years older than I was, and from Vienna. At sixteen, he and a friend went on a ship, the *Patria*. When the English wouldn't let them into Palestine, they jumped into the water. He couldn't swim, but was saved on land. I never knew my parents-in-law. They were taken away. My husband knew, but I don't know how he found out. He never talked about himself. He kept it all in.

He also didn't want to go to Germany. But then he had so much trouble with the people he worked for. He worked at the fishery at the harbor, but he didn't get paid, he was stiffed. Looking for something inland wasn't possible. There was no work. And when he came home, I was always tear-stained because I'd received another letter in which my mother complained and complained about how much she longed to see me.

My parents had already gone back to Berlin in the first half of the 1950s. When they heard that they were supposed to file a request for reparations. Papa did that, even for me. He had even found us an apartment when we arrived. We could simply have taken the reparations and gone back to Israel. But my parents felt more comfortable here. Mama worked as a cleaner in Israel and Papa worked with oranges. Then he worked in a laundry, so that's why we also opened a laundry here later.

My husband and I had been to visit three times and had always considered going there, too. But it wasn't an easy decision. But then a letter came from my mother that said, "Imagine if something happened to us, then you couldn't come in time." If someone dies today, you can fly there the next day. That wasn't the case then, first you had to apply for a visa.

I was both happy and sad to go back. Back to the country of those responsible. And many of my friends asked me,

"Why did you do that?"

That was later, when I was visiting in Israel.

"Maybe I saved my son's life by doing it," I answered.

Because that's when things got started with the military and he would have had to go into it. People got so upset with me for saying that. They all had children in the military. It was a bit thoughtless of me, but no one broke off contact with me. One friend has already been here a few times, he wants to come to Berlin every year. He feels really comfortable here. But he would never leave that country, and besides, he has children and grandchildren there. That makes it harder to leave the country. I managed the jump, because my son was so young. He was six years old when we came over here in 1958. We were already on the bus and ready to leave, and he said,

"Just let me ride around on my bike one more time."

It was so sweet, I'll never forget it. It was very strange, in Israel he always said to me,

"If we are out, don't speak German to me."

So, I didn't. Then we were there on the German border and he didn't call me *Ima* anymore, like we did over there, but instead, he called me "Mama." And I would have been so glad if he had continued calling me *Ima*. No, it was Germany, so he spoke German. At home, the three of us had spoken German, even with *Oma* and *Opa*. We lived in Berlin on Fasanenstrasse and sent him to school there, not to a Jewish school, but to a German one. The first worship services were held on Fasanenstrasse, then they were held on Pestalozzistrasse. That's where he had his *Bar Mitzvah*, and our second son did too.

He came into the world in 1962. We had opened a laundry the year before, and then I got pregnant. It happens. If it were up to my husband, it would have continued to happen. He loved children. But I couldn't, because I was working. The laundry was on Olivaer Platz, which is a good area. And it was hard work because we did everything ourselves. It was doubly hard because we didn't use our own money to take over the store.

Once it finally started getting better for us, my husband died in 1987. I was married for 38 years and never once was my husband sick. And then one time he wasn't feeling well. It was a heart attack. I was with him every day and then I got a call from the hospital one night,

"We had to move your husband back into the intensive care unit. Can you please come? But do not come alone."

I knew what was happening. It was bad. It was very bad. We had our anniversary on the 5th of March, and on the 8th of March he died. All of Olivaer Platz mourned because he was known to be a hard worker. If it was hot out he would be in the store at five, or five thirty, so that most of the machines were washed during the summer.

I continued to work until May. Then I couldn't do it anymore and we sold the store. My sons didn't want me to go into the Jewish old-age home, but I wanted to.

I went to Israel two times with my husband and once more alone. It was nice. So nice. And it was very hard to leave there again. The strange thing is that my husband adjusted to life in Germany better than I did. Going back to Israel never came up again. Andreas, our younger son, only got to know Israel as a tourist. He is interested in the country and goes there nearly every year. He only speaks a few words of Hebrew. Tuvia, our eldest, does speak it. He is a policeman and occasionally has to be called on to translate. He is also very pro-Israel. But they both live in Berlin and have children and grandchildren.

One of my grandchildren is studying Jewish Studies and found out for me where my parents-in-law were killed and about my cousin, his wife and children. Auschwitz. I already knew I'd lost him and friends anyway. How did we find out? They didn't come back.

I am very happy that she's pursuing Jewish Studies. And that she knows everything about what happened. Even my daughter-in-law knows more about it than my children. They get upset about that today. I tell them,

"She asked me. And I answered with whatever I knew."

My children have never asked about it. It was like that in many families. People didn't talk about it. It happened and that's it.

RUTH SCHLESINGER

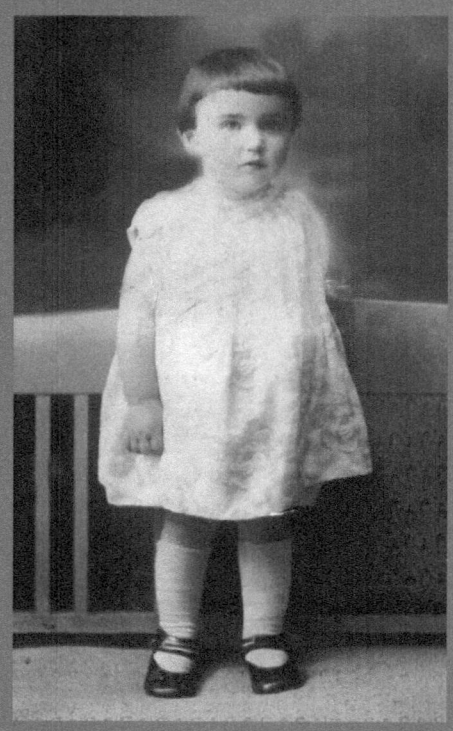

Ruth Hacohen

born Irmgard Ruth Scheuer on October 10, 1923

“ I have suppressed a lot. Otherwise I couldn't live here. Back when I received the definitive news that my parents were dead, it was 1947 and I was pregnant with my first daughter, Irith. I tried to kill myself. ”

I'm a country bumpkin. I was born in a village near Alzey. Our family had lived there for generations. We don't know where we originated. It could be that my father's forebears came from Spain, and so we were Sephardim. But my mother was light blond with green eyes, so someone must have mixed in somehow. She was born in Nordenstadt and grew up in Wiesbaden.

We had a winery with many vineyards. It was wonderful in the fall. Girlfriends would come to the harvest, we ate together and played. Even relatives and friends would come out from the city. Those are my fondest memories.

I was a happy child and known throughout town in Framersheim (see page 245). I went to school there for nearly four years. My siblings were already in *Gymnasium* (secondary school) in Alzey. My sister, Gertrud, was nine years older than me, and my brother was 8 years older. I was the baby and so I was also spoiled by the entire family. My father was not only very sweet, but he was also a very smart man. His father died young, so he couldn't study because he had to feed his sisters and mother. He also supported the poorer Jews in the area as well, anonymously. And he was a representative in Rheinhessen for the People's Party, which is now the FDP. I am still very political today because my father took me everywhere with him, even to assembly meetings.

One day, I had said to my mother in the morning that I was going to a girlfriend's house after school. Suddenly our neighbor picked me up from there and just told me I shouldn't be afraid. I came home and my father wasn't there. He was often not at home, because he had a thousand businesses. No one was there at all, until my mother and brother came back from the town hall. They were interrogated because they arrested my father due to his political activities and took him to the Brown Building. The Brown Building is where the Hitler Youth and the SA had their meetings. That was in 1933, right after Hitler was appointed as Chancellor.

First they locked up my father and a friend, who had also been arrested, in a pig sty. From there they could see that they had put a chair on a dung heap—they wanted to kill them. So my father took

Ruth Scheuer around 1925 in Framersheim, Germany.

out his pocket knife to kill himself. He didn't want to let them shoot him on a dung heap. But his friend said,

"Don't you do that. Let them."

They didn't do it, and after a while, the two were brought into a room in the Brown Building and left there overnight. On the next day, the SA people (one of my neighbors among them) accompanied my father home. I saw how they had beaten him totally black and blue. They took him again and brought him to the jail in Alzey. Protection. From whom did they want to protect him? My mother and my brother were not allowed to visit him, but I went on my bicycle to the jail. I can still remember today what that looked like. And then he went to the Osthofen (see page 258) concentration camp, which was an old factory. They released him after a month. But he didn't return to Framersheim because he knew that they would slaughter him. I intentionally say slaughter because they had done it before. He went underground, and went from place to place, here and there. My mother did get news of him, we did have a telephone—number 37.

One time, he came back at night. And on that night, they shot at us and threw stones in the windows. It was terrible. But we received a warning and had, therefore, already placed a ladder at the barn window. So we climbed out and ran over to the neighbors, who were also Jews and distant relatives. From that night on, we did not sleep at home.

After that, my parents decided they were leaving to go to Mainz. They still had money. But we weren't permitted to sell—we were forced to sell for cheap. First the vineyards. Everyone made a little money. Later we received reparations, but only for the house. It had two floors and twelve rooms. They gave us 4,000 marks for it.

My sister went to Cologne, she got engaged there. My brother came with us. I was nine years old, but didn't go to school for the first year in Mainz. I couldn't because my father was underground. Then I started in the fourth grade. My teacher was a real Nazi. And I sat there feeling lost. It was all strange to me. Six months later, I was still attending the Höhere Töchterschule (school for upper-class daughters). Today there is a bust of Anne Frank in the school and my younger daughter Dorith posed as the model for it because the artist thought she resembled her a lot. Even there, the people never let me forget that I was Jewish. Until my father said,

"That's it. You're going to the Jewish school."

And it was nice there. We had a lot of freedom, with boys and girls together and the best teachers. Our director was Professor Mannheimer. He and his wife killed themselves before the deportation. Then it was November 1938. I saw how the synagogues burned. I wanted to go to school, by then I was in 9th grade, and there were flames everywhere. But I must say one thing, it was so quiet. Hundreds of people stood there, but they didn't scream "hallelujah." Not one word. You could hear nothing but the flames. I think they were in shock. Who would have thought of that? We believed everything, even that we had to leave, but not that. I just stood there, no one recognized that I was a Jew. I didn't even think at all about the danger. No one from my class was there, although we all lived in that neighborhood. Hindenburgstrasse was a Jewish area, just as the Westend in Frankfurt was Jewish.

They did not arrest my father, but they took two of my friends, who were two years older, to Buchenwald. They came back after a while. But one friend from Alzey, they killed him by throwing him into the latrine.

It was time to go. But who would take us in? One day the son of the Jewish hospital director asked me,

"Ruth, there are so many refugees with us. Can you help?"

"Of course, I'll help."

My mother bought me a white coat and I worked eight or nine hours every day at the hospital. Women, men, child, baggage—everything sat there. It was full, they emptied out the villages and concentrated the people in larger cities. Perhaps they had already planned to deport us.

Then they organized *Kindertransports*. The English took in 10,000 children and the Swiss took 80. My father tried to get me a place on the transport to Switzerland, but couldn't because I was already 15. They would have taken the neighbor's girl, but then her mother got her affidavit for America, for her and her daughter. And there was a spot free! My father told the Rabbi, and he said,

"Ruth is too old. But we'll take her because she helped in the hospital."

So, I went with them to Heiden in Appenzell in Switzerland. With a backpack and a suitcase and ten marks. They wouldn't allow us to take more. Later, my brother sometimes sent me money. I used it to buy my first bra and chocolate for everyone. There were 40 of us children and the other 40 were in Basel already. We were housed in a Jewish children's home and they were so horrible to the three or four of us girls, who were a bit older than the young ones. We had to get up early in the mornings, make the fire in the kitchen, and wash dishes and clean. That was our "nice" family. No lessons, no school, nothing. It wasn't thought of as a stopover for Palestine. They thought the parents would be able to come and take their children back to Germany at some point.

I was friends with a boy who was already in college. He asked me to marry him and I wrote home that, "I'm getting married." I believed that I could save my parents by marrying a Swiss Christian. My father wrote back, "A girl who wants to marry at 16 can also still marry later." I listened to him.

At the beginning of 1940, a representative from the Youth *Aliyah* (see page 237) raved to us about Palestine and about the *Kibbutz*. At the end he asked,

"Who wants to go to Palestine?"

Everyone, young and old, said they wanted to go. Including me.

After two months, they called me into the office and said,

"You may go to Palestine."

No one else. Why only me? I didn't care. In April 1939, just before Italy entered the war on the German side, I got on the boat. Any later and I wouldn't have been able to go anymore. We sang and danced on board, it was really nice. I was happy that I got away.

My brother was in South Africa already and went straight into the military. My sister's fiancé was already in America, but she still had no affidavit. Then the Cubans gave out affidavits, so she went there by ship and once there they wouldn't let her debark because the affidavits weren't valid. The consulate who had given them out had put the money in his own pocket. The people stood on the ship for days, it wasn't allowed in the harbor. Then they tried it in America, they went to New York, but they also stood in the water there for days. Roosevelt said "no." No one took them in. No one. They had to come back. Some of the people were lucky and ended up in England or Holland. And the rest ended up in concentration camps. My sister ended up in Holland. And when the Germans invaded, she lived underground. She lived through hard times. In the last 14 days before the Nazis left Holland, the *Gestapo* caught her. She was locked up, interrogated about others and tortured. She believed they were going to kill her. One day, the door of her cell was open a crack. But she didn't want to leave because she thought she would be shot on the spot. She waited. At some point she did go out and look around and there wasn't a single sound to be heard in the other cells. She gathered her strength and nerve and left. The Canadians were standing downstairs! They sent her fiancé a telegram. He had just been stationed in Austria as an American soldier. Before he came, his brother, who was in the British military and stationed in Holland, brought her the first proper food she'd had in a while. She was so thin! She then got married in Holland, and went back to America with other soldier's brides to wait for her husband. Later she stayed in America.

I stayed in contact with my parents while I was in Switzerland. Then lost contact in Palestine. I simply heard nothing more from them, nor did I receive a Red Cross letter. I had always thought that I would see my parents again. Until the end. Then my sister told me,

"Our parents were deported."

But what and where, we didn't know those things at all at the time. It took years before it all came out. My father, Edmund, was born in 1876. My mother, Hedwig, was born in 1887. He was still a forced laborer near Erdal in Mainz, then was briefly in a brickyard. The last that I heard from them was that they were living with another family in an apartment. They were deported to Theresienstadt, and they were taken to Auschwitz on the very last transport. They say the ovens were already destroyed by then, so they used gas to kill them in the trains.

 I have suppressed a lot. Otherwise, I couldn't live here. Back when I received the definitive news that my parents were dead, it was 1947 and I was pregnant with my first daughter, Irith, I tried to kill myself.

 I don't even want to know how many family members I lost. Sometimes I think about this person, or that one. For example, Aunt Jenny, she lived underground in Wiesbaden. On the last day when they bombed the town she came out of her hiding place and wanted to go into the basement shelter. And the milk maid recognized her and went to the *Gestapo.* They shot her on the street. And one cousin who was pretty as a picture, with large blue eyes and blond hair, they deported her to Berlin. She was even younger than I. In Berlin she was forced to lay tracks during the day and work as a prostitute at night. She killed herself. She lay down on the train track so the train would run her over. I can understand why.

 No normal person can possibly imagine what happened back then. And the Germans shrink from it because they feel guilty. They ask themselves: How could this happen here? We did such a thing? Hitler? Yeah, I heard him on the bridge in Mainz and everyone raised their hands. I didn't raise mine, I went right to the back. But the people certainly heard what he said. And that they didn't know anything isn't correct. But they wanted to forget, just like we wanted to forget somewhat. Otherwise we couldn't keep on living. Especially not those people who were in concentration camps.

 We arrived in Haifa, spent the night in Beth Olim and were divided up into kibbutz settlements and schools. I went to *Kibbutz* Usha, which was a very young Polish *kibbutz.* I wrote in a letter to my brother in South Africa, "There are very intelligent people

here. They all speak German, it's broken, but they speak German."
It was Yiddish, but I didn't know what that was. How would I?
Where would I have heard Yiddish? But there were very good people.
Our *Madrich* spoke perfect German. He was our tutor. Anytime we
needed something, if we were homesick or such, he was there. He
was really great.

I stayed in Usha for two and half years. During that time, a
group came from another *kibbutz* that closed down. The man I
married later was also with them. When he came into the dining
room for the first time, I was sitting by the radio, and he said to his
friend,

"See that girl? She is going to be my wife."

I didn't know right away that I would marry him. I didn't even
know him. And besides that, I was with someone else. But he kept
persisting until I said yes. We got married when I was 18. Very
young. But a lot of people got married young. Everyone tried to
find a home. The *kibbutz* gave us a pound for the rings and we paid
the rabbinate with the last money we still had. In Vienna, my
husband's name was Erich Kürt. In Palestine and later Israel, he
was called Uri Hacohen. His grandfather came from Bohemia
and his last name was Cohen, but when he went to Vienna, he
assimilated and changed his name to Kürt. So, my husband took it
too and when he went to Palestine in 1940, he changed it again to
Hacohen. In Austria, he was still on *Hachshara,* at a farmer's house,
and took leave for a few days to go home. That was right in 1938,
like the *Pogromnacht* (see page 259) was. He hid in the Vienna forest
and then went back.

"God, what luck that you weren't here," the farmer said. "They
deported all the boys."

Some of them came out again. And then they could go to
Palestine, but first they were in a camp in Bratislava until 1940, and
waited there for a ship. They went on four boats, down the Danube
and through the Black Sea. People died along the way, but there
was no room for the dead anywhere else, so my husband had to
sleep next to them. They only had enough coal to get to Crete and

Ruth Hacohen and her husband, Uri, during military service, Palestine 1943.

then they stayed there. There were people from the island who came and brought them food and coal. In Haifa, the English interred them on a ship, it was called the *Patria* and they wanted to ship them to Mauritius. But the *Haganah* set a bomb to stop the ship. It sank and 270 people died. But 30 people jumped into the sea beforehand, my husband among them. He had to leave everything on the ship. He only had swimming trunks on. The British military got them out of the water.

"The way you catch a fish," my husband always said.

They were taken prisoner and were even beaten. Then they took them to Atlit (see page 238). He was there for 13 months. The first thing the girls there sewed for him (he was always around girls, he was a very good looking man and charming, so Viennese, right?) were trousers, because he didn't even have trousers. That's also where he learned Hebrew, from a rabbi. People didn't understand him when he got out and asked for directions on the street. He spoke literary Hebrew.

I learned Hebrew in the *kibbutz*. My husband and I never spoke to each other in German. We had books in Hebrew and English. No German.

We were both in the military. As you can imagine, we were also both in the *Haganah* before that. No one talked about it, but the *kibbutz* knew, of course. We learned everything we could, for example, shooting and throwing grenades. People came to the *kibbutz* to train us. We didn't have a lot of weapons. After all, how many could we hide? We had a *tsrif*, a corrugated iron container, which had tools in it. We hid the weapons underneath it. If the English had caught us, we would all have been taken to the Atlit camp. But it was obvious that we went to the *Haganah*. There was no need to explain why: to be trained in case the Arabs attacked. The translation of *Haganah* is "the defense."

We did have Arab friends. But mostly it wasn't peaceful, they attacked often. My best friend in Germany had a brother in the Yagur *kibbutz* and I was supposed to send greetings from her to him. I walked from Usha to Yagur and back on foot at night (it was still early on). And there were Arabs along the way who shot at me. I didn't tell anyone at the *kibbutz* that I was going, because I thought, I'm free to do as I please here. But I had no idea about the Arabs. They looked everywhere for me. They sent out the riders, even from the neighboring *kibbutz*, Ramat Yochanan. They all yelled at me so much—and then congratulated me for making it!

I was in the military for four years until 1946. We girls were first taken down to a monastery in Bat Galim near Haifa, then to a camp. If my husband came, then they all had to get out of my tent so that he could sleep there. We always saw each other somehow. It was a funny relationship. My mother would have been beside herself with horror and my father would have laughed. When I told them I was going to Palestine, my mother wrote, "Dear child, stay in Switzerland! What do you want in Palestine? It's a desert. And you have to work in a field in the sun!" I wish my parents would also have gone to Palestine. To Rishon LeTsiyon, the vineyard, my father could have...

Then I was in Egypt, in the middle of the desert near Isma'ilia, at a camp with 2,000 girls from Cyprus and England and Palestine. Women weren't allowed on the front back then and I worked in a big warehouse for tanks. And I stole ball bearings every day. It wasn't just me, everyone who was in the *Haganah*. My husband was in Egypt at the same time. And my brother was in Cairo, in charge of the

Ruth Hacohen during military service, Egypt 1945.

military, and if we all had time off work, we would meet at his place.

My husband was transferred to Italy and wounded there. He lost an ear. He was operated on in Egypt and couldn't go back to Italy. He became an educator and paymaster in Rechovot, it was a military and discharge camp. One day, members of the underground organization, *Etzel*, raided them, put everyone against the wall (even officers like my husband), and took their weapons. And once it was over, the English major said,

"A good sport!"

The English always respected such actions, but otherwise they monitored the people like crazy. Because almost everyone was in the underground.

I saved up during my military time so that we'd have something when we got out—200 pounds that I always had on me. One day my husband accompanied me, putting the money in his jacket, and an Arab stole everything from him. I didn't even have enough money to get something to drink on the way. I had to take out a loan to buy a wardrobe and table. That was the first and last time in my entire life that I borrowed money. Then I furnished my home for 100 pounds. Just 100 pounds! We lived north of Haifa in Qiryat Haim, where they had built extra accommodations for former soldiers. Two families in each, one per room.

My husband came home from the military at the end of 1947, having received an order from the *Haganah* to work for the English making entries in the land registry. After he fought in the War of Independence in 1948 and 1949, he was a secretary at the *Histradrut* (see page 248) for a year. Back then, nearly all the factories were under the control of the labor union.

We moved when we got an apartment for immigrants in Qiryat Anavim, west of Jerusalem, with a large room and a good kitchen. Meanwhile, Irith was born in 1947 and Dorith in 1949. Then they offered my husband a place to work at the largest social housing association and we lived in Zfat. And then he was supposed to go to Be'er Sheva (Beersheba, see page 239) for them. The entire Negev desert belonged to it, from Ashkelon down to Elat. So, we went to Be'er Sheva at the end of 1953 and stayed there until the end, until 1960. We loved it there.

My husband got very sick in 1956. A brain tumor. He was at a meeting. He went to the bathroom and didn't come back. His secretary found him. He was lying on the floor. He'd had a fit. He was an epileptic and was operated on in Yerushalayim (Jerusalem).

I drove back and forth frequently. The children were in Be'er Sheva. Then I took an apartment in Yerushalayim for three months and the children went to school there.

The doctor said, "He will live seven months at the most."

I thought I would have a heart attack. I loved my husband very much. It was terrible for me. But what is God's will? He lived longer than the seven months, but they made it really difficult for him at the office. "Then we'll go back to Germany," I said. "But only for one year."

We arrived in November 1960. We went to see doctors, in Switzerland as well. But they all said there was nothing left to be done. If they had operated on him again, he would have been paralyzed. I wouldn't have cared about that, but he wouldn't have survived it. He did try to take his own life. There was a mosque with a tower, he went up to the top and wanted to jump.

We also went back to Germany because as returnees we could get a better health plan than in Israel. We spent the first two or three months in Framersheim, then we moved to Mainz where the community center gave us a room. My husband worked there briefly, he translated text books from English into German. He was doing really well. But there was no cure. It got worse and worse. He threw plates and came at me with a knife. He couldn't help it, the tumor put pressure on his brain cells and he hallucinated. I was scared to be with him. In Be'er Sheva it wasn't a problem, we had friends everywhere. But not in Germany.

Then I started working. The employment office arranged a position for me at Kaufhof (department store chain). As boring as it was there, I simply couldn't go back even though I needed the money. In Israel, I took a few classes in career counseling and someone told the director of social work at the Central Welfare Office. They needed someone in Frankfurt and I became the head of the social department of the Jewish community center from 1962. I was Jewish, spoke standard German and Yiddish. I learned that in Israel.

Every day I drove to Frankfurt, came back in the evenings, and had to leave my husband alone in the apartment. But I had people who always checked in on him. One day he was in the bathtub in cold water and didn't get out, so the father of Peter Feldmann, the current mayor of Frankfurt, went to Mainz with someone and pulled him out of the water. Everything was horrible. The children also suffered. Then we all moved to Frankfurt, and three months later that is where he died, in July 1963. In the end and under morphine, he thought he was in Israel.

The children were 16 and 14, and I wasn't even 40. But I stood on two feet, I was always a positive person. I continued to work at the community center. Then the offer came to take over the social department in the Jewish community center in Zurich. I went there in 1970 and worked there for eleven years. Irith came too, and so did Dorith with her daughter.

When Dorith was 29, she developed multiple sclerosis. She couldn't speak anymore. She couldn't see anymore. She couldn't move anymore. She died in December of 1993. My husband died at 44 and so did she.

After that, I returned to Germany in 1994. To Frankfurt.

When we first came back to Germany, I didn't want to stay. I wanted to go back to Israel, but that was impossible with my husband. But I am very attached to Israel, even to this day. I feel like I am Israeli. But my roots are here. I am German and Israeli.

* * *

"My mother," Irith says, "loves Israel. She helped build Israel, she gave her blood for Israel. Because Israel saved her. She also lived in Switzerland and Germany for Israel. She collected donations for soldiers, was on committees for Israel, worked with Holocaust survivors, and fought for their reparations. She did a lot for the Frankfurt community center and she was politically active. And she rebuilt a life here in Germany, which deep down she had never left. To then pack a suitcase and go back to Israel again is hard. But I believe that she never really processed what happened in Germany back then. Otherwise she never would have stayed here. For years friends were always asking her, "How can you live there again?" But even my father was European, through and through. He went to Midnight Mass on Christmas. He was a music fanatic, he had even conducted and took his music book to the opera house for concerts. There isn't a single instrument we didn't have—violin, mandolin, piano. The first thing my sister and I got when we moved to Be'er Sheva was piano lessons. Everywhere people heard classical music coming from the houses—in the middle of the desert.

Our upraising was very yeckish. Ten pfennig were set aside out of every mark. And we never had debt. Never. My mother furnished the apartment the way a German woman would, and cooked the way they do in Rhineland-Palatinate. We never had falafel or pita at our house. But there was also no German literature. We also never spoke German. Israel was everything for us children and for my parents. It was our world.

My sister and I didn't know about the Holocaust. We never learned anything about it in classes, and it never came up at home. And we never asked about it. We had no grandparents, but almost none of my friends had grandparents. The Israelis around us, mostly of European origin, were our family."

RUTH HACOHEN

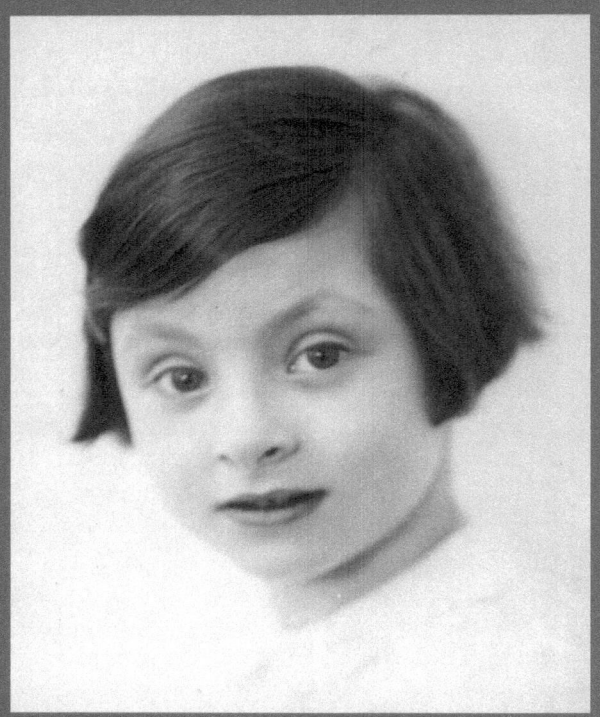

Dr. Alice Ilian-Botan
born Alice Braunstein on June 20, 1924

" I believe that fate wanted me to return in old age to the land where I was born. I never would have thought I would, after everything that happened during the war. I was able to come back here and work as a doctor and that was, naturally, a big step in my life. A triumph. "

I was eight years old when we went to Romania. My father had predicted what would happen in Germany, because the Nazis were already holding rallies. Yes, my father had this feeling that we have to go, nothing good awaits us. That's why we moved from Berlin to Bucharest. They were two different worlds. And traumatic for me—uprooting.

My childhood in Berlin? It was wonderful. We had an apartment on Düsseldorfer Strasse in Wilmersdorf. I played in Preussenpark, there was a field of grass there and you could take a blanket and eat your supper in the green field. At six years old, I was put in a private school, where my brother, Egon, also went. We were only a few students per classroom. My parents wanted the teachers to give us more attention than we would get at a public school, where there were 30 children to a classroom. I felt cared for by my parents and never wanted for anything. My childhood years in Berlin were happy. And I never imagined it would be different one day.

I had absolutely no idea why we left Germany at the time. I was too young to understand. And because both parents came with me, it was somehow a consolation that I was not alone. But I cried the entire time over my brother, who stayed behind. Because as a girl eight years younger, I was attached to my brother. I worshiped him. Because he was so big, so smart and knew so much.

We left in October 1932, before Hitler came into power. My brother only had one more year until his *Abitur* and that's why my parents left him with my mother's brother. But after Hitler took power and the Reichstag fire, they had him come to Bucharest right away. He lost a school year like I did, but had luck in that the high school there finished after seven years and not eight. He needed to go to school for one more year and then graduated and went to study at university.

We had private lessons with a teacher, my brother and I each separately, because we were not at the same level. I really resisted learning the language, because I was totally convinced that we were going back to Berlin. I couldn't do anything with it, it had nothing in common with German. The pronunciation was terribly difficult

Alice Braunstein in Berlin, 1928.

Alice Braunstein (right) with a friend, Berlin, 1931.

for me and everyone knew immediately that I was a German speaker. It took years for me to lose my accent and to really speak Romanian in such a way that no one noticed anymore that it wasn't my mother tongue. In the end, I spent all my school years there, graduated, studied medicine for six years and worked for twenty—all in Romanian. It became my second native language.

But the language wasn't the only hurdle in the beginning. I couldn't adjust at all. There was such a great contrast between Germany and Romania, and I felt that even as a young child. Bucharest was still just a big village. It wasn't until 1933 that they started to build apartment buildings. Until then, each family had their own little house with a garden out front and a yard in back. It was rural and was teeming with cats and dogs on the streets and chickens in the yards. When you went outside in Berlin, there were clean, asphalt streets and the buildings stood in a row.

Alice Braunstein with her father, Salomon, and brother, Egon, Bavaria around 1928.

My mother dreamed of having a little house with a garden. But my father disagreed and so we always lived in apartment buildings. With time, even the little houses disappeared and large apartment buildings were built, because the population grew. Even before the war, many people came from the backward provincial areas into the capital city.

My father was born in Romania and studied in Germany, so he

could speak perfect German but he went back after his studies. My mother also came from Romania, but from the Austrian part. The families knew each other, brought the two together and said,

"Now you two will marry."

My father was a man who really enjoyed life and had no desire to get married up to that point. But when he met my mother, he became a very good husband. The wedding was in Berlin because my mother lived there. She had been there since she was two years old and felt like a woman from Berlin.

So, my mother couldn't speak a word of Romanian, but my father could speak such good German that they spoke to each other in German, until we went to Romania. As in Berlin, my father was a building engineer in Bucharest. It wasn't a problem because he worked with his own capital. He got contracts from the state, hired workers and ordered the materials. And once the construction was done, he presented an invoice and was reimbursed for everything he put in, plus a charge for his services. It went well at first. Then later it didn't anymore.

I was "the German girl" in my class at first. Then I became "the Jewish girl." Romania joined the war on the side of the Germans, so the anti-Semitic laws came there, too. From 1939 my father couldn't work anymore, my brother had to stop his studies, and I wasn't allowed to go to school anymore. When my father went to enroll me for the next school year, he was turned away.

"We cannot keep your daughter here anymore, because she is a Jew," the director told him as she cried.

She regretted it so much because the Jewish children were the best students in all the classes. The teachers got no satisfaction from the fact that we were turned away from school. On the contrary, they were very sorry about it. Most of the teachers were not inclined to be anti-Semitic. Only one teacher sponsored a student who was a member of the Nazi party. Officially, students were prohibited from joining a political party, but this girl wore the cross around her neck regardless. She was the only one, the others didn't approve of her comments against us. In the end, there were only two of us Jewish girls left in the class.

We didn't have to wear the yellow Star of David, but of course we felt alienated by the fact that we couldn't go to the Romanian school anymore. The community center in Bucharest set up schools for us and for the Jewish teachers, who had also been thrown out. So, we stayed among ourselves, among Jewish children in the Jewish school. I completed my last three years and took the *Abitur* there.

Alice Braunstein after finishing the Abitur, Bucharest, 1944.

In addition to the fact that Jews couldn't work after 1939, they weren't allowed to go to school or college anymore, and weren't hired anymore. They were also dispossessed of their property. In 1913, my grandfather had a very beautiful, large house built in Iasi, in northern Moldavia. It was called *Palais Braunstein* and the location where it stood was very valuable because it was right in the middle of the city. My father would have inherited a portion of this family property as the youngest of seven children. But it was taken from us, without compensation even to this day. The Romanians gave the apartments back after the war, but not the houses. I saw ours for the first and last time in the fifties.

Once my father wasn't allowed to work anymore, he also lost his capital. And so everything with any value was sold. Everything that we once had was eaten up during the time of the war. We had to be very, very frugal with our funds. To which nothing was added, but only ever spent. They were hungry years during the war in Romania.

My father wasn't at all inclined to be political, my mother even less so, and I wasn't either. My brother studied architecture and wasn't allowed to complete his degree. Someone hired him at the railroad. Through that job he made contacts to the illegal communist party and joined. We had no idea, because it was kept totally silent. Thank God no one caught him. Otherwise he would have gone to jail. Who knows what they would've done with him. Later his party membership served him well and he became secretary of the communist government. I was surprised they put him, a Jew, in such a position.

After the war, I was also in the communist party for a while. No one had a choice, you only advanced if you danced along to the music. We were also convinced that communism was good. It brings us equality, there is no anti-Semitism anymore, everyone is paid according to his ability. We only realized they were empty words later. My brother was naturally the most deeply disappointed, although he could have had a career in communism. But then he saw that it was all lies and deception, that they had betrayed the people.

The war was over for Romania on August 23, 1944, but the end of the war wasn't fun for us. The Germans were still in Romania, they occupied it. Then the Americans came and bombed us to chase the Germans away. And likewise, the Germans bombed us to keep the Americans back. Then Romania allied with Russia, which ended the German occupation. Instead we had the Russians.

The anti-Semitic laws were abolished and we could live a normal life again. If you can call life after the war normal. I finished my first year of medicine at the Jewish college. It was recognized because I could prove that we were taught the same material and took the same exams as my colleagues in the Romanian school. It did allow us to go directly into the next year of medicine, but we were less prepared. The basic subjects of the first two years are anatomy, physiology, chemistry—and you need labs and dissecting rooms for that. But we didn't have any and we, therefore, couldn't work on corpses. So the Romanians were ahead of us. But we Jewish students had colossal ambition. We bought corpse parts from pathology and brought them to a colleague. Her family had a large house with unheated rooms. It was winter and the five or six of us worked in the cold in our coats. One of us had the anatomy book and read aloud and one would dissect. The others looked on.

Our new fellow students reacted differently to us. One of the girls was of German descent, she never spoke to me. Not one word. That was painful. But the others were nice. One of my classmates was a very nice boy, from a Boyar family. Boyars were the large estate owners. His conduct was impeccable. We took all our exams together the entire year and that really connected us.

After the end of the war, what happened in the camps reached us. They showed us films, Russian films, because we were still occupied by the Russians. We saw what happened in Germany. We didn't lose any relatives. Other than my father, no one else in his family was still in Romania. Many managed to emigrate before the war, so I have relatives in Italy, France, Switzerland and Brazil. We stayed in Bucharest, however, because we weren't allowed to leave. We also didn't have anywhere we could have gone. My parents weren't Zionists. Those who tried to go to Palestine back then were caught at the border. Everything was taken from them and then they threw them in jail.

When I took the state exam, I married my first husband in 1949. We were classmates, we both prepared for the clinical laboratory, both did a specialization course in microbiology and chemistry and then did scientific work. When people were qualified in the field like that, they could lay claim to a job working at a lab in Bucharest. That was forced upon us both. We wanted to be internists. But then, they would have sent us straight to the country. And if you were out there, it was over. I got my doctorate in 1952, but I could work before then. During communism, there were naturally no private practices, but instead there were outpatient clinics and everyone was only ever just a hired doctor. I was an assistant in epidemiology. That was nice. But after three years they let me go, so then I worked in a clinical laboratory.

In 1969, 200 doctors in Bucharest were cut from their positions. The government made jobs available out in rural areas because they wanted people to go there. The problem with that is that some of those jobs only existed on paper. But anyone who didn't go was without a job and without an income. That wasn't just against the Jews, their own people were affected too, but it also affected Jewish doctors, of course. Including me. I went home with tears running down my face. I was 44 and was supposed to just cross my fingers. I ran into a Jewish colleague by chance, who was also affected.

Alice Ilian-Botan and her husband, Felix Botan, Bucharest, 1963.

"You're crying? So, you don't know? We can emigrate to Israel!" he said.

It was like a light that appeared to me. A way, a path I could take, to finally get out of Romania. We had permission to go to Israel because the Romanians got good money from the Americans for us. Suddenly they couldn't wait to see us leave. That was in 1971.

I was 32 and my husband 34 when we divorced after seven years. He had long remarried and emigrated to Israel a little before

I did.

I was with my second husband for 20 years, married for ten of them. He had begun studying law, but then anti-Semitism came to the universities. It was particularly bad in the field of law, they even beat the Jews. He was forced to withdraw. He was very intelligent, spoke five languages and later earned a living as a translator. When Israel came up, he said, "What should I do in Israel? I'm an old man." He was 64 back then and I was 44.

"Israel is not a communist country," I told him. "And with your language skills, you can survive anywhere in the world. You'll see." And he got a job before I did, in fact! He found a job with a newspaper (there were Romanian newspapers, there were a lot of Romanians in Israel) at a leather factory doing bookkeeping. His boss was Romanian, so he didn't have to learn the Hebrew language anymore. And I worked incredibly hard until I could speak it. There was an intensive language course in the *Ulpan* (see page 267) available to people with academic titles and we also didn't have to pay for it. Israel needed us, they had too few doctors and the population was growing. I didn't just have to learn the language, I also had to get to know Israeli medications. That took me three months of work in a hospital in Afula. It took a while before I got a job as a general practitioner at an outpatient clinic. That was finally what I'd always wanted to do! Although it was under conditions I never dreamed of—every patient spoke another language. But working in Israel wasn't a problem. Romanian doctors were appreciated. As opposed to those who came from Russia, they were often *feldshers* (see page 244) or nurses who bought diplomas and went to Israel as doctors.

We initially lived in Nazareth. We were only interested in living in northern Israel. Then a spot at that outpatient clinic opened up in Qiryat Haim, where we already had an apartment. My husband had to take two buses to get to his job. But he managed and was very proud that he had a job before I did. He opened our first bank account with his pay. That's important to a man. We had support from the state in the beginning and this apartment in a

Alice Ilian-Botan in Tel Aviv, 1981.

new building. The beach and the sea were out front! After renting the apartment for one year, we could buy it. We paid the price in installments and they were less than the rent. We also had 20 years to pay it off. When my husband died in 1980 (he had Parkinson's disease) and I went to Germany a year later, I kept the apartment for another ten years. I went back every year. Then it just turned out that I was going to stay here forever, so I sold it. It was very hard for me. I cried. I really cried.

My first homeland was Germany. I was born and grew up there. German is my native language. But Israel is my second home because that country brought me out of the misery that I experienced in Romania. And I felt very comfortable—finally a country where there is no anti-Semitism. In Romania, you never knew what the Romanian person sitting next to you was thinking. Things were worse during communism than before the war. Life with communism was a prison. Much worse than in East Germany. I met Germans from the German Democratic Republic who came to Romania for vacation. For me, these encounters with German people were overwhelming. My parents' best friends, from before the war, were a German couple who lived in the same building as us in Berlin. The woman couldn't bear children and when I came into the world, she was so crazy about me that she said to my mother,

"Give me the little one! You already have one child. And I have no children!"

Of course, she didn't give me up. But that's how close the friendship was. That always stuck with me, friendship with German people. Back then, there was no "you're a Jew, I'm a Christian." Of course, people have totally negative feelings toward the people who carried out the genocide against the Jews, but my childhood is connected to a Germany that was different from Hitler's Germany.

I grew up without knowing what Jews and Christians were. We celebrated the Christian holidays, Easter and Christmas. I knew almost nothing about the Jewish holidays, like what significance they have, which I didn't learn until I was in Israel. My father only went to the synagogue once a year, and that was on the new year. My mother didn't go, and we children were not urged to do it either. When I got to know the Jewish traditions in Israel, I was sorry that I hadn't already learned anything about it in my parent's home.

Germany, Romania, Israel, Germany—the circle is complete. But I could have done without Romania. Romania was never my homeland, although I spent half of my life there and spoke the language like a second mother tongue. Even today there is no reason for me to go back there. Because I don't have anyone there anymore. And I'll never forgive the Romanians for the meanness of stripping me of my pension when we left. How could they do that to a person? To punish them for leaving the country? Twenty years of work and not one penny of a pension.

But even with an Israeli pension, I couldn't live in Israel. I worked there for ten years and got a minimal pension. So, the alternative was to go to Germany to work for a few more years. When I did in fact come in 1981, it never occurred to me that I would stay. They were looking for doctors here. Fate ensured that a position would become available in a city where some friends from Israel had also settled, Bad Oeynhausen in North Rhine-Westphalia. I worked there as an internist at a wellness clinic. I was paid much better than in Israel and that was good for my budget. But after three years, I developed labyrinthine hearing loss, losing 50% of my ability to hear and had to give the job up. A lawyer told me that I could receive a pension in Germany too, but,

"To do that, you need to attain German citizenship. And then you have to relinquish your Israeli citizenship."

Giving up my Israeli passport was horrible. I had my apartment and my friends in Israel. But what was I supposed to do? So, I said yes, and there were no difficulties because I could prove that I was born in Germany. I went to Munich. I didn't want to go to Berlin, because it's such a big city, I would have felt lost. It probably also would have depressed me that I don't have anyone there anymore.

I believe that fate wanted me to return in old age to the land where I was born. I never would have thought I would, after everything that happened during the war. I was able to come back here and work as a doctor, and that was naturally a big step in my life. A triumph. My life was definitely an odyssey. I have so often stood on the edge of a precipice. But I've learned over the course of my life that somewhere there is someone to thank for protecting me. First of all, for the fact that we left Germany and that we survived. I have my father to thank, because in doing that he saved us from certain death. Second, that we spent that time during the war in

Romania without anyone coming to any harm, that is, apart from being so reduced to poverty that we were down to our last penny. But in spite of that, I was able to study and was allowed to choose my profession. Third, that I was able to leave Romania and go to Israel where there was freedom. And that I was then able to go to Germany—again, a step forward. I can actually be happy that fate saved me so many times. That is why I'm not bitter. I'm grateful for my fate. Even though a lot of unjust things happened to me in life.

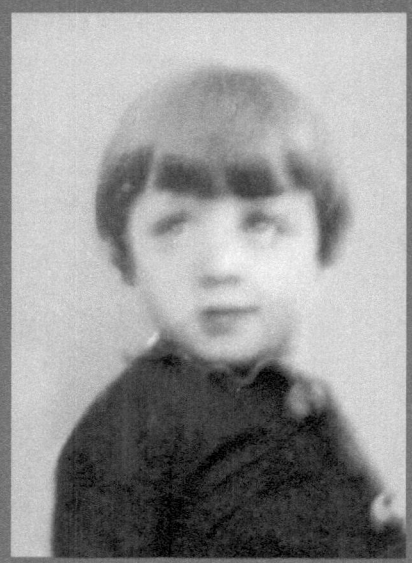

Ruth Stadnik Goldstein
born Ruth Kochmann on January 9, 1936

> "Be happy that Adolf Hitler was here," said a woman to me. "He did something good for you. Now you can speak so many languages, because you went all over the world." I was shocked. But that's how it was. That was about 30 years ago, but if someone had said that to me when I arrived in 1959, I would have left again.

In the middle of 1938, there was a great party with a lot of children and they were all running around with those nice swastika flags. I wanted a flag too, but my parents wouldn't let me. I cried bitter tears and couldn't understand why not. At the end of 1938 I also didn't understand why I couldn't go to the *Kindergarten* in Schillerstrasse anymore. The director called my mother in and told her that since I was Jewish, I wasn't allowed to go anymore.

"You'll stay home now," my *Mutti* said, "and you'll play with Marianne."

Marianne was my German nanny, who was very nice. I still remember her—tall, blond, blue eyes. And my father even had a servant—and this is important to mention, because it helped him in his work later in South America—who served food wearing white gloves. I was very seldom allowed to eat with my parents. I always ate with Marianne in the kitchen. My father was a banker and my mother was a physiotherapist in the Neukölln hospital. They married in the synagogue on Oranienburger Strasse at the beginning of 1935.

My father really loved playing Skat and always went to a bar and played a game. One day the proprietor suddenly told him,

"Herr Kochmann, raid! I can't stand up for you."

The SS came looking for Jews, and he hid in a garbage can. Thank God, they didn't find him. But he didn't come home. I didn't see him anymore, and I also no longer remember the explanation I was given.

Then my mother and I lived on Mommsenstrasse, on Uhlandstrasse and on Giesebrechtstrasse. That was very dangerous then, because many Jews lived there and there were often raids. The last three weeks before we went underground, we still lived in Zehlendorf, in my Aunt Friedel's villa. She was a Christian and my father's brother's housekeeper. They married, had two children and lived in the fantastic Schinkel-designed villa on the lake called Schlachtensee Lake. The house is still listed on a historical register. He was a director at Tietz (department store) and lost his job, of course. One

Ruth Kochmann in Berlin at the end of 1938.

morning he went to the Schlachtensee. He wasn't a swimmer. He went into the water and took his own life so as not to endanger his wife and children. That was at the end of 1936. The laws that also persecuted children from "mixed marriages" came later. His widow sent her son to London. He changed his name there and later went to America. But the daughter, Barbara, she was taken and killed in Theresienstadt.

Aunt Friedel always tried to help my grandparents with food. One day she wanted to go there and she saw that there was a raid on Rosenheimer Strasse (they must have been living in a Jewish building). They took everyone away. My grandmother made a discreet hand movement that Aunt Friedel shouldn't come any closer to keep her from getting into trouble. She told me all of this when I came to Berlin in 1959. She also hoarded everything, otherwise I would have nothing at all left, even photos.

At the beginning of 1939, I was three, and was taken from the villa to Marianne's. All she told me was that I would live with her now. My mother was hidden by a doctor from the Neukölln hospital. But she couldn't stay with him long, it would have been too big a risk for him. She had gotten word through another banker, who wasn't Jewish, that my father was able to flee to Marseille. He probably always had money on him and (I learned later) also diamonds hidden in a jam jar. We were supposed to follow. The same doctor helped us again and gave me anesthetic drops so that I wouldn't move. I had light hair and blue eyes, but my mother was dark and therefore wore a blond wig. There was a check point, but we were lucky. I don't know if she had fake papers, she never spoke about it again. These people suppressed everything. My father was haunted by it as long as he lived. But no one talked about it. They didn't tell any of us what happened here and what they went through. And how much family they lost.

We arrived in Marseille and went to a hotel. Everyone had a mattress and my parents put me in the middle so I wouldn't freeze. All of a sudden, my mother said,

"I'm itching! I'm itching!"

Bugs. We moved out and walked the whole night from one café to another one at the Arc de Triomphe. And I just cried. Then we went to the Jewish Agency, which arranged all the transports back then. At some point, there were two ships, one went to Palestine and one went to Argentina. My father was not a Zionist, a very good Jew maybe, but not a Zionist. I'm still sorry that we didn't go to Palestine. But he gave everything he still had to buy passage and a visa for Argentina. I told the people at the docks,

"Ruthy, shippy, Argentina."

We were on that ship for forty days. I always sat at my parents' table and ate really well. The captain was really delighted with me and my behavior, so much so that we didn't have to sleep with ten people in a cabin anymore, we got one just for us. Still, my mother was pretty distraught and didn't want to disembark. She kept saying,

"There are monkeys in Argentina."

What did we know about Argentina? There was an icy, wet cold in Buenos Aires and we had only the clothes on our backs. I had a little sailor jacket on. And the dress underneath, I wore that for three or four years. We had nothing, absolutely nothing.

The Jewish benevolent society housed my parents in a terrible room and me in a home for Jewish immigrant children who had come with the *Kindertransport*. I just remember that we were always standing in line, open mouth, spoon in, cod liver oil, open mouth, spoon in, cod liver oil. Eating was chaotic for me, coming from a refined family. That was not easy for me. My parents visited me on the weekends, and then I got a chocolate! We had an emigrant café in Buenos Aires and we went there every Saturday. My parents ordered coffee for themselves, but no cake so that Ruth could get a little piece of cake. Later, there was another café and a club in the summer. We were there as children. All of us were immigrants, all of us were Jews.

My father was thrown out of several jobs. He was a banker and couldn't work with his hands, but he did try. He worked with a glazier and every evening my mother pulled the shards and splinters from his fingers. He was distraught. Then he applied to the banks, but he had no Spanish skills. So, he started learning Spanish.

My mother had better luck. She went to the hotels where the rich Americans were and said she could do massages and could someone please just give her a chance. She sometimes gave six or seven full massages in the heat. And she could also administer intramuscular shots—in Argentina people had shots more than they took tablets. She bought herself a bicycle, such an old thing, and drove all over on it giving shots. She kept our heads just above water.

When my father sold shoelaces and candy at a stand, he earned a little bit of money. And then they pulled me out of the children's home. I was five and a half and very happy. We lived in one room and didn't even have a kitchen, just a *Primus*, a Bunsen burner. My father bought a suitcase, a really old one from a flea market. He took a handkerchief and laid it on top as a table cloth. And since we had no closet, we always put our stuff in that suitcase. That is emigration. He also worked as a waiter for a wealthy family, because he knew how to serve wearing white gloves. And he was allowed to take food home, one meal. There was little money, but we had food. Later we earned money together in the summers. He would put on a hat and stand with a llama and I would play the drums.

When I was still very young, the Argentinians called me "Alemanita," which means "little German girl."

"Alemanita baila—dance!"

And I danced, "Hänschen klein, Häschen in der Grube," I jumped and did it. Then they gave me *dulce de leche*, which is like Nutella. And the animal innards that they normally gave the cat. Argentina is the land of meat; they don't have to eat the innards. They always threw them away, but then they gave them to me, wrapped in newspaper, and I brought them to my parents. I was always very proud. And so, we occasionally ate these innards. I'll never forget that. I never would have eaten them in Berlin. I wouldn't have needed to. My parents also wouldn't have needed to eat on a suitcase, my father wouldn't have had to sell shoelaces and candy.

I did everything. I shined shoes at six or seven years old. In

Ruth Kochmann with her father, Hans, in Buenos Aires, 1956.

South America, there are shoe shiners with boxes and I had one, too. I had my cloth, my brush and I shined shoes. People always came to me—I was very bright and blond. Sometimes they gave me small tips, and I took that back home. How was it? It was necessary. That was life. There was something else that wasn't easy for me. We needed kerosene for the *Primus* stove, it was a reddish liquid. A big truck delivered it at 8 in the morning. There would be sixty people standing there to fill one bottle. Some people had bad luck, and everything was gone by the time they came to get some. I often stood there for two or three hours, freezing. It was cold and damp, and I was still very little. But then I was proud, I came home with my bottle and gave it to my parents and they turned on the little oven. Then we put a pot of water and put eucalyptus in it to make it smell good. There were still no heaters for poor people then. And no air conditioning in the summer. My parents lay there and were soaking wet, at 104 to 107 degrees. My mother dipped a sheet in alcohol and wrapped herself in it while the fan ran.

It was all difficult. Very difficult. We were very poor and sometimes lived with rats.

I went to the Pestalozzi school, a school for immigrants. I can only remember Jewish children; we didn't mix with the Argentinians. We all went to that school, it was free, and my father always said,

"We don't have any money, but you'll get a good education."

In the summer, we were sent to summer camps, which were also free. It was during Perón's time, and he said,

"The only privileged people in our country are the children."

We wore white overalls and little white hats and we were sad. Because it was far away and the school break lasted three months. That's how long we stayed. When I was 14 I worked as a nanny and looked after children. I also gave tutoring lessons in German and in mathematics in elementary school, which was six years there. When I was in fifth grade, I taught children from the second grade. And I cleaned, babysat and delivered flowers. I took on every job. Until it wasn't necessary anymore, but that took a long time.

Until then, we lived in a sublet with a man whose wife was a Christian and stayed in Germany. He emigrated with his daughter, and Marion is still my best friend in Argentina today. We moved into his small apartment and he gave us only one condition—that my mother took care of Marion as she did me. I grew up with her. There was a lot of noise, we argued often. But then we were like sisters. We lived there for at least three years, my parents and I in one room.

But when the Nazis went into the Netherlands, the Dutch bank in Bueno Aires wrote to my father that he should start working there. He did his training at a Dutch bank in Berlin. And when all the Germans in Argentina who weren't Jews were kicked out of the banks, he worked his way up, right up to being authorized signatory. That was in 1944 and my father was 34. My mother was 37 and continued to work giving shots and massages. Things were improving a little. We could finally afford a small two-room apartment.

Ruth Kochmann on the beach, Buenos Aires, 1955.

At 12 years old, I went to the English Belgrano Girl's School. I learned perfect English there and Spanish, and I also took my *Abitur* in Spanish. I always spoke to my parents in German at home. But not in public, my father didn't want that. He had no contact to Germany any more, but he always said,

"If a letter ever comes from Germany, call me at the bank."

And one day such a letter arrived, from the Red Cross. I called him. My father came immediately then said I should leave the room. After an hour, I went back in. He sat there and cried horribly. His parents. They didn't get out. Killed in Auschwitz. My *Oma*, she was an opera singer who had eight siblings—all killed in Auschwitz. And they had all laughed at first at my father for leaving. Their names are in the Jewish Museum in Berlin today.

My mother's father was a mason in the Humanitas lodge. They helped hide him and my grandmother and they got out of Germany in 1943 and came to us in Buenos Aires. They were in a Jewish old-age home there, but didn't live much longer. It was all too much for them.

I wanted to become a pediatrician, it was my passion. But in Argentina people don't get the same help that they get in Germany. So, there was no money available. My parents didn't have much themselves, so I didn't want to ask them for any. Then I considered learning to become a nurse at a German hospital, because that was the best training. I had already applied and met a man at a party there. He was a businessman and Jewish, his family was from Bamberg. We married in Buenos Aires in 1957. I was 21 and had meanwhile completed training as a preschool teacher. My daughter was born in January 1959. A half year later, we were on a ship, a freighter because it was cheaper, going to Germany.

I only wanted to visit. There was no way I wanted to come here to stay. I wanted to go back, definitely. We kept our apartment in Argentina. But my husband was speechless when he saw the economic wonder there. He was really excited, everything was great here, everything was marvelous. All of a sudden, he had a beautiful life, bought a car right away and a canoe. He was very charming and very good looking, so after another half year, he left me. The marriage fell apart in 1960. We had each received 3,000 German marks for returning. But I was naive. I was stupid. He put our 6,000 marks in an account at the Deutsche Bank in Hamburg. When I went there, they said,

"Your husband was here. He withdrew everything."

I had nothing. Nothing at all. I was pretty embittered. I was there all alone with my child and was finished with men. He went back to Argentina.

I then lived on Fuggerstrasse in Berlin, in a hotel room with a woman who was terrible to me. Finally, I went to the Jewish community center and met Herr Galinski.

"You're a preschool teacher? Brilliant! Can you stay?"

There were very few Jews in Berlin. But Heinz Galinski loved children, he wanted to start a Jewish kindergarten. We started with 16 children. Most of them were from Bolivia, Columbia and Brazil—these were children of emigrants who had come back. And

I could always bring my daughter, that's how she knows the families of the children she now has in kindergarten. She has been a kindergarten teacher there for more than 30 years.

Back then we were all on the fourth floor at Joachimsthaler Strasse 13, the kindergarten, the secretary, and Heinz Galinski had his office there. He was very respectable toward me. He even helped me get an apartment with two and a half rooms on Ansbacherstrasse. And after I worked at Joachimsthalerstrasse for three years, he gave me an opportunity to train on the job as a kindergarten teacher in the Pestalozzi-Fröbel building. When I was finished, I had a German certificate. I took that to the senate and worked hard to go from kindergarten teacher to the head of all early childhood day care in the Tiergarten district. I worked in the schools until I was 59 and then cared for older people until I was 69.

The fact that I am Jewish was never a secret. Most people were very nice to me in the beginning. Was it out of a guilty conscience? But I also had other experiences, like hearing,

"Ach, you're a Jew. The Jews all have brown hair. And you do have a hook nose."

Those are sentences that stick in my memory. I was sent to a wellness clinic and we sat around a table and talked. I talked about how I know more than one language.

"There, see? Be happy that Adolf Hitler was here," said a woman to me. "He did something good for you. Now you can speak so many languages because you went all over the world." I was shocked. But that kind of thing happened. That was about 30 years ago, but if someone had said that to me when I arrived in 1959, I would have left again. I also wouldn't have returned to Germany, had I known what happened here between 1933 and 1945. I did get more religious once I found out.

I also got more religious because we are a minority here. And I need to go to services! In Israel, I don't go to synagogue, I'm in the Jewish country. I always feel there like I do here on *Shabbat*. But here I need the unity, to know that the people around me are also Jewish. I always go very happily to *Shabbat* here on Fridays. Why?

Ruth Goldstein in Berlin, 1961.

Because we all sit together, have a nice meal, prayer, a rabbi comes, sings the songs, the men wear Kippas, and we are safe.

I've been to Israel a lot; the first time was in 1962. I would have stayed! But Heinz Galinski didn't want me to leave Germany, so I listened. Well, I did have a good income and a good Jewish life here. There was no anti-Semitism then, or I didn't sense it anyway. It probably existed though. But we were all happy and content. And one day, my friend said to me,

"Come with me! There's a Hanukkah Ball in Schöneberg."

And that's how I met my husband, Kasimir. It was 1963. I was 27 and he was 40. He was a businessman and always a good person. We have been living in a Jewish old-age home since 2009, in two apartments next to each other. I couldn't take care of him anymore. He needs insulin shots. He is originally from Russia, and he is very happy in the old-age home. Every week he meets with his veteran friends, these are the officers who came to Berlin at that time. And every May 1st they are all invited to the Russian embassy.

Back then, I came back to Germany to look at Berlin, where I was born, the streets where my kindergarten and my parents' apartment were. And because I wanted my reparations. But when I tried to get the reparations, the man responsible for administering them said to me,

"The deadline has passed."

How could he say that? He can say that when I'm dead.

"I'm alive," I said to him. "But I've been through enough and I have nothing."

"The deadline has passed."

I will never forget that sentence. That was the worst. If I'd known, I never would have come back.

I was born in Germany, but my homeland is Israel. Although I never went there to live. I was little, I wasn't consulted. We went to Argentina instead, and I feel like a part of that country. I am grateful that they didn't send us back. We were able to survive, even if we had a very difficult time. Many emigrants couldn't deal with such a difficult situation. They were lawyers, they were doctors, but they couldn't speak the language, or they would have had to study again. Many took their own lives. I'm living in Germany again, but I cannot feel like a German woman. I lost everything here. I was chased out of here. I have lived here since 1959, but I have no relationship with Germany. Especially not now, when it's become so bad with the extreme right and Islamists. We used to be free, today we live in the Jewish old-age home like it was a ghetto, behind a gate and protected by the police. When I was still working in the kindergarten we could take the children everywhere. If my daughter wants to take the children on a field trip today, she has to ask the police first if they have enough people to accompany them. And when the children take the bus home, the driver takes different routes. It's too risky.

I don't have any contact with the outside world anymore, especially not with Germans. I am only in contact with Jewish people. But there is no future for Jews here. At this moment, when the youth are no longer free to practice their religion, but are instead under threat—there is no future here. My grandson can't go out with his *kippah* (see page 252), or with his *tallit* (see page 265). He was in America and there it was all natural. He was very happy in New York. He put his *kippah* on in the airport. It also wasn't a problem in Argentina. But here it's dangerous. Who would have thought that we'd have to live through this anti-Semitism again in Germany?

Ruth Wolff-Stirner
born Ruth Wolff on December 27, 1946

" In Israel, we were stateless. When we came back to Germany my father was repatriated and I was naturalized. I have a German passport. But what I am, I don't know. What is my homeland? It's where my family is, but I don't have any left. "

I have no relatives, not one person. I definitely had a lot of family who died. But I can't research who they were, because I have no names. There is no one who can tell me where I come from.

My father was born in Maria Alois in 1883, which is currently in Poland. They were a Jewish family. I don't know whether, or not they were pious. I don't know anything about his family, I was just too young.

He was in several concentration camps until he got lucky and got out of the Dachau (see page 242) concentration camp. He was able to flee because there was a doctor. He had to buy medicine and took my father with him. He pressed a boat ticket in his hand and said,

"Get out of here!"

He took a transport ship to Shanghai and landed in the ghetto in Hongkou. He met my mother there, a woman from Berlin who was divorced from an American with whom she had lived in America, who then also went to Germany, but could no longer go back because she had a heart valve defect. They didn't let sick people in back then. She fled to Shanghai and had to stay there at first. The two of them married in the ghetto and, besides me, had a son. He was hit during an attack, while in the arms of my mother, or father, and died. I don't know if he was younger or older. I was two years old when we left there.

I still had two half-brothers from my father's first marriage. They lived in Hamburg and in Israel and were much older than I am because my father was 64 when he had me. They were going on 50 and weren't that interesting to me. I did meet them both, but I don't remember the one in Israel anymore because he wasn't especially friendly toward our family. We traveled from Shanghai to stay with him in 1948, when the country was founded. He wasn't happy to receive us, and then he even threw my mother and me out. My father was looking for work to be able to survive in Israel and his son threw us out of the house while he was gone. We waited until my father came back, mother and I, somewhere at a bus stop.

We went to Jerusalem because my father had found work there.

He was an interior decorator, even before the war. Where did we live? In the first house in no man's land. A section where there was absolutely nothing. Only barbed wire. We could see directly over it into Jordan.

I learned Hebrew on the streets and then later in school. My parents couldn't speak it. I spoke German with them. I also learned a little English. There was every kind of immigrant possible from different nations there. As a child, I never thought about which children to play with, we didn't care whether they came from Israel or Germany or Poland or Russia.

My mother became sick very quickly. Because of the unhygienic living conditions in Shanghai, her liver became infected and she died at the age of 46. That was in 1954 and I was eight. My father kept me away from her. I didn't see her anymore after she was taken to the hospital. He also didn't take me to the funeral because he thought I was too young.

I was a day student at a boarding school run by Finnish nuns and lived at home. It wasn't far from us. After my mother's death, I was taken in as a boarder. Israel was nice for as long as I was with my parents. I didn't do that well at boarding school. For example, I didn't want to eat spinach and was forced to do so there. I vomited onto the plate and then had to eat it again. And red beets, they disgusted me and I threw them up. The sisters told me I could not leave the table until I had eaten it. It was a disaster. No, it was not a good time. We also had earthquakes and were sitting in the cellar when the well in our courtyard collapsed. And then came the Sinai War. It was bad because we constantly had to hide somewhere. Even as a child I sensed the threat. I always saw my father on the weekends. He just worked, had to work here and there. I don't think he had any friends. I don't remember any. Or that people visited him. His family had died, his first wife died in Majdanek (see page 255). I don't know whether or how my parents heard about what had happened in Germany, what happened in the camps, after the war. I only know that my father definitely wanted to go back. That is what he always said to me: that we were going back to Germany again. Because it's so beautiful there. The landscape is so beautiful. He only waited until he had enough money saved up. He wanted to go to Munich and nowhere else. So close to Dachau, I could never grasp it later myself. What drove him there?

We left for Germany in 1957. I wasn't happy to leave Israel. By then I liked it. I had my friends there. But at some point, I had to say *auf Wiedersehen* to the children and nuns. We went by ship and traveled to Genoa, then took the train to Munich from there. We came into the train station on track 11. That was the track for immigrants for many years after our arrival. The long-distance trains came into track 11, bringing a whole lot of foreigners. There was an Inner Mission (religious social organization) for them, whose employees brought the people down and found housing for them. And that's how we were received as well.

My father went to the Jewish community center and received support from them in the beginning. We found a room right near the main train station. I was totally happy because the family from whom we sublet also had a girl and she and I quickly became playmates. There was another girl across the way with whom I also became friends. We walked home together from school and did our homework together as well. So, that worked out really nicely.

I was enrolled in a normal school. I could speak German, because I spoke German to my parents. I could speak it, but I wasn't so good at writing. But I didn't want to stay back a year and repeat the fourth grade again, I already finished it in Israel. I was permitted to start fifth grade, but had to promise that I could improve my German quickly. And I did, too. My father sat down with me and I studied hard. And I never stayed back a year, not once.

When our building was torn down, we moved right around the corner. We had another room we sublet there. I lived there until my father died. It happened in 1960, he was 77. He had an infection in both lungs. He'd had tuberculosis when he was in the concentration camp and was never really healthy again. When I realized how bad he was getting, I told him he should call a doctor. But he was terribly afraid of doctors. He didn't want a doctor. We had one in the school who examined us regularly. I went to him at some point and told him he had to come to my father. Naturally, he admitted him to a hospital. But for my father, a hospital was tantamount to death. He was sent home after 14 days. He had a relapse and went to another hospital. And that is where he actually died. I only have one memory from that time impressed upon my mind, my career choice. Because on his deathbed, he said,

"My God, what will become of you?"

He had always tried to get reparations. He did know that my mother was well off and that I had already received part of her wealth in Israel. We used it to leave.

"I cannot die in peace," he said. "I'm so worried about you."

So, I told him he didn't have to worry. I will go to our lawyer to train with her. I was always with him whenever he went to see her. And one day she told me that I should ask around my class if any of the girls would be interested in training to become a legal assistant after eighth grade, after getting a lower secondary school certificate. That was right before my father went into the hospital. Then I told him he shouldn't worry, I won't even ask the other girls first. I'll do the training myself. So, that's what I did, and at 13, I was the youngest trainee in Munich at the time. After three years, I was what we call a paralegal today.

I actually wanted to become a childcare worker. But I couldn't keep going to school. I had neither money nor anyone to motivate me. I had no other choice but to begin job training. I also couldn't continue living in our sublet room because I was a minor. Now the child welfare office was responsible for me because I had no one with parental authority anymore and needed a guardian.

When I asked my father why I wasn't baptized and why, whenever a question about religion came up, there was none assigned to me, while others were Protestant or Catholic, he said,

"That was deliberate. You will be able to choose which faith you would like to join for yourself at 14. You are totally independent in that regard. I do not want what happened to me to happen to you."

He was baptized as a Catholic out of pure fear that he would always be persecuted as a Jew. He hoped he wouldn't have to be afraid anymore. It didn't make a difference to him, of course. That's why he said he didn't want what happened to him to happen to me. He didn't want me to have the wrong faith and therefore be persecuted.

And so, I had no idea about Judaism. I have been in a synagogue, back in Israel. Only because my class went, although our boarding school was Christian. But they left it open for others to practice their faiths. But I never took any of that seriously. For me they were multifaceted events, and the stories that were told there were also interesting. But I never connected them with the feeling that I'm a Jewish woman. Not at all.

In the school in Munich I also had a free hour while everyone else was in religion class. There was no class taught on the Jewish religion. There were Protestant and Catholic classes. I went to either class during that school hour. I went to one faith or the other one—it didn't matter to me. Then in the end I liked the Catholic class better, because they'd just had the year with communion. Pretty white dresses and white candles and the children studied for the communion. I found that really great. That made an impression on me.

I was baptized Catholic when I was 12 or 13. I just wanted to belong. I also wanted to go to a confirmation and also to have a white dress and a candle. But I had never had communion. I had never in my life gone to confession. That was the condition though, that you had to confess to your sins first and then receive absolution with communion. I was baptized one or two days before, and through that had no more sins that I had to confess and was then allowed to receive communion at the confirmation. Because I liked everything so much and because I paid such good attention, the teacher, the catechist, took a special liking to me. She supported me after my father's death. Otherwise, I had no one. No adult person with whom I would have been friends. I only had a few school friends, and their parents didn't care about me. This teacher practically took me in hand and dealt with everything. And then she took over guardianship. That way I wouldn't have to have a stranger from the child welfare office as a guardian. She knew me all those years already and later, when it came out that my father had left me money, she set up a secure savings account for me.

I had to move into a girl's home then, also in Munich. I went to job training during the day and to the home at night. I was already familiar with dorm life from Israel. It wasn't that abnormal for me because I already knew how it was. The only thing I wasn't familiar with were the nuns. The Catholic sisters. But I also had a young, nice one who cared for me a lot. I really liked her a lot, I felt really secure with her. And I also had a lot of privileges. I don't know the reason. But if I asked for something, like that I'd like to go here and there, it was always, "yes." Naturally, I also lied, saying that I was invited to meet this or that person in the afternoon, and could I go. I really went dancing for two hours. People did things like that then. But the nuns had a terrific amount of trust in me and I actually rarely took advantage of that. I might have told a fib once in a while, but no more than that. Others were real problem children who ran away at night and were brought back by the police. Those things happened too. But not with me.

You just had to get to know these other girls first. I did get to know one, she went to the same class as I did at the vocational school, she had the same job as me. She was the only one with whom I had closer contact. Today, I don't remember any of the girls from that time. It was over once I left there.

I could rent my own room at 16. With the help of my guardian, she really helped me a lot. And then she went into a convent and transferred the entire guardianship to a friend of hers. Back then you didn't come of age until 21. She couldn't do it anymore because she was in a strict order and wasn't allowed to leave the convent.

I received very little money during my training. Starting with 50 German marks a month, then 75, then finally 90. My father left me 6,000 marks. The child welfare office kept some of it for my care during the three years that I spent in the home. But after I left the home, my guardian made sure that I could withdraw an allowance of 150 marks every month for my living expenses. I wouldn't have been able to survive on what I earned as a starting salary.

And then at 17, I had a breakdown. I wanted to see something of the world, to experience something, and went to my sister-in-law in Hamburg. My father completely cut off contact with his son in Israel after he threw my mother and me out. But we visited the son in Hamburg and the relationship was excellent. He died when I was 16, but I still had a good relationship with his wife. I settled in with her until she asked me a few months later if I needed to go home again at some point. I had to admit that I had left everything behind. That's why I don't have my one bag with pictures and a few files in it anymore. I never picked them up from my landlady. Meanwhile, she threw me out because I was three months behind in the rent and I was afraid that if I went back she would call the police, and that I would have to go back to a home.

Then I went back to Munich, looked for a new job because I also left my work suddenly. I started working at a personnel office that needed a paralegal who also had experience in labor law. One day, I ran into my former boss.

"Where did you go?" She asked me. "Why did you stop coming?"

I admitted in tears that I just needed to take some time off. And that I'm terribly unhappy in my new job.

"Come back," she said. "We'll be expecting you."

I was never happier and began working at the firm again. I could sleep on the couch the first few nights and made my breakfast in the kitchen. And the lawyer had looked for an apartment for me on the side. She found a one-room apartment, on the fifth floor, without an elevator. It was affordable back then, 80 marks. She also negotiated a contract for me so that I could be declared fully of age at 18, and then I could handle my affairs myself. I stayed at the firm for a few years, then changed to another one to improve my financial situation. I stopped in January 1, 2012, when I was 65. But I still work there just as before one or two days a week. It's wonderful.

I met my husband in 1981, and we married in 1982. We

were married in a Catholic service. But I became so angry about one Catholic priest that I left the church. That wasn't until later, because I worked for a very Catholic lawyer and thought that I couldn't afford to leave then because I might lose my job. When I didn't have that reason anymore, I left. There was a phase during which I was raised to be a strict Catholic by nuns. In the girls' home I lived in after my father died, I went to church every Sunday and prayed the rosary for the entire month of May. But that never really took root in me. There was always some doubt that surfaced about the stories they told, or that I read, and whether they were all so understandable.

I'm not in any parish today. I just live my life, which is so common here, and have no relationship with any religion. But I do believe that a higher power exists. And I also believe in all the saints and prophets, regardless of whether they are Catholic, Protestant, Jewish or Orthodox, or anything else. I pray too. I go to a synagogue, a mosque, or a church – it doesn't matter to me. And if there is no spiritual person to speak a few words of consolation at my funeral, there will be someone else.

At the end of 2002, I was indeed able to find out more about my family. My mother was pretty well off. My great-grandfather owned a factory in Berlin and had a large estate. When he died, my grandfather and my mother's two brothers became owners of the property.

After the Wall came down, there was a time frame in which you could file a claim with the government. If only I had known. But I didn't know that there was this property claim in the former East Germany. And when I did find out, the legal deadline had passed. It was still possible to submit a goodwill application for my great-grandfather's assets or his heirs. I am, according to the certificates of inheritance that were issued, the only heir after my uncles. Both were deported in 1942 and died childless, from the research. The Jewish Claims Conference accepted my claim and I received payment for a portion of my mother's claim to the property—but only a third of what I was entitled to, because according to the goodwill rules, grandnieces and grandnephews were not granted a claim.

When I was in Shanghai a few years ago, to see where I came from, I tried to find my birth certificate because I don't have one. But everything was lost during the Cultural Revolution, they said. Naturally, I had no memories of Shanghai. But I thought to myself that if we lived there, then things were not good for us. You could see that it was a very poor quarter. I understand why my parents didn't want to stay and why they went to Israel. Twenty seven years after we left Jerusalem, I went back there for the first time. And I still knew exactly where everything was.

In Israel, we were stateless. When we came back to Germany, my father was repatriated and I was naturalized. I have a German passport. But what I am, I don't know. What is my homeland? It's where my family is, but I don't have any left. So, my home can be anywhere.

No, I don't feel embittered. Some people have good fortune, others have it bad. I belong to those who were lucky that I didn't have to experience that time, but instead live in a very peaceful time now. There is no Jewish persecution here. I was able to take my life in my own hands and make something of it. I have a good life in Germany. I have no hatred. I never saw my parents express hatred or anger toward anyone. They didn't let me get a sense of their trauma. Or that they were very unhappy. I knew nothing as a child. My father had a hook nose. He was so badly beaten that the hook got bigger, he said. He had to work hard, that's what he told me. That I knew. But everything else, like the gas chambers, I didn't know about that. Even later, although I lived so close to Dachau, I didn't get it. Now I know what he suffered because I went to Dachau myself. To the concentration camp. To grasp what happened there. You can still see the gas chambers, where the gas came streaming in from above. I caught my breath.

I don't know when my internal change took place. Even ten years ago, the subject didn't interest me. Everything that had been written about the Holocaust bothered me so much that I always said,

"My God, that was 70 years ago, at some point it has to end."

But there can be no end. Now I watch all the films and read all the books. Now I'm moved by it. Terribly moved.

Anni Bober
born Anni Cohen on June 8, 1915

> " Do I feel German? More like Israeli. I have both passports. I would never give up my Israeli passport. But I have never considered going back to Israel. There was no longer any reason. My son was in school here. I had my reparations money. I had work. I came to Germany, however, purely for practical reasons and not out of conviction. "

"Children, go!" My mother said when she saw that it wasn't working out anymore. "Make sure, you get away."

We were all born two years apart, three girls and one boy. I am number four. My father, Hermann Cohen, had a clothing shop in Dinslaken. It was a real dump. So even my mother, Julie, said, "My children cannot grow up here."

So, in 1920, I was five, we moved to Barmen because my father could take over a shop for men's custom fitted clothing. It was on *Alter Markt*, and we lived in the same building. We moved out of the city center to a large art nouveau villa on Ringelstrasse in the mid-1920s.

There was no Jewish elementary school. Later, in the public girl's high school, there was a Jewish student in every class. Coincidence. We had such a bad teacher that after the tenth grade, part of what was called middle level (Mittlere Reife), only one student continued out of twenty. The others lost interest in school. But I had to stop anyway because I was Jewish.

I went to a type of women's school for one year, taking every course possible. I would have liked to be a neonatal nurse, but I wasn't accepted there. I went to a private tailor's course for one year, until the director told me one day that she couldn't keep me on anymore.

I went to the Netherlands in September 1936. To a *Hachscharah* in Polderland. We received training in agricultural activities in Joodse Camp in Wieringermeer. We learned to work! We were 120 boys and 30 girls between 18 and 25. Of course we women had to take over the cooking and cleaning, but some also worked in farming and in the chicken coop.

I came there through a Zionist youth group. My parents were not Zionists at all. I had a cousin who also became my brother-in-law after marrying my oldest sister, Hilde. He was a Zionist, and they had both already gone to Palestine in 1933 and came and got us all later. My brother was also in a *Hachscharah* group in Amsterdam and then at a factory in Utrecht. My sister Grete and I were both in Wieringemeer. I could have gone by myself though, we were raised

Anni Cohen in Wieringermeer in the Netherlands, 1936.

Anni Cohen in Barmen, 1930.

to be independent. Still, it was better to be together. Only, I didn't get along very well with that sister. She always put me down and I let myself be put down, strangely enough. When she was out of my sight, I forgot all about it and could do what I wanted and not what she wanted.

Otherwise it was a very lovely time—so many young people together. No danger, no alienation. But our goal was always Palestine from the moment we went to the *Hachscharah*. The Dutch gave us the land and the barracks. They were happy to have them be lived in and that the land was being worked. We were fully supported, the Dutch religious communities paid for it. My mother sent ten German marks every month. My sister received it one month, and the next month I would. We then had to budget those ten marks over two months.

I went back to Germany again, twice even. When my father's health got very bad in 1937, we all (except my sister in Palestine) went to Barmen and were also there for his funeral. That same year I went back for three months, because I could only receive a certificate of immigration to Palestine in Hamburg. After that, I stayed for another three weeks to pack. They drummed it into our heads that you don't need clothes, only tools. I arrived there without having one dress! I got fabric right away and sewed one. Later I sewed many, even for others, and earned a little bit of money that way.

I left from Cologne in January 1938 with an entire group. Saying goodbye to friends and especially my mother was hard. She actually wanted to come with me to visit and then come back home. But she couldn't get a passport anymore.

I arrived in Haifa and both of my sisters were standing on the dock to pick me up. Grete went a good year before me, to Nahalal to an agricultural school for girls. First, we both went to our older sister's in Pardes Hanna for a few days, not far from Hadera. And then I was assigned to an agricultural school in Petah Tiqva—horticulture and chicken farming. We were maybe 25 girls and two men for the hard work, and generated and sold at least, if not more than, what it cost to keep us. We lived three to a room, which had a door on both sides. One led out to the terrace and the other to the street. Both were a little bit open at the bottom and there was water in the room every time it rained. The mattresses were straw sacks and always damp and the wardrobe was a few shelves with no door. We hung a curtain on the front. One set of shelves for three people. We did it all. We did a lot. It was an adventure. We were young. And they drummed idealism into us,

"We'll make it! We'll do it!"

And we did. We resolved to live active lives. Of course, they did talk about Zionism. The school belonged to *Histadrut* and a lot of attention was given to bringing in their respective politics. Before the two years were up that people were expected to stay, I dropped everything. I ran away to my oldest sister, because my mother had arrived there.

She had lived through *Kristallnacht* in Germany, was with relatives in the Netherlands for a while, and came to us in Palestine just before the war broke out. She came with what was called a "parent's certificate" that we requested for her and on the very last ship that went through the Mediterranean. Before she came, she had to get rid of everything. Some old Nazi got the house for peanuts. She took the money and went shopping for us, buying clothes and underwear. She had everything packed up and shipped, and then the plates arrived in Palestine without cups. An entire set of plates and not one cup. And the underwear she bought for my brother was stolen. He had nothing, he came into Palestine illegally by land with one backpack. Then he ended up in a *kibbutz* near Hadera.

My oldest sister and her husband had a shoe store with a shoemaker. They lived behind the shop in one room with a kitchen and bath, you can't even imagine something like it at all anymore today. That was all. My mother and I stayed with friends who rented a three-room apartment. My mother, who came from a very big house, subletting in one room with her daughter! Although the climate was tough for her, she managed wonderfully. She was happy to have her fledglings around her. She was born in 1880 and when she came to us, she was 60 and took over my sister's household. She concerned herself with cooking and raising their children.

Then my other sister's marriage fell apart and we decided that I would go to Nahariya so that she would have someone from the family close by. I didn't live with her, but instead lived in a shipping container. They cut windows and doors into the containers and built a shower and outhouse somewhere. That was the best. You mustn't forget, we were raised in the Barmen youth movement. When we went traveling, we lived very primitively in tents and bathed in the creek. It was terrific preparation, a wonderful, friendly and educationally beneficial preparation. I feel sorry for the youth of today that they don't have something like that. They get on the bus and go wherever. We traveled on cattle trucks with farmers and their wares. That was the least expensive way.

Thank God it wasn't just idealism that was drummed into us, but also knowing how to deal with problems, if necessary. I had already been cleaning other people's apartments in Pardes Hanna (see page 258), and I did that in Nahariya also. For *Yekkes* (see page 270). There were a lot of Czechs there, but most of them were *Yekkes* and a whole lot of German-speaking Hungarians. They spoke German in Nahariya. I also spoke Hebrew, but never properly. It was enough for everyday life.

My husband, Kurt, was from Frankfurt. We met in the Penguin Café. He played music in coffee houses for the English, we were still under English occupation. He was often away, sometimes playing alone, with a trio, or with an orchestra. He had a thirteen-year-old son, who had just had his *Bar Mitzvah* when we met. When we got an apartment, two rooms of a four-room apartment, he lived with us and finally had a home. His mother didn't take much care of the boy.

We married in 1945. I can't say exactly when. I don't have any records of the day. You get the marriage certificate under the *Huppah*, but I can't find it anymore. It's buried somewhere. Afterward, we had to go to the English to have everything certified. They wrote in a completely different date. But I don't even have that certificate anymore. I can't prove in writing that I was married. It was recognized later in Germany for our pension claims, however, probably because of witness statements.

Anni Bober with her husband, Kurt, in Nahariya, 1945.

I was pregnant when Nahariya was locked down because of the unrest. The state was proclaimed on the 14th of May, 1948, and my son was born on the 28th of May, four weeks before he was due. He became afraid once the neighbors started sending us bombs, and so he came, so very tiny at 48 centimeters and 1.8 grams. On the second day after his birth, I got on a bus to get out of Nahariya. The midwife came with us, she sat on the floor with the child in her arms and said,

"If he catches a breath of wind, he's gone."

She rode with us until Qiryat Bialik, right before Haifa, because she had relatives there. They packed him into a laundry basket and wanted me to take him to the hospital in Haifa that specialized in childbirth. My sister Grete worked there. But I just howled and said,

"I don't want to! I want to go home! I want to go to my mother!"

I also knew a pediatrician in Pardes Hanna, who originally had a children's clinic in Hamburg. He heard that I was there with my child and came directly up. He rode his bike all over and then came two, three times a day to have a look at Dan. The *Yekkes'* children are all called Gad or Dan.

I got a room for myself, the child, and the dog. It was a sheepdog, a magnificent animal and the best nanny that you could imagine. It

Anni Bober with her son, Dan, in Nahariya, January 1950.

wouldn't let a fly touch the child. After a half year, at the end of 1948, I went back to Nahariya. Poison had been laid out against jackals, and the dog fell victim to it.

I started working again right away after my child was born. My husband brought little money home. I was just happy if he earned what he needed. I earned, more or less, enough to feed the family—the two children and me. But there was no problem—it worked out. We also had nothing to buy, so we didn't need money. It was the worst time during *Tzena* (austerity measures). That was after the war. During the Second World War, we were supported by the Allies. Then once they were gone, everything was rationed. One egg per small child, not for the adults, per week. One egg a week! 100 grams of butter a week. That was tough. But we always had enough greens, tomatoes and cucumbers. It got better as they were able to increase farming. Then things started being imported.

Somehow, we always had news from Germany, including through the Red Cross. There was airmail, thin, small things that you could only read with a magnifying glass. They aren't around anymore. I guess they disintegrated. They were letters that came out of the camps. We had news from my husband's sister. From Theresienstadt. They were pre-written cards. She was sent ten marks through a representative of the family, and then cards came saying "money received." The cards eventually stopped coming.

I lost dozens of aunts and uncles. One uncle went to the Netherlands in 1913, became very wealthy there and sent for his entire family. A whole lot of them were killed. All older people. The younger ones were hidden. The one was with a very strict Catholic family and when she went back to relatives (her parents were no longer living) they first had to tell her that she shouldn't pray under the cross. I found one branch of those relatives who had gone to the Netherlands at the cemetery in Diemen, near Amsterdam. In Amsterdam, Jews were rounded up in a former variety theater and deported. It's a museum today. There are chalkboards with the names of the people, but only the last names. And a whole row of my relatives are listed there as well. My father's siblings with their spouses and children – my generation. We rarely spoke of the losses in the family. And yet, what happened? People would like to know. But when you read the names, you go quiet.

My parents-in-law survived in London. They came to Nahariya. I don't know what they lived on, we didn't have anything either. My mother-in-law died after six months. Then my father-in-law became horribly sick and was in a nursing home. When the documents for the compensation office in Germany came, they had to be signed by him. My husband drove there and got the signature. His father died the next night. He knew "my son has something now" and he departed. If he hadn't been able to sign, everything would have been gone.

A little while later, my husband went to Frankfurt to take care of the money. And then he became so sick with malaria that he couldn't travel back to Israel. I could have said I'm not coming to Frankfurt, but I didn't want to leave my husband alone. So, I packed up the child and suitcases and went. It was difficult for me to go to Germany. I would never have come here if he weren't sick.

It was weird to tread on German soil for the first time again. My husband knew I didn't want to. He picked us up on the ship dock in Genoa. From there, we took a train to Zurich. Friends picked us up in a car so we had a fantastic trip through the Black Forest to Frankfurt. It was a long trip, but it was good and that made it easier for me. There was already snow on the ground in the Black Forest, in what must have been the final days of October.

"What is that?" asked my son.

He was eight and half. He had never seen snow and really wanted to get out of the car to see what it was. We always spoke German with him, but he spoke especially fluent Hebrew, he had already started school. It did matter to him that we had to leave Israel, he wanted to see his father.

My husband held out for another six months here, then he died, in May 1957 at 51. And there I was alone with the child with things left uncertain. In a city that I didn't know. In a country that I didn't want to be in. I felt a little despair, yes. That was a hard time, psychologically. I didn't have any family here either. And no money. I don't know where I got bread from. When we came back to Germany, we received 5,000 marks, to have a start. That was a lot of money, we could set up an entire apartment. I probably lived off that money. And I went to my landlord and said,

"I can't pay the rent."

It was 71 marks for a three-room apartment, imagine that. It was given to my husband as a persecuted Jew after his arrival.

"That doesn't matter, we know that you will eventually," he said.

They were decent people of a building society that belonged to the Evangelical church. For several months I didn't pay the rent, but then I paid it all at once. It took a while, but slowly money came in. And as I calmed down a little bit, I slowed down. I collapsed. I couldn't do it anymore. I didn't go to a hospital. I had a great doctor who treated me with strophanthin. They don't use it anymore, it really built up the heart and body. I was home for three weeks, and then he said to me,

"I'm sending you to a wellness clinic."

"But I'm not going," I said. "Work will be better for me."

And then I got better. There was a clothing company here and the people had heard that I needed work. They called me (I had a telephone) and asked if I could sew buttons on 100 coats. Of course, I could. That was how I started working in Frankfurt. I stayed seven years in that shop, sewing, modifying model clothes, and even helped in sales. When the boss died, the company closed and I went, for another seven years, to work in the office at a mail-order company. After that went bust, I spent eleven years at a clothing manufacturer. And when I stopped working in 1983, I was 68 years old. I liked working.

My boy was in private school at first, because I thought he needed to learn German properly. I was wrong, the public schools would have done just as well. He was in school until four and we came home together. Or he would come to wherever I was working. He quit right before the *Abitur* because of math. But could feed his family without it. First, he did a course in bookkeeping, then he trained at a hotel and catering company. He got work in Wiesbaden with the state welfare association and he's still there. He has a son who is studying at the university, he wants to be a teacher.

I moved into the Budge Foundation (see page 241) in November 1998. I was sure that I really wanted to be in this Judeo-Christian old-age home, because it's more cosmopolitan. There is a Jewish one in Frankfurt, but today there are more Russians than *Yekkes*, and that's a completely different culture. We always have people who come here for a few days to try out living here. I didn't need to. I had no choice. And even if I come from a totally liberal family, I go to synagogue. Not to pray, but because of a feeling of belonging. Thanks to the rejection back then, today you get a feeling of belonging together. We have things in common.

Do I feel German? More like Israeli. I have both passports. I would never give up my Israeli passport. But I have never considered going back to Israel. There was no longer any reason. My son was in school here. I had my reparations money. I had work. I came to Germany, however, purely for practical reasons and not out of conviction.

There is anti-Semitism again. Today I have more fear than I did then. Back then it was much simpler, even for my son. The boy came running in from the street, crying that another boy had called him a "nasty Jew." I just told him,

"Go down there and beat him up."

Shortly after that, his mother came and complained, wanting to know what that was about.

"Ask your son what's wrong," I said to her. "My son doesn't have to take that."

And then everything was peaceful.

Eva Fröhlich
born Eva Beutler on June 15, 1922

❝ Why should I go to Germany? To Nazi Germany? Okay, it wasn't Nazi Germany anymore, but I didn't actually have to go back. I lived in South America for 55 years. We were doing well in Brazil. But for my husband, Germany was his country. […] With a heavy heart, I gave in. ❞

I knew that I am a Jew. I always knew it and never denied it. But for children it was never an issue. We were all together, and there was a very good relationship with the others. My parents kept *Shabbat* and went to synagogue and, as we got older, they took us with them.

My father was a book auditor; what people today would call an accountant. But when I was seven and my brother was eight, he became sick. He had served in the First World War, received the Iron Cross as recognition (which was later no longer acknowledged) and he got dysentery, a bad infectious disease that broke out again so badly that he had to rest for a long time.

My mother had to start working. As a young girl, she made hats—millinery, they called it. And then she began tailoring. She worked at home and put a small display box with her children's clothes in it in front of the door. She got customers right away from doing that. When I was twelve, I learned to embroider and smock and always helped her after school. We did that in South America, too.

I was born near Alexanderplatz, at Magazinstrasse 1, and I went to a public school starting in 1928. Then we moved to Wilmersdorf and I enrolled in the Hohenzollern-Lyceum. But only for about three quarters of a year. When Hitler came to power in 1933, Jewish girls had to leave. There were six or seven of us in my class, and we had to go. Just go. Schools were then set up in the synagogues, and I went to the one on Prinzregentenstrasse. There were Jewish teachers, and we had classes just as before. I wasn't afraid to walk to school, and I wasn't verbally accosted. Maybe I didn't look that Jewish. Meanwhile, my brother was in Marburg, he was supposed to prepare for his *Bar Mitzvah*. He was excited about Marburg and life there. It was a small town compared to Berlin, of course, but he thought it was great. And I thought Berlin was great. We actually never left Berlin, except for vacation. Then we went where everyone from Berlin went, to the Baltic Sea. So, I wasn't familiar with anywhere else. Warnemünde, Swinemünde, Kolberg and Heringsdorf—those were the places I went to.

Eva Beutler in Berlin during the summer of 1928.

Eva Beutler (second from left) with grandparents, parents and brother, Lutz, at the Baltic Sea around 1925.

We emigrated in good time because my father saw it coming. He had taken a course in 1935 to become a chartered accountant, which he completed with honors. And one of the examiners said,

"We can't avoid giving a Jew a diploma."

My mother would have liked to stay. She always thought, like many others did, that it wouldn't get so bad. She didn't have a store and could continue working at home, she was never harassed. No one ever said to her, "You Jew, I won't buy anything from you." It didn't happen. People still had money to buy handmade dresses.

My mother had a brother who had emigrated in 1936. His wife owned a shop on the Kurfürstendamm, called *Mode-Kunst* (English: fashion-art). She sewed really well, and the greatest singers and dancers in the opera were her clients. And so was the wife of the Uruguayan Consulate. One day my uncle met the Consulate by chance in the shop. They started talking—at that point, people were not supposed to buy from Jews—and he said,

"If you want to emigrate, we'll gladly take you! We are a very small country. Why don't you come to Montevideo?"

"Yes," my uncle said, "that would be good thing." It was still easy then. Before 1940, it was still easy.

My father's youngest sister went with her family to Shanghai. They weren't accepted by any other country. They left with the last emigrants and had to wait out the war there. Things there were hopeless, difficult and primitive. It's unbelievable what they had to go through.

My father's eldest brother stayed with his wife and their daughter. They said the nightmare would soon be over. Then they couldn't get out anymore. They were deported. My father never found out what happened to them.

We left from Hamburg in 1937. We wanted to go through Morocco, but the ship ran into a sandbank off of France, and we had to wait in a hotel in Le Havre for another one to be chartered. The trip was endless. It was a nice trip, but we weren't in the right frame of mind to enjoy it. We were supposed to be there at the end of September, but didn't arrive until the 2nd of November. The sun was shining—November is spring there—and it was fascinating. Montevideo is a very beautiful city, spread out wide, with very few tall buildings. Uruguayans are proud of their sea, which isn't a sea, but rather the Rio de la Plata. Buenos Aires, Argentina is on the other side. But you can't see it and that's why it's a sea to them and not a river.

We stayed with my uncle and his family for the first two weeks. Until we found something that we could rent. Everyone was only allowed to take ten German marks out of Germany. Everything else, what people had in the bank anyway, was confiscated. We packed a big box that contained my mother's sewing machine and a porcelain china set that we had to sell quickly because we needed money. And clothing, what we would need at the start. Only people with large shipping containers could take furniture. But you couldn't sell it in Germany anymore either. Who would have bought it? Christians weren't allowed to buy from Jews anymore, and Jews were busy with their emigration plans and didn't buy anything more either. People left everything behind. My mother had a *Berliner Zimmer*, which was only opened up if there was a party. The neighbors probably took the large, beautiful furniture as soon as possible.

We moved into an apartment in a small building. It was a good area with people who had money, and South Americans spent everything on children. We had a number of requests for smocked work, shift dresses with puff sleeves or with long sleeves. I helped do the embroidery.

My father and I were always interested in languages, we learned the basic concepts in two months with a private teacher. My mother wasn't interested, she had her needlework, and that spoke for itself. And my brother Lutz didn't take any lessons.

"I'll learn it eventually," he said.

And he did. He trained with a carpenter and worked with him for a few years, until he could do it independently. Then he got married. In Uruguay. He had a daughter, who lives in Israel now and doesn't have a Jewish mother. My brother's wife is Catholic and from a very good family. A delightful woman with whom I still chat today. I got a laptop for my 90th birthday because I could type. I took classes to become a typist in Montevideo. And at night I had class to improve my Spanish language skills. I would have liked to study psychology. Or something with art—painting. That I couldn't do the *Abitur*—that's the one thing I very much regretted when we were leaving Germany. I liked learning, it was easy for me.

After I couldn't study anymore, my thought was always to become a teacher. I took an evening course for two years with a friend. When we were finished, we had to give a one-hour lesson in front of a class. But then the day before they said,

"The director of the school will be there."

"Oh, my God, I'm not doing it. I can't. I'll be so nervous that I won't be able to say a word."

But because I wanted to teach so badly, I was so well prepared and, to me, it was like he wasn't even there. He was a tall, older gentleman, and we all respected him. And then he came to me when I was finished.

"Miss Bjutl"—Beutler—, "you are a born teacher!"

I thought that was so fantastic! They hired me to teach right away at the institute. From then on, I gave children and adults lessons in English. I was 26 already. I had given private lessons so that I had money for the course.

I always liked languages. We could choose a language at the Jewish school in Berlin, and I chose English. We also learned Hebrew. I can't translate it, but I can read it. I follow along with all of the text in the synagogue. But in Uruguay I didn't speak any Hebrew, only Spanish. The Jewish community center wasn't founded until 1940 or 1941, as more and more Jews were there. A lot of people from Frankfurt came later, they came together and built a very nice synagogue. In the beginning, there was only a prayer hall, like everywhere. They kept *Shabbat* and the holidays. And they even founded a youth group so that we could get together and dance. Naturally, we made friends with German immigrants at first. But over time, there was a mix and it resulted in this Youth Forum. We were between 18 and 21 and spoke to each other in Spanish.

I still lived with my parents. I couldn't afford my own apartment. And I also helped my mother. In the meantime, she rented a shop and we lived behind it in two rooms. The money was thrown into a pot, everything my father, my mother, my brother and I earned.

My father didn't find work right away. He took money for an association, making collections. He also delivered rolls. You took what you could get. But no one was embittered. People were just glad they got out of Germany, that they could save their own lives. And life in Uruguay was very good, very comfortable. They said that Montevideo is a nice city for retirees. My father was especially excited. He was so funny. If we were on the beach he would say the air is magnificent. They're always singing praises about the air in Berlin, but he said,

"No, this air here is no comparison to the air in Berlin."

He was always an optimist; he didn't sit around like an old grouch mourning. My mother did mourn for Germany a little. I didn't miss it at all, I was far away. Young people adjust to life quickly. You don't think much about whether or not you like it. But we did like it.

We knew about the war in Europe, we saw it in the newspapers. We also knew about the concentration camps afterward. The newspapers also published that. But it wasn't like what we saw later in films. That people were forced onto livestock cars like cattle. We didn't know they were deported. We also didn't know that Germany had been divided up. And that so many people were in Russian captivity—I didn't find that out until I was here again. The Nazis came to Montevideo later. Two couples lived on our street. They rented or bought a house. They all had money. When they went by, we said, "Look, there go the Nazis."

We were above them, because we had been in the country a long time. They weren't these great masters anymore either, they were diminished. They had to be pretty good, they especially didn't want to bring any attention to themselves. A lot of Nazis resettled in South America, mainly in Argentina. But they also went underground in Uruguay. But, of course, they weren't Nazis anymore. They never had been. But everyone knew, whichever Germans went there after the war, they could only be Nazis, and they couldn't keep it quiet.

My mother had a cousin, who had gone from Berlin to Rio de Janeiro. She invited my mother to visit, she should definitely come to Rio, get out of Uruguay and see something else. My mother preferred being at home though and said no.

"Well, then send your daughter."

And her daughter didn't want to go at first either because she wasn't used to traveling. I was always a homebody and worked with my mother. But then I did end up going because Rio, at the time, was said to be the most beautiful city in the world.

One day I went to the yacht club with my aunt and her husband. He had just become the president of the Jewish lodge, *B'nai B'rith*, and met a member there who was also invited to accompany us to Petropolis the next day. Arthur accepted the invitation and we all went to this former imperial residence. A very beautiful city, high in the mountains. After that, Arthur and I went on a date.

He and his brother had a shop further inland, with electronic equipment. He was in Rio for a year to build a mail-order company for radio equipment. It went really well and he wanted to stay in Rio. But he did tell me that he might have to go back to Cachoeiro de Itapemirim. It was far away, in the state of Espírito Santo. There were no airports there, just a field where a small plane could land. There was a train in fact, but if it was on-time it was the train from the day before. That was Brazil back in 1956.

"There's no point with you in Montevideo and me here," Arthur soon said. "Then we can barely see each other. I would really like to marry you. But I don't even know your parents. So, either we get married and set a date, or nothing is going to happen."

I had barely known him for two weeks! So, then I stayed another week in Rio and he introduced me to his rabbi. After I went back, he showed up a week later in Montevideo. My mother was not thrilled, she didn't want to let me go to Brazil. But she was pretty thrilled with him.

He came from a pious house where his father didn't turn on any lights on *Shabbat* or open any mail. The mail carrier did it for him and then laid it down. When he was 15, my husband had to go to *shul* (see page 264) to study the Torah.

"I can't relate," I told Arthur. "We were raised free. Am I supposed to cook kosher?"

"No! Not at all!"

The wedding was in June of 1956, on my 34th birthday. He was ten years older than me. We had to marry in Brazil because his mother was very ill and couldn't travel anymore. My mother would have loved to have had the wedding in Montevideo because that's where our friends were. And people constantly wanted to introduce me to men there. You know the way Jewish women are, "What, there's a Jewish girl? Well then, let's just see if...!" I said no to them all.

I worked with my husband in his office in Rio. At first, I only spoke Spanish—Brazilians understand it. The other way around is tougher, going from Portuguese to Spanish.

After three years, we moved inland. I gave children private

Eva Fröhlich in the 60s, Cachoeiro de Itapemirim, Brazil.

English lessons in Cachoeiro. My husband worked and was in the Rotary club. There wasn't much else in this small town. The Rotary wives took me right in. They referred to me as *a alemã*. It was a somewhat pejorative word for "the German" and meant "you are the newcomer, you need to become Brazilian, you have to become an implant." I got the naturalization papers at the consulate in Rio. Thanks to Hitler, I was stateless and never naturalized in Uruguay because I had to prove that I had worked for, I believe, six years. So, I became Brazilian in Rio and got a Brazilian passport.

For a while, we lived in a house on the river, on the Itapemirim. There was flooding practically every year. My first time, an employee of Arthur's came up in his *camioneta*, that was like a delivery truck, and said,

"Your husband sent me. I'm supposed to drive you around."

"What, now?" I asked. "In this flood?"

"Yeah, yeah, you'll see!"

Then he showed me the areas that were hit the hardest. When I got back home, I called my sister-in-law up,

"How are you doing?"

"Really great!"

"Let's meet at such and such bakery," she said.

"Yeah, but it's under water!"

"Yeah, that's exactly what's nice about it. We'll be in water up to our knees. Make sure you're prepared."

That was an event there. It was all so strange to me, the experience that we had. There was no winter, but sometimes the air was a little cooler. That was good for us naturally. It was tropical air otherwise and I felt like I was in an oven.

We were there from 1959 to 1971. We left because my husband and his brother closed the shop. They were robbed by a long-time employee. They fired her, but it was already too late because someone else was also stealing. They liquidated everything. And the warehouse, which was huge, became a supermarket.

We moved to Rio again. That was wonderful for me, the best thing that could happen to me. I did not enjoy living in a small town. It was so boring. And Rio is wonderful. We lived a little outside in a suburb where people with a lot of money lived. I had a group of private students right away. The Brazilians placed value on having their children learn another language.

My husband took on sales contracts for radio equipment and

orthopedic materials, and then also for water beds. It was during a time when they were very popular, and he sold a lot. He was already retired by then.

We stayed until 1977. Then we bought a little apartment in the mountain town of Teresópolis, not far from Petropolis. That was magnificent. It was a tourist town and the population tripled in the summer.

I really enjoyed living in Brazil. I didn't want to leave. But my husband's friend was already in Germany. And that was my tough luck. My husband let himself be talked into it.

"Come back," he said. "You have everything here. Community colleges, concerts, and it is affordable for people in retirement."

He made it sound so good that my husband finally said, "Ok, we'll come!"

He didn't think about me. When he told me, I said,

"Wait, I have something to say about it too. I'm not going!"

Then my husband applied pressure, saying he was getting depressed in this small town. Our friends used to always come to their vacation houses every summer, when their children were young. But when they grew up, they didn't come any more and sold their houses.

"Then we're going back to Rio," he said.

But the heat there is murderous, humid heat. You're always wet. I didn't want to go back to Rio. But why should I go to Germany? To Nazi Germany? Okay, it wasn't Nazi Germany anymore, but I didn't actually have to go back. I lived in South America for 55 years. We were doing well in Brazil. But for my husband, Germany was his country—the country where he was born. And he was a citizen of Frankfurt with all his heart and soul, although he adjusted well to life in Brazil. If he hadn't spoken the language well, couldn't really gain a foothold, didn't have any friends, or had been lonely, then I might actually have been able to understand. But that wasn't it. My husband's old German roots sprouted again when he got older. That wasn't the case with me. I was born here, so I'm automatically German. But in my heart, I'm more South

American. I would have stayed there. Nothing at all pulled me to leave. Different from back then, in the thirties, when we were happy that we could get out of Germany.

With a heavy heart, I gave in. We went back in 1992.

Ruth Thorsch

born Ruth Jaffe on December 27, 1923

> " I was never happy to be in Palestine and always badly yearned for Germany. Because I never had a bad experience there. [...] We went back then. Why? Too much fighting! The War of Independence in 1948, the Sinai Campaign in 1956. It was obvious to us that there would always be fighting. So, we thought, "Go!" And I haven't regretted it for one minute. "

The strange thing is that I really welcomed the fact that Hitler came to power. He did the right thing, in the beginning. When I went with my mother to the Tauentzienstrasse in Berlin to shop, I noticed the beggars were gone! Hitler took the beggars off the street. I didn't know anything else about him. When he came to power, I was nine years old and still went to public school for one and a quarter years. That was a typical public school on Nachodstrasse. We didn't say "Heil Hitler" there.

They didn't have the ubiquitous "Heil Hitler" until I went to the Rückert Oberlyzeum in Schöneberg in 1934. Okay, everything was new to me, and that was also just as new. On the second day, I read what stood outside the class in the school. And there "O1", the *Oberprima* (final year in school), was crossed out. The Oberprima didn't exist anymore, Hitler got rid of it. That was the right thing to do! It was totally unnecessary. Not everything that Hitler did was bad. He just took care of the excesses.

We didn't sing any Hitler songs. We sang, *Die Gedanken sind frei* (thoughts are free), that's a song from the Middle Ages that prisoners sang. It has
nothing to do with Hitler. Then we sang, *Freiheit, die ich meine, die mein Herz erfüllt* (Freedom that I mean, that fills my heart). That has nothing to do with Hitler either. The other girls went to the BdM (Bund Deutscher Mädel or League of German Girls), and they taught me how to make sailor's knots. And I said to my father,

"Papa, I want to go to the BdM, too."

"Sorry, you can't do that. You're going to *HaShomer Haza'ir*."

The Rückert-Oberlyzeum was a public school. Everyone knew that I was Jewish. There was one other Jewish girl who then had to leave because her father hadn't fought on the Front. We were allowed to stay (my brother was born a year after me), our father had fought on the Front in the First World War. They called us front fighter kids.

I didn't have any Christian girlfriends. It also wasn't common back then for them to come to our house. Birthdays were only celebrated with cousins. But one time when I was supposed to go to my cousin Ursula's birthday party, I went to a piano lesson. My parents worked themselves up, you never knew with a Jewish kid where he or she was. It was horrible at home, actually. I left school ten minutes late because I had to exchange a book still. My mother was completely undone. Big drama. My parents were afraid because they knew very well what was happening, especially my father. He was an attorney and notary in the courts. Those people knew a lot more about the politics than the little guy. You want to know why so many Jews were murdered? Because a lot of people said,

"Stay here. Hitler won't last long."

On a Sunday in 1935, the telephone rang at home. My mother answered it, went totally pale and said to my father,

"Max, Hitler took away your notaryship."

I knew what that meant. That he would earn a lot less. My father wanted to send us to Ben Shemen, to the youth village. But my mother didn't want to be separated from us children. So, because of that, we essentially saved our parents. Because now my father had to come with us. What was left for us there? We all emigrated, legally, in 1936. We got an affidavit for Palestine.

The first year there, I always asked,

"Papa, what's in the newspapers? Is Hitler gone yet? I want to go home again. To Berlin."

Eventually I understood that it wasn't an option. And when I heard that the synagogues were burning in Germany, I became afraid.

"What will we do to the German Christians here out of pure anger and rage?" I asked my father.

Nothing happened to them, no one paid attention to them. Only later, when Rommel moved closer, did they intern them all. They put them together in a German town near Haifa. There were other German towns in Palestine, too. Wilhelma, near Tel Aviv and so named in honor of Wilhelm II. Or Sarona, north of Jaffa. By 1939, Hitler had sent a ship for all the German men fit for military service. They were fresh, happy and had their Swastika and the black, white and red flags. We lived in Ramat Gan, a family of four in a two-room apartment, just as before. On Saturdays, we often went to Sarona, because we heard German there. We children waited in front of the single classroom school until it let out, and then we played whatever German children usually play. The girls played with the jump rope, and the boys played soccer. My mother exchanged recipes with the other women. We liked being with Christians. And if it was too hot, we sat in the small church, all together, and marbles rolled along the floor. In the middle of Hitler's time in office, there were Jews and Christians sitting comfortably 2,000 kilometers away from Germany, playing marbles. Fact! And by the time I was 14 years old, I thought this politics stuff was totally crazy. There is no hatred between Jews and Christians. There are simply decent and indecent people.

My father couldn't work as an attorney. He would have had to retake the exams in English and Hebrew. He couldn't do it at 53. First, we had a grocery store. Naturally, it went bust. Later he became a coffee salesman. He would set off mornings with a backpack and two heavy bags to the grocery stores. He brought coffee and got food stamps and money. It wasn't that easy. My father was driven by his depression. He wasn't the only one. Everyone was in the same boat. You had to be happy you were spared. And somehow everyone muddled through.

I was never happy to be in Palestine and always badly yearned for Germany, because I never had a bad experience there and because Palestine was totally foreign to me. I went to school with boys for the first time. That was a miserable thing. And then a foreign language on top of it. I can't describe what it's like when you're sitting there and barely understand a thing, you have to experience it for yourself. I understood a few words, but in the seventh grade, which I was in, you really have to be able to speak a little more. After one year, the teacher said to me,

"You still can't speak Hebrew! You have to repeat the year."

I wouldn't learn Hebrew that way, I thought, and stopped going to school completely. I sat myself down in the park, which was totally empty, because who had time to go to the park?—I took a German book with me and picked up my friend around one. I was exposed when the teacher was standing in our grocery store one day and asked my father,

"Why doesn't Ruth come to school anymore? Is she sick?"

At that point my father made progress with the teacher, agreeing that I would take a retest after the summer break and would get tutored for it. Hebrew doesn't fall from the sky! You have to sit and study. But at some point, the penny will drop, you just have to pay attention when it does. I passed the test, and so after the eighth grade, I was able to change from public school to the Balfour-Gymnasium in Tel Aviv. After four years and only eight and half months before I got my *Abitur*, I had to leave, because my father said,

"You don't need an *Abitur*, you're going to work as a cleaning lady."

That was horrible. And sad. I wanted so much to keep learning. My brother couldn't finish his education either, he got polio when he was 20. He was paralyzed in a wheel chair for 65 years. Our destiny—not exactly easy.

When I was 16, I went to the *Haganah*, in the medical unit. I did a lot of what the non-military service providers do today in Germany. I served in the hospital, as an assistant to the nurses. And when the Arab gentlemen had their fun and games, I had to ride along in an ambulance and we would drive out to the fields and collect all the wounded men.

I spent eight years in the *Haganah* and two years in the military because I had to. I was drafted once the state was founded. Nothing changed during my service. The sad thing, though, was that once the state was founded, the war started—the War of Independence in 1948. During the entire World War II there was no problem with the Arabs. We could go over the Allenby Bridge into Transjordan. We were in Abu Gosh, near Jerusalem. We were in Ramallah. Everywhere. Glad to see it. Peace with Arabs ran deep. An everlasting peace would have been possible then.

We had already known about what happened in Germany during the war, because the English had a very good news service. The only things we didn't know were who was killed and who remained alive.

One of my father's brothers went to Tel Aviv in 1933, with his wife and both daughters, Vera and Eva. And then Vera died when she was eight from meningitis. There was an epidemic in Tel Aviv at the time. Then Uncle Martin moved out to Herzliya and later went to fight in the war. He was stationed in Isma'ilia and fought against the Germans. It wasn't uncommon to see people who had fought on the German side during the First World War fight on the British side during the Second. In addition to my father, his five brothers had all fought on the Front in the First World War. Uncle Alfred was really badly wounded. He couldn't get himself or his family out of Germany anymore at some point because they had no money. My father and Uncle Martin wrote to him that he should send his daughter, Ursula, to us in Palestine. My cousin Eva and I looked forward to seeing Ursula.

"We'll teach her Hebrew, we'll play with her. And she'll sleep in Vera's bed."

"We will not be separated from our only child," her parents wrote back. All three of them, she and her parents, were murdered in Dachau. Ursula could still be alive today. That selfishness—we will not be separated from our only child. Incomprehensible, you could see what was going on.

My Aunt Paula was in Theresienstadt, but no one told me about it. And I was always afraid to ask my relatives more about it. I think you shouldn't do that, stir up those days.

My husband's father also fought on the Front for the Germans during the First World War. And then he was murdered by the Nazis. Both of my parents-in-law were murdered in Treblinka. My husband came to the country illegally and at the last minute. He embarked on a ship with others in Odessa, and then they were shot at by the English off the coast of Palestine. It was 1939, shortly before the war broke out. He got tuberculosis from the hardship suffered in that country, people starved during that time. He lay in a tuberculosis clinic for four and half months. All around him patients died, but he wasn't that badly infected.

When he got better, he came to Ramat Gan, where I met him. He was Czech and a textile engineer and worked over in a textile factory. We married in 1944. The first child came in 1951. It took that long, because I didn't want to have children so soon. I married at 21! Does it have to be so soon? I didn't think so. We continued to live in Ramat Gan in a shack – people lived that way then. We got an apartment in 1954.

My husband was very embittered after his parents were murdered. Understandable. But with him, it was really not very nice. I told him often that he should go to psychotherapy. There is a lot in life that can't be worked through alone, so you get help. But he said,

"No doctor can help me!"

We went back then. Why? Too much fighting! The War of Independence in 1948, the Sinai Campaign in 1956. It was obvious to us that there would always be fighting. So, we thought, "Go!" And I haven't regretted it for one minute.

Not to mention that Ben-Gurion, who instead of fostering contacts with the wealthy Jews in America who want to invest in Israel, demanded that everyone should be pioneers and live as modestly as he did. But that was his private business. We wanted to get out of our holes in the end and live. And so, the majority of Americans invested nothing at all, and they had to move my husband's textile factory to Dimona, for example. The nuclear reactor was in Dimona, and my husband was certain that's where the bombs would fall first. So, a few different things led us to leave the country.

I was initially here alone, to see how I liked it. My former neighbors from Israel, who were already in Frankfurt, took me down to a woman who rented rooms out. An overnight stay with breakfast was five German marks—those were the prices in 1960.

On the first morning, she asked me,

"Do you want to eat rolls? Then you have to get them yourself. Here is a shopping bag. The grocery store is over there. Bring a newspaper back up here, the *Frankfurther Rundschau*."

I stared in amazement at a tram, which I hadn't seen in 25 years! In the grocery store I turned over the money in my hand, and they thought "she's crazy!" But I had also not seen German money in 25 years. Then convention guests came and the woman said,

"I can't just give your room away."

"What is that supposed to mean?" I answered. "It brings in money!"

So, I slept in the living room with her and her husband and woke up mornings, tied on an apron, and asked the guests,

"What would you folks like?"

Yes, I served Germans and I was enthusiastic about it. I was glad to do it. Then my landlady sent me to the department store and to get health insurance. She couldn't have done better by me. If I were in a hotel, I wouldn't have known how anything was done. But I could adjust this way.

After I was here for a while, I took a room and sent for my boy. My husband came much later, he couldn't bear to leave from there for a long time. I always wanted to have two children and I thought if I study first and then have a baby, it will be too late, so I had my daughter in 1963. And when she went to the Kindergarten, I began my studies. I would have liked to study psychology, but didn't think I was smart enough. That was drummed into my head, you can't do anything, you are nothing. But I had taken piano lessons when we lived in Berlin. Not in Palestine anymore, who was supposed to have money for that? I couldn't do that to my parents. Later, in 1939, I found a Russian teacher from Moscow. She hired me to help the children, who were in their first year of lessons to practice on a quiet keyboard. And she gave me piano lessons in exchange. Very good lessons. And my mother noticed that I was really practicing.

"You don't need to play the piano! You need to work and hand over money!"

After that I practiced at a friend's house. Then my father said, "You don't play anymore! I'm selling the piano."

In Israel, it would have cost umpteen thousand dollars to put a child through university. I came to Germany and studied here. Here it is free, of course! I took state exams in two majors, piano and early musical education. I made it through three years of that—with two children. In 1970, I started working and gave lessons at the Youth Music School, a proper BAT position (civil servant job) until retirement.

What did my husband do? It's better you don't ask. He was such a ghetto Jew. He couldn't do anything but gripe. It's a shame. Everyone has to take their own destiny in hand. You can't wait for something to fall out of the clear blue sky. I fed the family. It was a hard life.

My parents stayed in Israel when we went to Frankfurt. My father wanted to come back to Germany. He came and worked again as an attorney. But he didn't like it here anymore and he went back to Ramat Gan. He died at 72. I visited my mother later when I earned enough money. I couldn't allow myself to go before earning enough money.

And today? I can't walk anymore. I live in a three-room apartment for 634 euros. I have my pension and the pension my husband left behind. He was 9 years older than I was and died in 1991. He had dementia in the end and lived in the Jewish old-age home for three years.

I go there once a week myself. The Jewish atmosphere appeals to me. The Jewish holidays are celebrated there. I come from a pious house, my family went to synagogue. Meanwhile, I've become totally anti-religious. I don't care much for piety. But just as I had a Jewish upbringing, I also gave my children a Jewish upbringing. My daughter married a Jewish man, and my son a Christian woman. That was inevitable here. Both children remained in Germany. He has three children, she has two, and they're all girls. When I came back to Germany, I did experience anti-Semitism. But I ended up working with people who had nothing to do with Hitler because they hadn't even been born then. A new generation always comes up.

Margot Wisch

born Margot Strauss on September 12, 1924

" A lot of people came back, which I can't understand. Why? I came here because my husband came here. But of course, I was born here. It's my language. It's my culture. I can't just shake it off. It's part of me. Everyone I meet says, "you're more German than the Germans." But I don't feel that way. "

What I remember best is that I was afraid. Of the screams on the streets, of the parades of people, the songs they sang like, *Wenn das Judenblut vom Messer spritzt*. Standing straight, arm raised. I always tried to avoid being noticed by anyone. And somehow it stayed with me. It took a long time to shake that off. Really, it took a very long time. I was already grown up. If possible, no one notices me. I'm there, but don't want to attract attention.

I actually only had Jewish girl friends except the one girl who also lived in the same building, one floor below us. We played together and until a particular date it was normal. Then she wasn't allowed to play with me anymore. From one day to the next. Her parents forbade it. Totally absurd! I can't remember what I thought at the time. But I assume that people were already familiar with these feelings. Somehow people were used to this situation. Even if it's perceived differently as a child. I was still pretty sheltered by my parents.

I was the only child. We lived in the east end of Frankfurt and I went to the Jewish elementary school and then to the Samson Raphael Hirsch school. We did notice that one or two people left the country. They said goodbye and were gone. But at least they could still say goodbye. The first went to the Netherlands. That wasn't good, no. One went to France, also not good. Four, five, six of my schoolmates emigrated to America and to Canada. But I don't know anything about the others.

One of my father's brothers had already emigrated with his wife to Brazil in 1933. Even my father mentioned early on that he didn't want to stay here. He was a salesman and his frequent travels took him all over Germany. And on his trips, he often found that he'd be sitting on the train and people were talking about Jews and how things would be best if they were gone. I have personally never experienced hostility toward me. But I can tell you something about how it went. I had a school friend, the daughter of a rabbi, a girl with little black pigtails, a cute little girl. And she was walking with her father, who as a rabbi wore black clothes, on the Friedberger

Margot Strauss in Santiago, Chile, in September 1937.

Margot Strauss (second from right) in first grade, Frankfurt, 1930.

Anlage (where the synagogue was) in Frankfurt. SA people came up to them and said,

"A German girl with this disgusting Jew! Go home now!"

No, I haven't had such bad experiences as others have. But the memories remain, and that's enough. I still can't understand today why people would suddenly be enemies with those they'd seen every day. Was that how they really felt inside? Or were they themselves scared so that they couldn't do anything different? For the time, around 1935 or 1936, I can't imagine it at all. But maybe the parents of that girl who I used to always play with, also weren't allowed to speak with my parents, although we lived in the same building.

So, my parents went up to Bremen to get their travel papers in order. I was terribly afraid that they were never coming back. Because people were so frightened after everything they did. Those were troubled times.

We went to Chile because my parents met a German who came to visit from Chile and told them that people could still go there easily. And they decided to go there along with one of my mother's brothers and his wife. We emigrated in 1936. We left from Bremen. It took three and half weeks.

My father learned Spanish before going, but there's a difference between learning and speaking. He still got accounts very quickly again, and a little later traveled around Chile. My mother was at home. We met a family of Frankfurt Jews with whom we then became very good friends. They had a boy my age, which was nice.

I adapted to Santiago very quickly. In Germany, I'd finished the sixth grade and half of the seventh. In Santiago, I went to a special class for the second half of the school year. It was a class where children were brought together who had come mid-year and weren't yet integrated, either into the school or into the country. So, every school age came together to study for this half year. It was an English school and we weren't allowed to speak anything but English, whether we understood it or not. That's how people learned it quickly. I learned Spanish on the streets and spoke German with my German-Jewish friends, until we could all speak Spanish. We only spoke German at home.

After my *Abitur*, I studied stenography and typing and then worked in an office. It was a Chilean-German company. There were a lot of Germans in Chile. Entire colonies, especially in the south. There were also a lot of Germans among my father's clients. During the time of the war, they weren't looked upon very well. But there was no hatred. Not even from the Jewish people toward the Germans. No one did anything to anyone. For example, we knew that the man in the family that lived diagonally across from us was absolutely German-friendly, a Nazi. But he was very kind, very nice to us. There was never an unfriendly word.

We heard little from Germany. People could still write in the beginning, then not anymore. We knew what they did there, but we had no idea how bad it was. People didn't know about the concentration camps yet. My parents wanted my grandmother to emigrate too. But she said,

"As long as my daughter is still here, I'm not leaving."

Margot Strauss (left) with two friends at the English school in Santiago around 1938.

My mother had seven siblings. The eldest brother died in 1914, right at the start of the war. One emigrated with us with his family. Another one with a wife and two children came later to Chile. One sister died naturally in Germany before we left. Three sisters and their husbands were killed. My *Oma* too. She lived with one of her daughters in Wiesbaden. My aunt was deported to Sobibor and *Oma* was sent to Theresienstadt. We found that out afterwards, through the Red Cross. Two memorial stones lie in front of the building they lived in.

I married very young, in 1943, at 19 years old. When I think about that today, it was too young. I met him in Santiago. He was also a German, born in Posen, but he'd lived with his family in Berlin. He was also a salesman and also traveled. Our first son was born in 1943, and the second was born in 1946. I stayed home with the children and didn't work anymore. I would have been happy to study something if I had been more confident. But even my girlfriends started working very young as a result of emigrating. Our parents weren't all doing that well, and that's why we all started working. But if I had said that I really wanted it, then it would have worked out. I always thought—doctor or midwife. That would have appealed to me. I would gladly have become one, but I wasn't assertive.

The marriage was good. But in 1972, I went to Israel alone, because my husband wanted to see how things were going to continue in Chile. This was during Allende's time. Many, many people left Chile, because they were afraid of the Communist regime. But it turned out to be over quickly. My older son married and stayed in Chile. But the younger one, in the meantime, was already in Israel with his wife. He really wanted to go there.

It was the first time I was in Israel. I lived with my son for a few months in the beginning, and then I started working. At a Jewish company in Haifa. I didn't speak Hebrew, but English was enough. Then my husband was also there, but he really wanted to go to Germany. His sister and her husband were already there, too.

My husband lived with his mother for a long time, his father had died much earlier. And his mother, sister and brother-in-law emigrated to Chile together. And then they went back again, all to Wiesbaden. Why Wiesbaden exactly, I can't really say.

A lot of people came back, which I can't understand. I came here because my husband came here. But of course, I was born here. It's my language. It's my culture. I can't just shake it off. It's part of me. Everyone I meet says,

"You're more German than the Germans."

But I don't feel that way. What am I? First and foremost, I'm Jewish—people ask about it all the time anyway. And I am German. The country that touches me the most is Israel. But if you ask me about love for a country, then it's Chile. It was always good to me. The time I spent there was a lovely experience, there are agreeable people and I had good friends. I am still in contact with one girlfriend. We talk on the telephone or Skype, which is nice, because at least we can see each other.

I could have imagined staying in Israel, too. I was there for four and half years. My husband went to Germany at about the same time. I was in Haifa and he was in Wiesbaden. I came one time to visit, that was in 1974 maybe, and to see how it was. That visit was the first time after the war that I came here. And my first thought, my very first feeling was everything is dead here. This is no life.

Everything looked so slow to me. Compared to Israel. And compared to Chile. I found everything so stiff and impersonal. Now I don't see it that way anymore, and things have changed a lot.

I initially went back to Israel. And then we decided that we would indeed live in Germany. My husband already had an apartment in Wiesbaden and I came in 1978. There was a large Chilean-Jewish colony here. The Hotel Rose was in the middle of the city. Everyone from Wiesbaden knows it, and today the state chancellery is inside of it. Back then, a lot of immigrants lived in that hotel. People were connected to it, it was a little like home. I didn't work at first. Not until my husband died. I started at the community center in 1982. I had already made connections there, and, since then, I do a little bit of everything. There is always work, something needs to be written, an eye kept on revenues. Then there are the holidays, those are special tasks. My hobby here is books. I'm responsible for seeking out new ones and buying them.

After my husband's death, I continued to live here with my mother. She was with me in Israel and she came with me to Wiesbaden. My father died long before in Chile. Both sons, in Chile and in Israel, have children and grandchildren. I have five grandsons, but I see them very seldom. Chile is really far away. The last time I was there was 2011. I was last in Israel in the year 2012. I have thought about going back to either Chile or Israel. But there's a moral conflict. If both of my sons lived in the same country, no matter where, I would be there. But the one is here and the other there.

I come from a very religious family. Whenever possible, I eat kosher. I don't buy meat, but I have a more liberal attitude with chicken. But I separate milk and meat, in any case. I'm not pious anymore, but I still live the traditions. And that's through the pretty Orthodox-led community center that I work in. And it has also created the conditions for my more Jewish than Christian circle of friends. But the people I knew from before—none of them are here anymore.

Gerda Rosenthal
born Gerda Freund on March 20, 1917

> "What? You're going to Germany? To the land of the perpetrators?" our friends asked when we left America. They really held it against us. There were even people who cut off contact with us. They couldn't understand that anyone would go back to Germany.

When they were young, my parents came to Germany from Galicia in Eastern Europe. For the same reason that people emigrate today, to have a better life. Poland was not fun for Jews. It was rife with anti-Semitism.

Both spoke good German and they went to Düsseldorf, where there was a type of transit camp, where they met and fell in love. They married in 1910 or so. My father was actually a watchmaker. He wanted to be independent though and heard that in Remscheid (a small city in the Rhineland) there was a shoe store for sale. You didn't need a lot of money. You could make a deposit and pay off the rest over time. That tempted my father. He didn't know anything about shoe shops, but you can learn fast, he thought. The store was on the main street and the entrance to the apartment that belonged to it was around the corner. A kitchen with a room that could be used as a bedroom. There was no bath. People went to the public baths every week to bathe. My brother came into the world in 1914 and I was born in 1917, the apartment became very small with two children. So my parents rented two rooms on the fourth floor as well. Every night of my entire youth we walked the four flights to go to our bedrooms. It was very high up and you could see the top of the Cologne Cathedral.

I was enrolled in the regular elementary school. There was no Jewish one. There were very few Jews living in Remscheid, but there were a few business people and there was the Tietz department store and a clothing store that belonged to Jews, as well. And my father had the shoe store, which is how the family was fed. He was popular, our store was popular, we had a lot of customers. Things weren't bad for us. We were always talking about getting a bigger apartment but we never did.

My childhood was carefree. The other girls at the *Lyceum*, back then they had the *Gymnasium* for boys and *Lyceum* for girls, found it interesting that I was Jewish. I wasn't the only one, there was another Jewish girl in the class above mine. And then came my cousin, our fathers were brothers. Her brother later spent the entire war in a concentration camp. He survived, because he had always

Gerda Freund, Jerusalem, 1939.

been a light eater, and that made life easier for him. He lives in Frankfurt today and visits me every week. We're the only survivors in our family.

Hitler came to power in 1933. He did, in fact, speak a lot against Jews, but at first he didn't do anything. Later, he had all the Jewish shop owners arrested, but that was more of a show for his supporters. My father told me they were in jail for half a day talking with the SS folks, but they were all friendly. Then they sent them all back home again.

The landlords also lived in the building where we rented our apartment. They had a boy and a girl, who were friends with my brother. Karl was a year and a half younger than I. "Der Karl und die Gerda," as we were called in the building, we were bosom buddies. Every morning Karl would set himself in a corner and wait patiently until I was finished and was permitted to get up from the table. And then we would both go out and play. Later we would always talk about what happened in my school and his school. One day, I said "Hello Karl" to him like always, but he just stared right through me as if he didn't even see me. And then he looked away. I didn't understand that. That's an experience that really hit me, and I told my mother. So she spoke with his mother and she explained that he had to join the Hitler Youth, because all his friends had. He couldn't be the only one who didn't. The Nazis were clever in how they started, they influenced the youth right away. There were field trips, *Kraft durch Freude* (English: Strength through Joy), and that's how they filled the youth with excitement for Hitler's ideas. While telling them at the same time that they were not permitted to speak with Jewish children.

Then the smear campaign against Jews began. The Nazis had showcases and they stood everywhere with signs saying, "The Jews are our misfortune!" That was the leitmotif of the newspaper *Stürmers*. It was a bad time. One day, it was April 1, 1933, I heard at school that there was a boycott against all Jewish businesses. So, against that of my parents as well. Out of pure fear, I began to cry. And my schoolmates consoled me and said,

"Gerda, that doesn't apply to you at all. You are decent Jews. That only applies to the profiteers and swindlers among the Jews."

They were definitely influenced. And I wondered who of our many Jewish acquaintances was actually a profiteer or a swindler? They were craftsmen or had little shops. My mother went to the director of the school and asked,

"Will Gerda be able to stay in the school?"

"Frau Freund, I assure you that as long as I am the director of this school, no Jewish student will have to leave the school," he told her.

But he wasn't the head of the school for much longer. There was a teacher who treated me like I wasn't there. But I didn't have any difficulties. On the contrary, the math teacher told me,

"Do not leave the school. Show them that you will overcome it. I will help you. Try to do your *Abitur* here. Then, if you have to emigrate, you'll have it much easier out in the world."

Most of the teachers were anti-Nazis. But because they wanted to keep their jobs, some wore the SA or SS uniform. And many came into the classroom with the German greeting, *Heil Hitler*. I used to think, no, I don't think I'll be able to stand it long enough to do the *Abitur*. It would have taken another three years. I was in the tenth grade and had a *Mittlere Reife* (school leaving certificate). And then there were people coming from Palestine with their own propaganda.

"Send your children to Palestine! Try to emigrate yourselves! Things here will end badly."

But my parents didn't really believe that at all because they had a lot of clients who were very friendly. Although they were saying, "don't buy from Jews," people were still coming to us.

My brother had already gone to Denmark for *Hachscharah* in 1933, in preparation for Palestine. At some point, he and a few young people there nabbed a boat and they just went. It was adventurous, he told me later. They nearly drowned after the boat capsized. They clung to the outside of the boat and sent out calls for help. A ship rescued them and took them to Palestine. And there were Jews there who took the refugees and hid them as soon as they came on shore. It was still the English Mandate. But the English didn't care about much, they just wanted peace. Sometimes they carried out raids to arrest people who were in the country illegally, but they didn't send them back. They turned a blind eye many times.

When my brother emigrated to Palestine, my parents registered me as a youth to make *Aliyah*. They had heard there was no oversight on a *kibbutz*, that boys and girls slept together. That didn't appeal to them and that's why they decided for the religious youth *Aliyah*. They weren't especially religious, but they did keep a kosher house. They were conscious Jews.

There was a big rush to sign up and I had to wait two years. In that time, I helped my parents in the store, because they also said, "don't work for Jews!" It was hard to find help. Then business got worse. My parents stayed above water because they financed some of the shoes they sold. So, I went out collecting every week from the people who paid 50 pfennigs or one mark. But my parents didn't want to go away. And you could only immigrate to Palestine if you were a "capitalist" with 1,000 pounds sterling each. They didn't have that because they put everything into the shop. Then they had to sell it and got a little money. The remaining money was supposed to be financed, but of course was never paid. After the war, we got a kind of compensation for it.

When it was my turn to go, I was 18. The youth *Aliyah* was actually for 14 to 17-year-olds. Nevertheless, I was able to get on the ship in Triest in 1935. I was sad, of course. I knew that I was leaving my parents behind to an uncertain future.

We were met by Henrietta Szold at the port in Palestine. She was old then. We celebrated her 75th birthday that year at the home where we were taken. The youth *Aliyah* had rented an old, abandoned Arab house outside of Jerusalem. We were about 80 girls from Germany, Austria and Poland, sleeping five to a room. It was very primitive at first, then we set up a vegetable garden and a flower garden. They told us beforehand that we could also be trained for a job there, but when I came I hadn't completed enough school. My cousin, who came two years after me, was able to train as a tailor. I only learned to cook, because I worked a lot in the kitchen. And Hebrew and Jewish history. I arrived in July 1935 and stayed until July 1937—then returned to Remscheid again, because my parents longed to see me. I had a return visa for Palestine, and I still remember how the English administrator said to me,

"You must be back on this day!"

Exactly one year, and if I had come just one day later, then the English wouldn't have let me in anymore. Before the year was up, I went back on the last ship in 1938. But before that, I tried to help my parents with emigration. We saw the danger the Nazis posed abroad better than they did from within the country. So I asked my pen pal in America if there was anything she could do for us. Then I won't go back to Palestine, I thought, I'll go instead with my parents to America. She was very nice, she really did file an application and declared that her family would sponsor us if we came to America. They would have had to set aside a lot of money as a guarantee.

But the option was gone once my parents became stateless. Stateless people can't go anywhere. When they left Poland, they became Germans. But the Nazis removed their citizenship. And the Poles didn't want them anymore. They were arrested and sent away. They were simply driven to the border and left there. They went to Zbąszyń, in no man's land, to a large camp for all the Jews expelled from Germany. As the war broke out, the Germans attacked it on the first day, killing everyone. That was the last day I heard anything from my parents. Later we researched it and learned that no one from that camp survived. They were murdered there. The only thing I received was a certified document saying that my parents died. Today, they read the names of the dead every year there. My parents are there and so are most of my family. During the war, I didn't know what happened to my parents. I kept holding onto hope.

Before I went back to Remscheid, I had met my husband. When I was walking one day in Jerusalem, I saw a young man who was holding a city map in his hand and looking at it. I thought at the time, oh, he's foreign, maybe he needs help. And I slowed my steps, but we could never agree later on what happened next. He thought he got my attention and asked me the way to the main street at that time,

"*Slicha geveret* (see page 264), where is King George Street?"

And I thought I said something to him, asking if I could help him. In any case, I told him,

"I'm just taking a stroll. I'll walk with you and show you King George Street."

We spoke Hebrew until we realized that we both speak better German. Alfred came from Frankfurt, but he was born in Hamburg in 1913. His father had been a respected banker there, but was killed in the First World War. Alfred was just a year old and his mother wasn't provided for, because she said that if she had taken out insurance on him, then it would have been bad luck and her husband wouldn't have returned. My mother-in-law then took all the money she had left and spent it to have him found. He had been missing and it wasn't until after the war that someone found his grave in an area that was inside Poland at the time. The Jewish community center set a stone for him there. We went there one time to see his grave.

We married in 1940. We moved to Tel Aviv and lived with his mother at first. At that time, there was an apartment shortage in Palestine due to the sudden waves of immigration. You could rent a larger apartment with one room and use of kitchen, and so that's what we did.

Alfred had a job, and with a German company even—Siemens Orient. During the year before the war started, a requirement came out of Germany that all employees had to sign all letters with *Heil Hitler*. So my husband said, *auf Wiedersehen*, and left the company. We were furious anyway, the swastika flag waved at the German consulate the entire time. It was the Hitler era. But when war was declared, the German flag was quickly torn down and burnt. That put an end to that.

He took on sales accounts, for example, one for rubber boots. There was no sewer system, and when it rained in Tel Aviv, it really poured. You couldn't cross the streets.

I worked in homes as a maid. My last position was with a family that were also from Germany and who had a young girl who I really liked. I heard later that when she was a soldier she was standing guard and an Arab came up from behind her and stuck a dagger in her back. It hit her heart and she was dead on the spot. I cried so hard over that girl.

After that, I worked at a German company. I was very happy there. I could do office work instead of working as a maid. But the company closed when war broke out. In the end, I baked brownies— I baked very good brownies—and sold them to bakeries and also privately.

I had my son Hanan in 1943. People named children after living grandparents, but we didn't know if my parents were still alive. And my husband's father's name was Hugo. Naturally, you can't name your kid Hugo in Palestine. So we looked for something that began with H. We named him Hanan. Our daughter, Noemi, was born in 1947. When I had my children, it made me think of my father who loved children so. Both of my parents did, but especially my father. I really thought a lot about how excited my parents would be over their grandchildren if they came to Palestine. It wasn't to be. I have often

Gerda Rosenthal with her son, Hanan, in Tel Aviv around 1945.

asked myself what their last moments must have probably been like. It still leaves an impression on me.

My husband was such a good son. His mother didn't want for anything, because "she had had such a hard life." Her husband was killed after seven years of a blissful marriage. She never got over it. She was a great strain on us. We couldn't go anywhere without her or she would immediately start complaining. She was always sick; she took refuge in her sickness. She always wanted you to feel sorry for her. Relatives of my husbands, who had gone to America, wrote to us "you'll never have a life of your own if you stay." They couldn't give us an affidavit, but then they persuaded other relatives to send us one. It was very nice of them to do that, because if we couldn't have fed ourselves, they would have had to take care of us.

In 1956, we made our way to America. My husband couldn't leave his mother alone, of course. So I said a little diplomatically, "When we are adjusted, we will send for her."

But it never came to that. On the way to America, we were in Germany again, because I wanted to find out more about my parents. It was the first time back after the war and we only wanted to stay a few weeks. But then the Sinai Campaign broke out in Israel. My husband was still in the military, he had to do his military service every year and was only on leave. If war broke out, he had to go back. And we didn't want that.

That's why we took on German citizenship again. We had seen that it was a different Germany. But even still, we didn't want to work for a German company. We both took a job with the USAFE, the United States Air Force in Europe, and moved to Wiesbaden. That's where they were headquartered. We were only ever around Americans. We didn't want to have anything to do with Germans. My husband thought about it even more than I did. He wondered with everyone, what were you doing back then? Nevertheless, we were here for almost a year and a half, waiting for our American visas. The children made it easier for us. They were both good students and adjusted very quickly. We spoke to them only in Hebrew in Israel. But we thought they should learn German, so we tried a German school. Noemi went into the third grade and was accompanied by a horde of cute little girls every morning.

"We have to pick Noemi up because she can't speak German very well. And so she might get lost on her way to school."

The school was on the same street. We lived in a nice area. This was before the large immigration waves from the East, so Noemi was the only foreigner.

We arrived in New York and stayed a week to go to the famous theaters. We wanted to use the time there well, having had no idea that we would live in New York for a while later. We thought we would never come back to the east coast.

Our goal was Portland, Oregon, where our relatives lived. We had a small house there, and my husband was a traveling salesman for a company selling work uniforms. The main sewing factory was in Los Angeles. He worked there in the summers and we took an apartment with the children during the long school break. The company paid for everything. But I didn't like it that much, that my husband had to travel. He started driving late in life, not taking his test until we were in America. He was constantly on the road in the car and he wasn't the best of drivers. I think I was the better driver.

I had a cousin who worked with her husband in a branch of the jewelry industry, selling cultured pearls. They both wanted to open a store in Chicago and they persuaded us to manage it. Okay, I thought, then Alfred won't have to travel anymore. So in the middle of the 1960s, we went from Oregon to Chicago. That was a big mistake, we really regretted it afterwards. The climate is murderous—too hot in the summer, too cold in the winter. Noemi continued to go to school and Hanan went to university. At some point though, my husband wanted to be independent. He was sick of always working for someone else.

"If we want to find a greener pasture, we have to open a franchise," he said.

We moved to New York and took over an ice cream parlor. It was in Queens, and Andy Steiman, who is the rabbi today in the Budge Foundation where I live now, always came to our Dairy Queen to buy his ice cream as a child. We only got chocolate and vanilla from the company, and we made over 30 kinds out of that. And we created ice cream cakes for kids' birthdays. It was very successful.

I have always liked to have books, that's why I worked in a book store for a few years. It was fun for me, but it became too much, I couldn't do both anymore. I still helped at night in the store, because we were open until midnight. We did tell ourselves that if we wanted to land in a greener pasture, we would definitely have to do a lot.

Back when we told my son that we were emigrating to America, but first we had to go to Germany, he began to cry.

"Where will I go to school?" he asked.

He just wanted to study. He was really gifted, he completed his doctorate in physics at 25. He died when he was 27. In an accident. In America. Someone drove into him in his car. He was thrown from the car. They told us it was a boy who didn't even have a license. He had borrowed a car from a friend and drove it. We would have sued him if his family had been wealthy, but they were poor people. So we thought, we are unhappy, we would just probably make another family unhappy. We let it go. We had Hanan cremated, brought the ashes back to Israel and buried them in the Dorot *Kibbutz* with which we had been connected all those years.

After that, we were so beaten down that we couldn't do all the hard work anymore. Even before that, the company had asked us if we would go to Germany for them.

At the time, we said, "Germany, never again!"

But when the accident happened, we thought maybe it would provide us with a distraction and we would power through it better. And so we did that. We went to Offenbach as employees.

"What? You're going to Germany? To the land of the perpetrators?" our friends asked when we left America.

They really held it against us. There were even people who cut off contact with us. They couldn't understand that anyone would go back to Germany.

When the store had to close after a few years, we wanted to go back to America. But then the folks from the Jewish community center came and said we should stay, they wanted to build a new center in Frankfurt. We gave up everything in America. Should we really start all over again? We decided to stay here in Germany, to try it. We took an apartment in a place that belonged to the center. We made friends through the center, but I also have Christian friends.

Later we moved into the senior home, where my husband died in 2009. We were always sure that we wanted to live a Jewish life. We are Jews. I go to the synagogue on Friday evenings. I eat in the kosher dining room. I'm not very religious; we fell out of the habit in Palestine where we often ate Arabic food.

Today I'm an American, and I feel like an American. I have an American passport, not a German one. I can't be a German anymore, because I gave up my German citizenship when I became an American. I was only permitted to hold onto one more citizenship. Since we had a lot of relatives in Israel back then and my brother lived there, I kept the Israeli citizenship. I also feel Israeli. I speak pretty good Hebrew. And the fact that I live in Germany again, is really by chance.

But in Palestine and later in Israel they called me Golda, a Jewish name. I never really liked Golda, I kept my own name. In my passports, it has always been Gerda.

Memorial stones that Gerda Rosenthal had laid in Remscheid for her parents, Israel and Cecelia Freund, who were deported to Poland in 1938 and murdered there.

GOING BACK

National Socialist (Nazi) Actions against Jews 1933 – 1945

(excerpted from about 2,000 rules)

March 29, 1933 Call for the systematic boycott of Jewish goods, Jewish doctors, and Jewish attorneys. Party members are required to participate in the boycott and with effect on April 1, 1933.

March 31, 1933 [...] Jewish judges and other Jewish attorneys who are working in court are to be forcefully put on leave. They are forbidden from entering the courthouses. [...]

April 7, 1933 Law for the Reestablishment of the Professional Civil Service: Government employees who are not of Aryan descent are pushed into retirement. Pro bono employees are dismissed from their jobs. This does not apply to employees who had already been employed since August 1, 1914 or those who had fought for the German Reich on the Front in World War I or those whose fathers or sons had died in World War I.

April 11, 1933 A non-Aryan is defined as anyone descended from non-Aryan, especially Jewish parents, or grandparents. One parent or grandparent is sufficient to be declared non-Aryan. [...]

April 22, 1933 The services of doctors of non-Aryan descent are no longer reimbursed under the national health plan, no new non-Aryan doctors are registered to be paid through the plan. Exception: Those who fought on the Front in World War I.

May 4, 1933 Private legal contracts with non-Aryan employees and workers for the Reich, the Länder [states], and unions, etc. are suspended with one month's notice. [...]

May 6, 1933 Non-Aryans are no longer allowed to work as tax consultants in general, and pending admissions are withdrawn. [...]

July 14, 1933 Naturalized citizenships attained between 11/9/1918 and 1/30/1933 could be revoked as "undesirable". [...]

July 26, 1933 The decision of whether naturalized citizenship is deemed "desirable" is based on racial and national principles. De-naturalization of especially Eastern European Jews followed. [...]

July 26, 1933 The government's desire for people of Jewish descent to emigrate is so high that it is not legally prevented. But the loss of able bodied workers reduced the tax base by leaving, requiring the increase of a large final payment—the Reich Flight Tax.

September 13, 1933 Genetics and racial anthropology is required learning in all schools; they are also compulsory test subjects for every student on all types of leaving exams.

July 12, 1934 Government employees who want to marry must provide proof of their future wives' Aryan descent before marriage.

September 15, 1935 Law to protect German blood and German honor: 1. Marriage between Jews and German citizens or those with German-related blood was forbidden; marriages performed in spite of this were nullified (punishment: prison). 2. Non-marital sexual relations between Jews and German citizens or those of German-related blood were forbidden (for men, this meant prison or jail). 3. Jewish men are prohibited from employing female German citizens or those with German-related blood under 45 in their households. [...]

November 14, 1935 Marriages between Jews and individuals of mixed blood [Mischlinge] who only have one Jewish grandparent and between Mischlinge themselves are also forbidden. [...]

November 14, 1935 Jews (i.e. who are descended from at least 3 fully Jewish grandparents by race, whereby fully Jewish is considered to refer to those who belong to the Jewish religious community or Mischlinge with 2 fully Jewish grandparents if the Mischling belongs to those who belong to the Jewish religious community by decree of law, joins it later, or by decree of law is married to a Jew, or marries a Jew, for example, after those offspring of Jews born out of wedlock from 6/31/36) cannot be citizens of the Reich, have no political voting rights and may not hold any public office. Jewish government employees retire with effect from 12/31/35. [...]

December 19, 1935 Only the Jews and the Roma are deemed foreign races in Europe

February 8, 1938 Reports must be made about every Jew who leaves Germany, giving full details about each person or their parents [...]. In all cases, Jews are to be deemed enemies of the state, even if there are no known facts that relate to previous subversive activity or punishable offenses.

April 26, 1938 Every Jew, and even their non-Jewish spouses, must assess and report all their domestic and foreign assets. [...]

June 14, 1938 [...] Also aim to cut Jews off from the economy as quickly as possible. Yet no one wants the savings accounts that come from Jews to be denied by savings banks. [...]

June 22, 1938 Finding a place for Jews in medical institutions must be carried out to avoid the danger of a racial scandal. Jews are to be taken to specific rooms.

July 23, 1938 Jews who are German citizens have until 12/31/38 to apply for an identity card that displays reference to the trait of being a Jew. Jews must show the identity card without being asked during any personal requests to an authority. In written requests, they must refer to their trait as Jews using their identification place, number and card.

August 17, 1938 Jews [...] must use the names "Israel" and "Sara" as first names from 1/1/39 onward.

September 27, 1938 Jews are forbidden from working as attorneys [...]

October 5, 1938 All German passports that are held by Jews are declared invalid. Any previously issued passports must be turned back in. Foreign passports shall be valid again after they are stamped with a "J."

October 26, 1938 Because of the intention of the Polish government not to allow Jews with Polish citizenship re-entry, an order is given for Polish Jews to leave the Reich territory by 10/29/38.

November 9, 1938 All Jewish shops were immediately destroyed by SA men in uniform, with SA guards watching to make sure that absolutely no valuables are looted. The press is called in. Synagogues were immediately set on fire, Jewish symbols were placed in safety. Only residential buildings with Aryans in them were protected by the fire department, but they also protected Jewish residential buildings next door. However, the Jews had to move out anyway so that Aryan citizens could move in shortly thereafter. The police are not permitted to make arrests. All Jews were disarmed and those who resisted were shot to death on the spot. [...]

November 12, 1938 [...] The entire Jewish population with German citizenship was charged with paying a contribution to the German Reich of 100,000,000 Reich Marks. [...]

November 12, 1938 Jews were forbidden from going to the theater, cinema, concerts, exhibits, etc.

November 15, 1938 [...] Jews are no longer permitted to attend German schools. They can only go to Jewish schools. [...]

December 3, 1938 Driver's licenses and vehicle registration documents held by Jews are declared invalid and are ordered to be turned over.

December 14, 1938 Jews are no longer permitted to lead companies that belong to them. [...]

January 28, 1939 Jews are forbidden to sell goods at marketplaces [...]

February 21, 1939 All Jews—except foreign citizens—are given two weeks to deliver any objects made of gold, platinum or silver as well as precious stones and pearls found in their possession to the public purchasing centers set up by the Reich.

July 4, 1939 The Reich Association of Jews in Germany is established. Its main purpose is to promote Jewish emigration. The Jewish school system and the independent Jewish welfare system also receive support from the Reich Association. All German and stateless Jews who reside or spend most of their time within the Reich borders belong to the Reich Association. Membership requirement exceptions exist for mixed marriages.

September 12, 1939 Jews are told to purchase their groceries from certain shops. Reintroduction of Jewish-only shops is out of the question. [...] Searches were carried out in places where small groups of Jews lived to find hoarded goods. If any Jew was found to be in possession of such goods, they were confiscated, and the person was taken into custody.

September 20, 1939 Jews with German citizenship and stateless Jews are forbidden to own a radio. [...]

December 7, 1939 Clothing ration cards, which had been distributed to Jews, are immediately taken back. This didn't apply to Jews living in mixed marriages if the offspring from the marriage were not considered Jewish.

March 11, 1940 Food ration cards for Jews are to be marked with the letter "J" on them. The basic rations for average people, such as the special allotments for children, are not reduced. Jews are excluded from receiving non-rationed and most not readily available food.

May 4, 1940 Jews are forbidden to leave their apartments during the time between 4/1 - 9/30 from the hours between 9 in the evening and 5 in the morning and during the time between 10/1 - 3/31 between 8 in the evening and 6 in the morning.

July 23, 1940 The Aryanization of Jewish businesses will be complete by the end of the year.

August 7, 1941 The distribution of food is further reduced for Jews.

September 1, 1941 Beginning on 9/15/41, Jews, who have reached the full age of six years are forbidden to show themselves in public without a Jewish star. Jews are forbidden to leave their neighborhoods without written or police permission [...]. This does not apply to spouses living in mixed marriages if there are offspring from the marriage who are not considered Jewish or if the only son was killed in battle, nor for Jewish wives in childless mixed marriages during the length of the marriage.

Early September 1941 The following Jews living in mixed marriages are considered privileged: 1. The Jewish spouse of a German woman, if one or more children result from it who are seen as first degree Mischlinge. 2. The Jewish wife of a German husband, if their children are deemed first degree Mischlinge or the marriage is childless.

September 18, 1941 Jews can get permission from police to leave the areas where they live and for rides on particular forms of transportation in those areas. They must always show their permission slips without being asked. Jews are banned from using the sleeping car and the dining car on the Reich rail and from excursion carriages and excursion boats. Jews are entitled to use the remaining public transportation only if there is room for them, but not at all during the times of greatest use, when not even all the non-Jews can find a seat. Jews can only ride in the lower classes and may only take seats when no other travelers are standing. [...]

October 23, 1941 The emigration of Jews from Germany is forbidden for the remainder of the war, without exception.

October 24, 1941 Order given for the deportation of approx. 50,000 Jews from the "Old Reich" (Germany), Austria as well as Bohemia and Moravia to the east.

November 4, 1941 Jews who are not working in industries important to the economy are deported to the eastern territories over the next few months. The property of the deported Jews is seized in favor of the German Reich, except for 100 RM [Reichmarks] and a 50-kg package per person. Before those Jews are deported, they must first submit a list of their property.[...]

November 13, 1941 All typewriters, calculators, copiers, bicycles, cameras and telescopes found in private possession of Jews is seized and turned over to the government. [...]

December 3, 1941 Every Jew who is confirmed for deportation must pay at least 25% of liquid assets to the Reich Association; these sums are deposited to special accounts and serve to finance the costs associated with deportation and transport.

January 3, 1942 In the face of the impending Final Solution to the Jewish question, emigration of German and stateless Jews from the German Reich was put to a stop. [...]

January 5, 1942 Jews who must wear the Jewish star in public have until 1/16/42 to turn over any fur and wool clothing as well as any skis, snow shoes or hiking shoes found in their possession. [...]

February 14, 1942 Bakeries and cafés are required to post signs indicating that cake will not be given to Jews or Poles. February 15, 1942 Jews are no longer permitted to keep pets.

March 3, 1942 Processing approvals for Jewish Mischlinge seeking marriage is discontinued for the duration of the war.

March 13, 1942 To prevent them from blending in, Jews are instructed to mark their homes with a black (other sources say, white) Jewish star on the front door.

March 30, 1942 Jews are forbidden from traveling through the Reich region.

April, 1942 Aryans and people living in mixed marriages are forbidden from visiting Jews in their homes.

May 12, 1942 Jews who are required to wear the Jewish star in public are not permitted to be served by non-Jewish hair dressers.

June 9, 1942 Jews must turn over all non-essential clothing items.

June 20, 1942 The Reich Association of Jews in Germany is instructed to close all Jewish schools with effect from 6/30/42, to provide a list of their members, and that from 7/1/42 teaching Jewish children, whether by paid or unpaid teachers, is forbidden.

June 22, 1942 Jews are no longer to receive cards that allow them to buy eggs.

July 10, 1942 Sending money or gifts of any kind in any form to deported Jews is forbidden.

July 15, 1942 Children of a Jewish father or a first-degree Jewish Mischling must be distinguished from children of a German-blooded father or a father with a negligible amount of Jewish blood through a process that determines their origins. Strict standards are applied in cases when the mother is also Jewish or is a Jewish Mischling.

July 16, 1942 Jews are forbidden to transfer securities under their ownership to non-Jews, even if done free of charge. [...]

July 30, 1942 Jewish religious objects made of precious metal must be turned in to the Reich Association. [...]

September 1, 1942 The estates of the prisoners who died in the concentration camps are seized for the benefit of the Reich.

September 18, 1942 The supply of meat, meat products, eggs, milk and other distributed groceries to Jews is discontinued. Grocery rations for Jewish children are reduced. [...]

September 24, 1942 According to a decision by the Führer, soldiers are forbidden from marrying women who were formerly married to a Jew.

October 7, 1942 Jews are forbidden from having any direct or indirect contact with foreign diplomatic representatives and non-Jewish foreigners.

October 23, 1942 [...] Jewish employees who carry the additional name of Israel or Sara must ask their employer to include these additional names in all documents that refer to them. [...]

Early November, 1942 All concentration camps within the Reich are to make themselves "Jew-free," and all Jews are to be deported to Auschwitz and Lublin.

March 26, 1943 All Jews still working in private companies are to be removed from their jobs and transferred into forced labor units or to deportation centers.

April 28, 1943 Jews who are still employed doing work important for the war are to be removed from their employment and required to find out if they are being evacuated to the east or if they were being moved to Theresienstadt. To prevent anyone fleeing, the Jews selected for transport are to be housed together. [...]

July 11, 1943 An order in agreement with the Führer was made that people should avoid talking about the Final Solution during a public discussion of the Jewish question: Jews were sent to work, en bloc and in appropriate ways.

December 18, 1943 Jewish spouses from marriages that no longer exist as well as those just considered Jews are to be sent to Theresienstadt.

January 12, 1944 Jews are not given time cards for correspondence with the rest of the world. [Without these cards, letters are not sent out of the country.]

January 13, 1945 All able-bodied German and stateless Jews living in mixed marriages are to be handed over to Theresienstadt as a working unit.

February 16, 1945 [...] If files with contents describing the anti-Jewish actions are not able to be transported out, they are to be destroyed so that they don't fall into enemy hands.

Taken from: Joseph Walk (publisher), Das Sonderrecht für die Juden im NS-Staat (The Special Laws for the Jew in the Nazi-State), 2nd ed., C. F. Müller, Verlagsgruppe Hüthig Jehle Rehm GmbH, Heidelberg 2013—printed with kind permission.

GOING BACK

Glossary

A

Abitur: German school leaving certificate that qualifies a student to enter university.

Abu Ghosh: Arabic village 10 kilometers (6.2 miles) west of Jerusalem; one of the few whose inhabitants (today approx. 7,000) voted for a life in the newly founded Israel during the War for Independence in 1948.

Affidavit: A declaration in lieu of an oath; necessary in this case for immigration, in which a resident guarantees they will be responsible for supporting the immigrant.

Afula: Northern Israeli city in the Jezreel Valley (also called Emek) between the mountains of Galilee and Samaria.

(Beth) Ahava: Hebrew for (house of) love; originally an orphanage on Auguststrasse in Berlin whose director, Beate Berger, opened a home of the same name in 1934 in Kiryat Bialik near Haifa, thereby saving 300 children from being deported.

Aliyah: Hebrew for going up; Immigration of Jews to Palestine or Israel.

Allenby Bridge or King Hussein Bridge: Spans the Jordan River and connects Jericho in the West Bank with Jordan.

Allende, Salvador (1908-1973): Doctor and President of Chile from 1970-1973.

Alzey: City in the southeastern part of the Rhineland-Palatinate region.

Aryan: Originally a designation for an Indo-European people; from the 19th century onward, it became a synonym for the supposedly superior races of white people; in National Socialism Aryan stands for non-Jew, and from 1935 it was replaced by "German-blooded."

Aryan paragraph: First appearing in the Law of Restoration of the Professional Civil Service (Gesetz zur Wiederherstellung des Berufsbeamtentums - BBG) from April 7th, 1933, it regulated exclusion of non-Aryans; consequently, those considered to be non-Aryan were those with Jewish parents or grandparents.

Aryanization: Nazi name for the alienation of German Jews from economic and professional life as well as for the expropriation of Jewish property and assets to the benefit of non-Jews.

Ashkelon: City on the Mediterranean in southern Israel first mentioned in writing in 1285 BCE.

Asti: City in northwest Italy in the Piedmont region.

Association of Persecutees of the Nazi Regime (German: Vereinigung der Verfolgten des Naziregimes—VVN): Association of victims' unions founded after the Second World War that declare resistance to fascism and war among their tenets.

Atlit: A town south of Haifa on the Mediterranean coast founded in 1903; during the Second World War the British Mandate government erect a detainee camp in which illegal Jewish immigrants were interned, who were then freed by the Haganah in October 1945.

Auschwitz: Oświęcim in Polish; the largest National Socialist extermination camp (with the Auschwitz, Auschwitz-Birkenau and Auschwitz-Monowitz camps, where over 1.1 million people were murdered) was established on the edge of the city beginning in 1940; Auschwitz became synonymous with the inhumanity of the Nazis.

Aussig: Ústí nad Labem in Czech; City in the North Bohemia region of the Czech Republic.

B
Baccalauréat: French; equivalent to the German Abitur

Bar Kochba (Berlin): The first Jewish sports center in the German empire founded in 1898; it had over 40,000 members in 1939, it closed after the November pogrom of 1938.

Barmen: A city in the eastern Rhineland until 1929; today it is a neighborhood of Wuppertal.

Bar Mitzvah: Hebrew for "son of commandment"; ceremony in which Jewish boys reach the age of religious maturity on the Sabbath after their 13th birthday and therefore become full members of the community; refers to the status as well as the day of celebration.

Bat Galim: Northern neighborhood of Haifa at the foot of Mount Carmel.

BAT—Bundes-Angestelltentarifvertrag [National Agreement for Public Sector White-Collar Workers]: Regulated payment of public civil servants from 1961 to 2006.

BBC—British Broadcasting Corporation: Independent radio broadcaster founded in London in 1922; the most important source of foreign information for German listeners during the Second World War.

BdM—Bund deutscher Mädel (League of German Girls): All young females in the German Reich were conscripted members by law, beginning on December 1, 1936, and as such the BdM became the largest female youth organization in the world with 4.5 million members in 1944; the uniform was a dark blue skirt, white blouse, and black neckerchief with a leather slide.

Be'er Sheva [Beersheba]: City in southern Israel; lying on the perimeter, it's considered the capital of the Negev Desert.

Belgrade: The capital of Serbia today, then part of Yugoslavia.

Ben Gurion, David (1886-1973): Born as David Grün in the Vistula Land; emigrated to Palestine in 1918, he was head of the Histadrut (trade union) and co-founder of Haganah as well as founder of the Mapai (Zionist socialist worker's party); he read out the Israeli Declaration of Independence on May 14, 1948 and became Israel's first prime minister (1949-1954 and 1955-1963).

Ben Shemen: A home founded for Russian orphans in 1906 between Tel Aviv and Jerusalem; it has been a boarding school since 1927 and, from 1933, the center of Youth Aliyah.

Bergen-Belsen: Concentration camp in Bergen (near Celle) that originally served as a camp for prisoners of war; until it was liberated by British troops in April 1945, more than 50,000 people died there, and for many, it was a stopover to an extermination camp.

Berliner Zimmer: A living room that connects the front of a building with the back of the building; a particular feature of Berlin apartment buildings in the 19th and early 20th centuries.

Beth Olim: Hebrew for house of immigrants; immigrant home.

Bialik: See Kiryat Bialik.

Bialystock: Polish city approx. 180 kilometers north of Warsaw; formerly a significant Jewish center.

Black-white-red: From 1867, the (colors of the) flag for the North German Confederation as well as of the German Reich from 1871 to 1919 and from 1933 to 1945.

Bloomingdale's: A clothing store founded in New York in 1860; today an American department store chain for high-end goods.

B'nai B'rith: Hebrew for Children of the Covenant; founded in 1843 in New York as a secret lodge for German immigrants for the advancement of tolerance, humanity, and welfare as well as for teaching and educating about Judaism; one of the largest Jewish organizations today.

Bojars: Former noblemen below the level of a prince or tsar in some eastern countries; the ruling class of big owners in Romania until 1945.

Bornplatz synagogue: Dedicated as the largest synagogue in northern Europe in the Hamburg Grindel quarter in 1906; the internal fittings were destroyed during the November pogrom of 1938, the building was torn down in 1940.

Bratislava: Pressburg in German; today the capital of Slovakia.

Breslau: Wrocław in Polish; fourth largest city in Poland and capital of the Lower Silesia District.

(Castle) Brüningslinden: Country seat of the Regiment Commander Ernst von Brüning built in 1911/1912; commandeered by the U.S. Army after the end of the Second World War and used partly as a summer camp for Jewish children.

Buber, Martin (1878-1965): Born in Vienna, a religious philosopher who taught at Frankfurt University until 1933 and emigrated to Jerusalem in 1938.

Buchenwald: Concentration camp on the Ettersberg River near Weimar in which around 250,000 people were imprisoned, with about 56,000 of them dying, between July 1937 and April 1945.

(Henry and Emma) Budge Foundation: Foundation established in 1920 by the Jewish couple Henry and Emma Budge with a goal of supporting elderly people, committed to Judeo-Christian equality across Europe as per its Articles of Association; today it is also the name of a senior home in Frankfurt run on that principle.

C

Cachoeiro de Itapemirim: A city founded in 1890 in the Brazilian state of Espírito Santo.

Carabinieri: Police station in Italy.

Carlebach, Joseph Zwi (1883-1942): The last head rabbi in Hamburg, where he was deported in December 1941 to the Jungfernhof concentration camp and shot in the forest near Riga with his wife and three youngest daughters in March 1942; the five older children were saved by emigrating to England, while the youngest son survived nine concentration camps.

Carmel: Mountain in northern Israel, on the north slope of which the city of Haifa lies.

Central Welfare Board of Jews in Germany Zentralerohlfahtstelle de Judan in Deutschland (ZWST): An umbrella organization of Jewish unions and agricultural associations focusing on social work with a main office in Frankfurt the was founded in 1917, closed in 1939 by the Nazis, and reestablished in 1951.

(Capitalist) Certificate: Permission to immigrate to Palestine given out by the British Mandate for payment of 1,000 pounds.

Chełmno, also known as Kulmhof: Nazi extermination camp in Poland in which many Jews and Roma were killed in gas chambers from December 1941 until March 1943 as well as in summer 1944.

Chuppah: Canopy used in Jewish weddings under which the couple is married.

Civil Rights Congress: An American civil rights organization founded in 1946 in Detroit, Michigan and disbanded in 1956.

Cohen, Yardena (1910-2012): Israeli dancer who became famous in Haifa for her dance studio, where she still taught as a centenarian.

Coolie: East Asian day laborer or porter.

Cultural Revolution (in China): Political campaign led by Mao Tse-tung (1893-1976) in which massive human rights abuses were carried out and 20 million people were killed.

D

Dachau: Concentration camp erected in March 1933 in which about 200,000 people were imprisoned and about 41,500 died until it was liberated by American troops in April 1945; while countless prisoners were deported to extermination camps

Star of David: In Hebrew, Magen David (David's shield); six-pointed star that is considered the symbol of Judaism and the people of Israel as well as the emblem on the flag.

Der Führer schenkt den Juden eine Stadt [The Führer Gives a City to the Jews]: Mentioned in the memories of the survivors of the Theresienstadt concentration camp, what was called and became the famous title for a film whose original title was "Theresienstadt.

Ein Dokumentarfilm aus dem jüdischen Siedlungsgebiet" [Theresienstadt: A Documentary Film from the Jewish Settlement Area]; the Nazi propaganda film made in August/September of 1944 under the forced supervision of the director, Kurt Gerron, who was later murdered in Auschwitz, supposedly showing the ostensibly good conditions in the ghetto of that name.

Dimona: Israeli city founded in 1955 in the northern part of the Negev Desert, which is best known for its nuclear reactor.

Displaced Persons (DPs): Designation for civilians who were kept from their homelands in the Second World War and after the war ended were brought to live temporarily in what were called DP camps belonging to the Allies.

Dora Mittelbau or KZ Mittelbau Dora: Made as a sub-camp to Buchenwald in August 1943, mainly to provide labor for building the V1 and V2 "vengeance" or V weapons mainly in the tunnels protected from air raids near Nordhausen; the entire complex extends out over the entire Harz mountain range with nearly 40 sub-camps; 20,000 out of 60,000 prisoners died due to the extreme work and living conditions.

Dorot: A kibbutz in southern Israel founded by German immigrants in 1941.

Dysentery: A disease affecting the colon that occurs predominately in areas with poor hygiene care; mild cases are treatable, but more serious cases can be deadly.

E

Eger: Erlau in German; city in northern Hungary.

Eichmann, Karl Adolf (1906-62): As the head of the Section of the Reichssicherheitshauptamt (RSHA) or Reich Main Security Office responsible for the dispossession and deportation of Jews, SS Obersturmbannführer (Lt. Col.) Adolf Eichmann was one of the main perpetrators of the Holocaust and jointly responsible for the murder of 6 million Jews.

Elat: City in the southern Negev desert on the southern tip of Israel; the only access point to the Red Sea from the country

Emek: Hebrew for valley; refers to the Jezreel Valley between the mountains of Galilee and Samaria in the northern Israel.

Epidemic Typhoid: The correct designation is spotted fever; symptoms are fever, pain in head and limbs, and impaired consciousness; carried by lice, mites, etc. and occurs predominately in tropical and subtropical areas.

Epidemiology: The science of the origin, spread and control as well as the social consequences of epidemics. Etzel (also Irgun): Underground organization founded in Jerusalem by former Haganah members in 1931, its commander, Menachem Begin (1913-1992), later became Prime Minister.

F
Fabrikaktion [Factory Action]: Large scale raid by the Gestapo and SS on February 27, 1943, in which the last of the Berlin Jews from armament factories were arrested and transported to a collection point; most members of the Jewish community imprisoned on Rosenstrasse were freed after protests from their non-Jewish relatives, most of those imprisoned in other collection points were deported to Auschwitz and murdered.

Falafel: Fried balls of pureed chickpeas; originally Arabic cuisine, today it is the Israeli national dish.

Fascism: Original designation for the right-wing movement, led in Italy by Benito Mussolini (1883-1945) from 1922 to 1943; also used for post-1920s extreme right, totalitarian and nationalistic dictators, especially the German National Socialists.

Feldsher: Originally an unskilled country doctor, later the lowest rank of military doctor; still common in the Russian army today.

Framersheim: Town in the Alzey-Worms district in Rhineland-Palatinate.

French Concession: Elegant section of Shanghai (currently the neighborhoods of Luwan and Xuhui) that was established by French business people and traders who moved there in the 19th century.

Fifth column: A subversively active group aimed at overthrowing an existing order on behalf of a foreign power; during the Second World War, it refers to the German National Socialists in Shanghai.

Fuhlsbüttel: A concentration camp set up in 1933 in part of the building complex of a Hamburg prison, which existed until 1945.

G

Galinski, Heinz (1912-1992): Born in Marianburg (West Prussia) and living in Berlin as a textile salesman. He, his wife and his mother were deported to Auschwitz, where both women were murdered; from there he was dragged to and forced into labor in the Mittlebau-Dora concentration camp and later in Bergen-Belsen concentration camp; after he returned, he became the head of the Jewish community center in Berlin (1949–1992) as well as the first (1954–1963) and fourth (1988–1992) president of the Central Council of Jews in Germany [Zentralrat der Juden in Deutschland].

Galicia: Region of West Ukraine (East Galicia) and South Poland (West Galicia); part of Austria-Hungary until 1918.

Garrison town: Town in which military units, troops or offices are permanently stationed.

Gestapo: Secret state police; political police force during the Nazi era.

Ghetto: Segregated living quarters; the first ghetto was established in 1516 in a neighborhood the Jewish community were restricted to in Venice; during the Second World War the Nazis create Jewish ghettos from which to deport them to extermination camps; there were around 1,150 ghettos in eastern Europe between 1939 and 1944.

Givat Haim: A kibbutz founded by European immigrants between Tel Aviv and Haifa in 1932.

Glowworm (Glühwürmchen): Broučci in Chech; children's singing game that was learned and performed, along with the more famous piece Brundibár in Theresienstadt concentration camp.

Gospić: City in Croatia where a concentration camp was run by the Ustascha (Croatian nationalist movement with a close connection to the German Nazis).

Grindelviertel (Grindel quarter): Neighborhood in Hamburg, which was heavily characterized as a Jewish center up until the Nazi era with its Tora Talmud school and Bornplatz synagogue.

Große Hamburger Straße: A street in central Berlin; used here as a synonym for the assembly camp erected by the Gestapo in the former Jewish school and the Jewish old-age home, and from which tens of thousands of Jews were deported to Auschwitz and Theresienstadt.

(Camp de) Gurs: The largest internment camp for Jews, among others, during the German occupation of northern France in the Second World War; 6,538 German Jews were deported to Gurs on October 22nd, 1940, of which about 2,000 died there; in 1942, the people interned there were expelled and deported to extermination camps.

H

Hachschara: Hebrew for "the preparation;" courses during the 1920s and '30s that prepared German and Austrian Jewish youth for agricultural trade and for settling Palestine; the Nazis closed down these facilities or turned them into forced labor camps in early 1941.

Hadar (HaCarmel): Central part of the city of Haifa, built on the slope of Mount Carmel.

Hadera: City founded in 1890 by Russian and East European immigrants in the Sharon Valley between Tel Aviv and Haifa.

Haganah: Hebrew for "the defense;" Zionist underground paramilitary organization in Palestine during the British Mandate period (1920–1948), which later merged into the newly founded Israeli army.

Haifa: Israel's third largest city behind Jerusalem and Tel Aviv; located in the northern party of the country on the northern slope of Mount Carmel and on the Mediterranean, it is also Israel's largest port.

Hakoah: Hebrew for "the power;" name of multiple Jewish sport clubs.

HaMahanot HaOlim: Youth movement founded in 1927 by students at the Tel Aviv Herzliya Gymnasium, marked by socialist Zionism and supporting equal opportunity.

Hanukkah: Hebrew for dedication; eight-day holiday to remember the re-dedication of the second temple in Jerusalem in the year 164 BCE; it begins the 25th day of the month of Kislev (November/December).

Harbin: Manchurian city in northeast China founded by Russians in 1898.

HaShomer Hazair: Hebrew for "the young guard;" founded in Galicia in 1913 or 1914 as a boy scout movement, today it's a socialist Zionist youth organization.

Hatikvah: Hebrew for "hope;" title of Israel's national anthem.

Hefzibah: A kibbutz in northern Israel founded by German and Czech immigrants in 1922.

Heiden: Municipality in the Swiss canton of Appenzell Ausserrhoden

Hershey chocolate: Hershey's is one of the oldest (founded 1894) and best known chocolate producers in the United States.

Herzliya: An Israeli city, 15 kilometers north of Tel Aviv in the Sharon Valley, founded in 1924 and named after Theodor Herzl.

Hindenburg, Paul von (1847-1934): German general field marshal and politician, who as the second Reich's president (1925–1934)

of the Weimar Republic appointed Adolf Hitler to be the Reich's Chancellor on January 30, 1933.

Hiroshima: Port city in the southwest of the Japanese island Honshū; the target of the world's first atom bomb dropped on August 6, 1945.

Histadrut: Hebrew for "union;" umbrella organization for Israeli unions founded by David Ben Gurion in Haifa in 1920.

Hitachdut Olej Germania: Hebrew for "association of immigrants from Germany" (in Palestine, or Israel)

Hitler Youth—(Hitlerjugend): Youth organization founded in 1926 by the Nazi Party; comprised of German Jungvolk (boys, aged 10-14), German Jungmädel (girls, aged 10-14), the actual Hitler Youth (aged 14–18) and Bund deutscher Mädel (aged 14–18); membership was compulsory from 1939, so that at one point they claimed 8.7 million youth members.

Höfs, Else (1876-1945): Politician in the SPD party and member of the German Weimar National Assembly; head of Worker's Welfare Association from 1919-1933 in Pomerania.

(Jewish) High holidays: On Rosh HaShana (first day of the year), on the 1st of the month of Tishri (September/October), people take account of their actions, and on the tenth day afterward is the highest holiday, Yom Kippur (day of atonement), where they can ask God's forgiveness through repentance.

Hongkou: Section of Shanghai; a refuge for many European Jewish immigrants in the 1930s and 1940s.

House Committee on Un-American Activities: Former committee in the House of Representatives that investigated possible threats of infiltration by groups like the Communists and worked on bills against them.

Humanitas: Grand lodge of freemasonry for men and women.

I

Iaşi: University in northeastern Romania; today the cultural capital of the country, formerly the main area where Romanian Jews settled.

Ida Ehre School: Former elementary, now a middle school, built in 1934 in Hamburg, that has been named after the Jewish actress and theater general manager (1900-1989) since 2001.

Ima: Hebrew for mama.

Iron Cross: War medal, first awarded by the Prussian king, Friedrich Wilhelm III, in 1813; was permitted to be worn again (after the Second World War and without the swastika) only after 1958.

Isaaksohn, Rolf (1921; 1957 declared dead): Jewish passport counterfeiter in Berlin during the 1940s who collaborated with the Gestapo as a "catcher," seeking out and denouncing Jews in hiding; worked with the most famous "catcher," Stella Goldschlag (1922-1994), as her second husband.

Isma'ilia: City in northern Egypt.

Israelitische Töchterschule (Jewish girls school): A Jewish school in the Karolinenviertel (Karonlinen quarter) in Hamburg from 1884 until its closure in May, 1942; today it is a memorial and educational institution. It was renamed as the Dr. Alberto Jonas building in 1998, in honor of the last school director.

Ivrit: Modern Hebrew: Semitic language and Israel's official language.

J

Jaffa: Yafo in Hebrew; a port city in modern Israel in existence since antiquity, with the suburb of Tel Aviv, originally founded in 1909; both cities were united as Tel Aviv-Jaffa in 1950.

Jahn, Dr. Friedrich Ludwig (1778-1852): German educator and member of the Frankfurt Parliament as well as the initiator of the "gym movement", and thus called "Turnvater Jahn" (father of gymnastics).

Jewish Agency: Sochnut in Hebrew; agency for Jews founded in 1929 at the World Zionist Congress and during the British

Mandate era responsible for domestic concerns of Jews living in Palestine; today it is Israel's official immigration organization.

Jewish Claims Conference—JCC: A union of Jewish organizations founded in 1951 that represented the claims of damage of Jewish victims of National Socialism.

Joachimsthaler Straße 13: Originally a building for the Jewish B'nai B'rith lodge in Berlin; during the post-war years, it was the office of the head of the Jewish Community, and today also houses offices of Jewish Organizations like WIZO (Women's International Zionist Organization).

Joint–JDC (American Jewish Distribution Committee): An American Jewish organization mainly active in Europe since 1914 that was originally founded to provide support for Jewish victims of the First World War.

Jonas, Dr. Alberto (1889-1942): Director of the Israelitische Töchterschule in Hamburg from 1924 who accompanied several Kindertransports to England and returned to Germany every time until 1940, when he was no longer permitted to travel and was deported with his family to Theresienstadt, where he died soon after; the former school building bears his name today.

Jonas, Dr. Marie Anna (1893-1944), née Levinsohn: Worked as a school doctor at the Israelitische Töchterschule in Hamburg where her husband was director until she was no longer allowed to practice medicine; she was deported to Theresienstadt with her husband and their daughter Esther (Bauer) in 1942 and killed in Auschwitz in 1944; a square was named after her in Eppendorf, a neighborhood in Hamburg in 2003.

Joodse: Dutch for "Jewish".

Juchacz, Marie (1879-1956): Member of the Weimar National Assembly as a representative of the SPD since 1919, founded the Workers' Welfare Association (Arbeiterwohlfahrt, AWO) that same year, emigrated to New York in 1933 where she founded the welfare organization Arbeiterwohlfahrt USA to help victims of National

Socialism in 1945, and moved back to Germany in 1949.

Jewish Studies: Study of Judaism.

Jewish Hospital, Berlin: Founded as the first "Jewish (military) hospital" in Berlin on Oranienburgerstrasse; in 1914 it moved to Iranische Strasse, which was later renamed Heinz-Galinski-Strasse; from March 1944, part of the building was used as a collection point for deporting Berlin Jews; hospital services for Jews and non-Jews resumed in 1945.

Jewish House: In the fall of 1939, Jews were moved to former Jewish apartment buildings by order of the Gestapo and lived there under extremely restricted conditions; on one hand, this measure had the effect of further discriminating against Jews, while on the other hand, it worked to house the so-called "German blooded" population.

Jungfernhof: Concentration camp in the village of Jumpravmuiza near the Latvian capital Riga, built from December 1941, to March 1942 to temporarily house German and Austrian Jews; many of them were shot to death in a nearby forest and buried in mass shallow graves.

K

(Hamburg) Kammerspiele: Theater founded in 1918 that accommodated the Jewish lodge B'nai B'rith from 1904-1937 and the Cultural Federation of German Jews until 1941; after the theater was closed, the building became a collection point where Jews were deported to extermination camps in July 1942; the theater was re-opened in 1945 under the directorship of concentration camp survivor Ida Ehre.

Kapo: A prisoner functionary in a concentration camp who supervised the work of other prisoners for the SS or the camp administration and received special privileges.

Katamon: A neighborhood in south Jerusalem that arose in 1914.

Kibbutz, Kibbutzim (Pl): Hebrew for "collection, assembly;" agricultural settlement collective in Israel with common property and a basic democratic structure; the first kibbutz is Dganya Alef, founded in 1910 on the Sea of Galilee, which preceded about 270 others and played a decisive role in the Jewish settlement of Israel.

Kibbutznik, Kibbutzniks (Pl): Member(s) of a kibbutz.

Kindertransports: Departure of around 12,500 Jewish children from Germany, Austria, Poland and Czechoslovakia between the end of November 1938 and September 1, 1939. England took about 10,000 of them, the others were divided between the Netherlands, Sweden, Belgium, France, Switzerland and the United States; these children were often the only members of their families to survive the Holocaust.

Kippah: Hebrew for little cap; little circular hat worn by religious Jewish men.

Kiryat Anavim: The first kibbutz in the Judean hills west of Jerusalem, founded in 1920 by Ukrainian immigrants.

Kiryat Bialik: Israeli city northeast of Haifa founded in 1939 by German immigrants, named for the national poet, Chaim Nachman Bialik.

Kiryat Haim: City north of Haifa founded in 1933, named after the Zionist leader, Haim Arlozorov, who was murdered in the same year.

Korean War: Conducted from June 1950, to July 1953 between North Korea and China on one side and South Korea and the United Nations, especially the United States, on the other, because each Korean government wanted to force reunification of the country under their own leadership.

Kosher: Hebrew for "pure;" relates to food that is considered edible by Jewish dietary laws, so for example, meat from mammals or fowl cannot be made with milk; orthodox Jews therefore use different plates and flatware.

Kraft durch Freude—KdF [Strength through Joy]: Nazi organization that existed from 1933 until 1945 (but its activity had long since discontinued by 1939) to shape and supervise the free time of Germans; coincidentally, it was the largest tour operator during those years.

Krakow: Kraków in Polish; the second largest city in Poland, in the southern part of the country; German Nazis built a ghetto in the city, and they built the Auschwitz, Auschwitz-Birkenau, Auschwitz-Monowitz and Plaszow concentration camps not far outside the city.

(Reichs-)Kristallnacht, Pogromnacht: Nazis destroyed 1,400 synagogues and houses of worship as well as Jewish businesses, apartments and cemeteries in Germany on the night of November 9, 1938; around 30,000 Jewish men were deported to concentration camps, hundreds of which were murdered or died from being held prisoner.

L

Latrun, Battles of Latrun: Area of what is today the West Bank, 15 kilometers west of Jerusalem where there were skirmishes between the Israeli and Jordanian armies as well as Palestinian militias from May to July of 1948; Israel failed in their attempt to take the strategically important area, which controls the road between Tel Aviv and Jerusalem.

Le Prese: Town on the Lago di Poschiavo in the Swiss canton of Grisons.

League of Jewish Women: Organization founded in 1904 by Bertha Pappenheim (1859-1936) that pursued feminist goals, like strengthening women's rights, as well as traditional Jewish goals, like charity as God's commandment; it was closed down by the Nazis in 1939.

Leitmeritz: Litoměřice in Czech; city in the Czech Republic, six kilometers north of Theresienstadt (Terezín); during the Second World War the Nazis built a satellite camp for the Flossenbürg concentration camp near the city.

Leo Baeck School or Leo Baeck Education Center—LBEC: School founded in Haifa in 1939 and rooted in the tradition of liberal

Judaism; today it is known all over Israel as an educational institution for Jewish and Arabic children from kindergarten through high school.

Lette House or Lette Verein (Lette Society): Founded in 1866 in Berlin by Wilhelm Adolf Lette (1799–1868) for the advancement of women's ability to work; today it is a foundation and responsible authority of three vocational colleges and two schools.

Lindenfels: City in the Odenwald forest where the American military built a camp for Jewish displaced persons after the Second World War that was closed in November, 1948.

Lions: Founded in 1917, today it is the largest service club in the world with over 1,347 million members; its motto "We Serve" compels each member to place service to others above personal profit; LIONS is also the acronym for the slogan "Liberty, Intelligence, Our Nation's Safety".

Lod: Today a city in the Central District of Israel, about 20 kilometers east of Tel Aviv; in 1921 the Jews living there were expelled by the Arabs; in 1944 approx. 17,000 Arabs lived there who left the city after it was occupied by the Israeli troops during the Independence War (May 1948–July 1949).

Lodz: Łódźin Polish, called Litzmannstadt from 1940–1945; third largest city in Poland, located in the center of the country; in February 1940, the Nazis built one of the largest ghettos there, and most of the Jews who were imprisoned there were later deported and murdered; a youth concentration camp was built in one area that had been cleared in December 1942 where, according to estimations, 12,000-20,000 children were imprisoned for up to two years.

Lublin: City in eastern Poland; it was occupied by the Germans from 1939-1944 and served as the headquarters for "Operation Reinhard," with the mission of murdering every Jew in Poland.

Lviv: Lwiw in Ukrainian; today a city in western Ukraine; from 1918-39 it was Polish (Lwów) with Jewish residents totaling more than 50 percent of the population; a ghetto and a forced labor camp were built there during the Nazi era.

M

Machtergreifung (Hitler's seizure of power): Term commonly used to refer to January 30, 1933, when Hitler was named Chancellor and the resulting Nazi Party abolishment of democracy, securing its power.

Macy's: New York department store founded in 1858; today it is the largest department store operator in the United States, with nearly 800 branches.

Madrich, Madricha: Hebrew for "teacher".

Majdanek: The first German concentration camp in occupied Poland (near Lublin), which existed from October 1941 until its liberation by the Russian army in July 1944; there is no exact given number of victims, but estimates are around 78,000 people.

Marienburg: Malbork in Polish; city in what was formerly West Prussia, currently in northern Poland.

Matzo, Matzot (Pl): Unleavened flat bread, which is eaten by religious Jews during Passover as a reminder of the Israelite exodus from Egypt.

Mauthausen: Largest concentration camp in Austria, to which nearly 200,000 people were deported from all over Europe, with about half of them killed from August 1938 up to its liberation by American troops in May 1945.

McCarthy Era: Period of time (1946–1957) named for American Senator Joseph McCarthy (1907–1957) that was marked heavily by anti-communist sentiment the United States, which lead to (among other things) naming political suspects with subpoenas and interrogations in front of congressional investigative committees.

Minsk: Capital of Belarus; the largest Jewish community in Russia with 30% of the total 240,000 inhabitants before the Second World War; from July 1941, one of the largest ghettos, in which 60,000

Jews were imprisoned inside two square kilometers.

(Privileged) Mixed Marriage: Nazi designation for a marriage between an "Aryan" and "non-Aryan" partners; differentiation exists between "non-privileged mixed marriage" of a "German-blooded" person with a Jewish husband without baptized children or with Jewish children and "privileged mixed marriage" of a "German-blooded" man with a Jewish wife with or without baptized children. Death of the non-Jewish husband or divorce meant deportation for the Jewish partners. In the fall of 1944, the Jewish husbands in existing "mixed marriages" were also deported to work camps, and in 1945 to Theresienstadt.

Moldavia: Romanian Moldavia; Region in northeast Romania, also called Western Moldavia, is not to be confused with the Republic of Moldova.

Moshav, Moshavim (Pl): Agricultural association where members have greater independence than on a kibbutz, according to the principle that everyone is self-employed, but purchasing and operations are organized at the association level.

Mozartkugel [Mozart ball]: Bite-sized candy made with pistachio marzipan and nougat covered in dark chocolate.

N
NAACP – National Association for Advancement of Colored People: Founded in 1909, one of the oldest and most influential black civil rights organizations in the United States.

Nahalal: Founded in 1921, the first moshav west of Nazareth in northern Israel; planned by the Frankfurt architect, Richard Kaufmann (1887-1957), who emigrated to Palestine in 1920

Nahariya: A coastal city on the Mediterranean in northern Israel founded by German emigrants in the 1930s.

Nansen Passport: Travel document drawn up in 1922 and introduced that same year by Fridtjof Nansen, High Commissioner of the League of Nations, for stateless refugees; valid for one year, though it could be extended, it allowed the return to the country of issue and was last accepted by 53 nations; in 1946, it was replaced by a corresponding document of the Geneva Convention on Refugees.

Napola—Nationalpolitische Lehranstalt [National Political Institute of Teaching]: An elite school where the next generation of Nazis were educated; criteria for entrance into these boarding schools included quality of race, character, physical shape, and apparently last on the list, intellect.

Nazareth: City in Galilee in the northern district of Israel, which today is largely populated by Muslims and Christians, whereas its sister city, Nazareth-Illit, founded in 1957, is Jewish.

Negev: Desert in southern Israel that takes up 60% of the country with 12,000 square kilometers, but is only inhabited by nearly ten percent of the population.

Nesthäkchen: Series of children's or youth books with ten volumes by the Jewish author, Else Ury (1877–1943), who was killed in Auschwitz.

Neue Dammtorsynagoge: Synagogue built in 1894–1895 on what today is called Allendeplatz in Hamburg; the interior was completely destroyed during the Kristallnacht in November 1938, but rebuilt through private donations so that services could be held until it was seized in June 1943; shortly after being seized, it was hit by a bomb and destroyed.

Niedergebra: Municipality in the district of Nordhausen in Thuringia.

Nordenstadt: Formerly a village in Hessen, it has been a municipal district of Wiesbaden since 1977.

NSGWP—National Socialist German Worker's Party [Nazi Party]: Political party founded in 1920, and the only one permitted in Germany from 1933 until it was forbidden as a criminal organization in 1945.

Nuremberg (Race) Laws: The law to "protect the German blood and German honor" among others and forbade marriage and extra-marital relations between Jews and non-Jews was unanimously passed at the 7th Nazi party rally on September 15, 1935. Violations were punished as "racial defilement" with time in jail or prison.

O

Odenwaldschule: Boarding school founded in 1910 in the Hessen town of Heppenheim (Bergstrasse), which was occasionally considered a model school for the reform education movement.

Odessa: Ukrainian port city on the Black Sea.

Opfer des Faschismus—OdF [Victims of Fascism]: Term (used especially in former East Germany) for those who were murdered as well as for the surviving victims of Nazi persecution.

Opium Wars: The first war (1839–1842, Great Britain vs. China) ended with the defeat of China and its forced toleration of opium trade. The second war (1856–1860, Great Britain and France vs. China) ended with the same result, and the opium trade was legalized.

Ostróda: Osterode in German; city in former East Prussia and currently in northeastern Poland.

Osthofen: City near Worms where one of the first concentration camps for Nazi political enemies was built between March 1933 and July 1934.

P

Palestine Office: Official representative of the Zionist World Organization, whose German office was established at Meinekestrasse 10 in Berlin in 1924, which helped around 50,000 Jews emigrate until it was closed in 1941.

Pappataci Fever: Disease found predominately in the Mediterranean area, which is transmitted by the sand fly and is accompanied by high fever lasting days.

Pardes Hanna-Karkur: City in northern Israel founded in 1929.

(SS) Patria: Refugee ship that was supposed to transport thousands of illegal Jewish Palestinian immigrants from Haifa to the island of

Mauritius; to force their immigration, Haganah blew up the ship on November 25, 1940; 270 people died, most of those rescued were interned in the Atlit camp.

Paymaster: Former designation for someone who keeps accounts, for example in the military.

Pearl Harbor: Port on the island of O'ahu (Hawaii); here it is a synonym for the Japanese air attack on the American fleet anchored at Pearl Harbor on the 7th of December, 1941, which prompted the United States to enter the war.

Peres, Shimon (1923): Born Szymon Perski in the Polish town of Vishnyeva; Israeli Prime Minister (1984–86 and 1995–96) and President (2007–2014).

Perón, Juan Domingo (1895–1974): Two-time president of Argentina (1946–1955 and 1973–1974) who led a string of social reforms and was celebrated by his followers as a hero of the working class even before his presidency.

Pesach: Central celebration in Judaism that commemorates the Israelite exodus from Egypt, or freedom from slavery there; it is celebrated during the week of the 15th through 22nd of the month of Nisan (from mid-March).

Petah Tikva: Founded as an agricultural settlement in 1878, a city east of Tel Aviv.

Petrópolis: City in Brazil, founded by German-speaking immigrants in 1825, around 60 kilometers north of Rio De Janeiro.

Pita: Flat bread made from leavened dough.

Pogrom: Violent riots against people who are classified as belonging to a certain political, religious or ethnic group by the perpetrators; the term was formerly used only for violent acts against Jews.

Pogromnacht: See Kristallnacht.

Polder: Low lying area near water, which is protected from flooding by dikes.

Polenaktion: Without warning on the 28th of October, 1938, the

German police moved around 17,000 Polish Jews to Poland, where they were denied entry so that they had to camp for several weeks on the border in Zbąszyń and other places; for Herschel Grynspan, whose parents were affected, this was the incident that prompted him to shoot German diplomat Ernst vom Rath, whereupon the Nazis carried out violence against Jews throughout the German Reich on Pogromnacht (November 9th–10th, 1938).

Poschiavo: Municipality in the Swiss canton of Grisons.

Posen (Posnan): City in western Poland.

Potaznia (Maria Alois in German, 1815–1918 and 1933–1945): Maria Alois is a place that belonged to the German Empire before the Versailles Treaty and was situated in the administrative region of Schildberg (Ostrzeszów), about 130 kilometers southeast of Posen (Poznań) and 100 kilometers northeast of Breslau (Wrocław). The place is now called Potażnia and belongs to Poland.

Primus: A brass Bunsen burner.

Purim: Joyful Jewish holiday, celebrated on the 14th of Adar (February/March) that commemorates the rescue of the Jewish people in the Persian diaspora.

Q
Quaker: Member of the Quaker religion, a sect of Christianity.

R
Rabbinate: Position of a rabbi.

Rabbi: Spiritual leader of a Jewish community.

Race Laws: See Nuremberg Race Laws.

Ramallah: City in the Palestinian autonomous region of the West Bank, 15 kilometers north of Jerusalem.

Ramat Gan: City east of Tel Aviv, originally founded as a moshav in 1921.

Ramat Yohanan: Kibbutz in northern Israel 15 kilometers east of

Haifa, founded by native and immigrant Jews from the United States in 1932.

Ramlah (Arabic) or Ramla (Hebrew): Capital of the central district in Israel, 20 kilometers southeast of Tel Aviv.

Ravensbrück: Concentration camp 100 kilometers north of Berlin, which, from 1939 up until it was liberated by Russian troops in April 1945, became the largest concentration camp for women, 28,000 people died there.

Rehovot: City located 20 kilometers south of Tel Aviv, founded in 1890 by Polish and Russian immigrants.

Reichstag Fire: Fire that burned the Berlin Reichstag building during the night of February 27, 1933; on February 28, 1933, the "Order of the Reich President for the Protection of the People and State" legalized Nazi Party persecution of political enemies using the police and SA.

Righteous Among the Nations: Honorary title for non-Jews who risked their own lives under National Socialism to save Jews from being sent to their deaths.

Rishon LeTsiyon: City south of Tel Aviv, originally founded as a moshav in 1882.

Rommel, Erwin (1891–1944): German General Field Marshall during the Second World War, who has his action on the African front to thank for the nickname "Desert Fox".

Roosevelt, Franklin Delano (1882–1945): 32nd President of the United States of America (1933–1945).

Rosenstrasse: Street in Berlin; here a synonym for the largest protest during the Nazi era against the arrest of Jews from "mixed marriages," who were arrested during the Fabrikaktion on the 27th of February and locked up at Rosenstrasse 2-4; "Aryan" relatives gathered for days in front of the buildings and demanded their release, and in fact nearly all 2,000 prisoners were set free.

Rosh HaShana: Hebrew for "head of the year"; New Year's Day on the 1st of Tishri, the seventh month of the Jewish calendar (September/October), which are the high holidays with the Day of Atonement (Yom Kippur) following ten days later.

Rotary (Club): Founded in Chicago in 1905 as a community with shared values, in which everyone supports each other's abilities; today the oldest service club in the world with 34,000 clubs in 200 countries with the goal of providing humanitarian services and a mission of peace and understanding between nations.

Red Cross Letter: In 1936, the International Red Cross set up a communication service to give emigrants the option to stay in contact with their relatives who had remained in Germany or were already deported; only a maximum of 25 words was permitted on the form used for the message.

Reparations or German Reparations Policy: State measures to receive material compensation through the Persecutees of the Nazi Regime.

Ruma: Current capital of Serbia, formerly part of Yugoslavia.

S

SA—Sturmabteilung [Assault Division, aka Brown Shirts]: Nazi combat organization during the Weimar Republic; after the Nazis seized power it was temporarily set up as auxiliary police and then forbidden in 1945.

Saba: Hebrew for grandfather.

Sabre, Sabres (Pl): Hebrew for "prickly pear;" term for native born Jewish Israelis, who were described as prickly on the outside, but with a soft inner core.

Sachsenhausen: Concentration camp built in 1936 near Oranienburg, which because of its proximity to Berlin held special status and became a training camp for concentration camp commanders and guards; until it was closed in 1945, more than 200,000 people from 40 countries were imprisoned there, of which tens of thousands died.

Safed: City in Galilee in the Northern District of Israel, considered one of the four holy cities of Judaism, next to Jerusalem, Tiberius and Hebron, and the spiritual center of the Kabbalah (mystical tradition of Judaism).

Samson Raphael Hirsch Schule: Orthodox Jewish school founded in 1953 in Frankfurt that was closed by the Nazis in 1939.

Sarona: Piece of land purchased and developed by members of the German Templers in 1871 in a neighborhood of Tel Aviv that was renamed to HaKirya in 1950 after the Templers were deported; the area has been rehabilitated in recent years and carries its original name again.

Schindler, Oskar (1908-1974): Sudeten German industrialist who protected Jewish forced laborers employed in his factory in Krakow, Poland during the Nazi era and saved around 1,200 from being deported and murdered.

Schlachtensee: Lake in southwest Berlin along the edge of the Grunewald forest.

Schleich, Josef (1902-1949): Austrian smuggler who until 1941 helped Jews for a payment of 670 Reichsmarks find refuge in Yugoslavia, thereby saving hundreds of lives.

Sepharde, Sephardim (Pl): Jews who lived originally in Portugal and Spain and also settled in the Ottoman Empire and northwest Africa (Maghrib) as well as in northern Europe, such as in Amsterdam and Hamburg, and in America, India, and Africa.

Shabbat: In Judaism, the seventh day; day of rest that begins at sunset on Friday evening and ends at sunset on Saturday evening.

Shabbat lamp: Hanging, oil-filled lamp above the table, used in Jewish homes on the evening of Shabbat.

Shanghai fever or dengue fever: One of the most widely spread infectious diseases; caused by a virus carried by mosquitoes and is accompanied by severe headache and muscle pain.

Shanghai ghetto: Beginning on the 15th of November, 1942, the Japanese occupying forces ghettoized the Jews in Shanghai; although Japan was under pressure from Nazi Germany to hand over or kill the Jews, Japan did not give in despite an alliance between the two countries; the ghetto was liberated on September 3, 1945; nearly all of the Jews left the city when the state of Israel was founded.

Shul: Yiddish for synagogue.

Shuk HaCarmel: Market in Tel Aviv open every day (except Saturday).

Sinai Campaign: Israel invaded Egypt with the support of England and France from October 29th to November 5th, 1956, capturing the Gaza Strip and the Sinai in response to Egypt's blockade of the Suez Canal and its military alliance with Syria and Jordan.

Slicha geveret: Hebrew for, "excuse me, Madame".

Sobibor: Concentration camp built in 1942 in southeastern Poland that served as an extermination camp for "Operation Reinhardt" along with the Belzec and Treblinka camps, with a mission of killing all Jews in Poland; according to estimates, 250,000 people died in the gas chambers.

Split: Today the second largest city in Croatia, formerly part of Yugoslavia.

SS—Schutzstaffel: Founded in 1925 as a special organization of the Nazi Party for the personal protection of Adolf Hitler; from 1934 an independent paramilitary organization of the Nazi Party, which later played a decisive role in the Holocaust.

Standartenführer: Rank in the SS and SA during the Nazi era.

Stettin: Szczecin in Polish; city in the former West Pomerania, 120 kilometers northeast of Berlin.

Stolpersteine (literally "stumbling stones," metaphorically a "stumbling block" or a stone to "stumble upon"): Rectangular commemorative plaques made of brass, that are laid like paving stones in front of the last self-selected residences of those people driven to suicide or who were deported by the Nazis; a project of the artist Gunter Demnig, who has laid stones engraved with names and biographical data in Germany and in 17 European countries since the year 2000.

Strauss, Ludwig (1892–1953): Aachen-born author who was relieved of his duties as a Jewish professor in 1933 and emigrated to Palestine in 1935, where he worked as a teacher for a time in the youth village Ben Shemen.

Strophanthin: Medication formerly used in the treatment of heart diseases.

(Der) Stürmer (the stormer): Anti-Semitic newspaper distributed by Julius Streicher from April 20, 1923 to February 22, 1945 that played a crucial role in agitating hatred of Jews and among other things, were publicly hung in boxes called *Stürmerkästen.*

Stutthof: Concentration camp built in August 1939, in the area of the annexed free city of Danzig and therefore the first outside the German borders, in which 110,000 people were imprisoned, of which 65,000 died.

Sukkah, Sukkot (Pl): Hebrew for "foliage hut'" or "Feast of the Tabernacles;" during the seven-day holiday (harvest appreciation) from the 15th to 21st of Tishri (seventh month of the Jewish calendar, falls in September or October), observant Jews build a foliage hut in which they also temporarily sleep.

Szold, Henrietta (1860–1945): Born in Baltimore, Maryland, she was a teacher, author, social worker and in 1914 the founder of the Hadassah (Zionist women's organization in the USA) as well as the head of the Children's and Youth Aliyah in Palestine.

T
Tallit: Jewish prayer shawl; rectangular, mostly white cloth with blue or black stripes, with long, knotted threads on each of the four corners that are there to remind the faithful to fulfill God's commandments.

Talmud Tora Schule: School in Hamburg in the Grindelviertel that existed from 1805-1942 and during its time was considered the largest Jewish school in northern Germany; the building was back under ownership of the Jewish community in 2004 and from 2007 is now once again used as a Jewish school.

Tanakh: The biblical texts that are regarded as binding for the Jewish religion; comprised of the three parts of the Torah (teaching), Nevi'im (prophets) and Ketuvim (writings); also the Old Testament and is also called the Jewish Bible.

Tatra Mountains: Mountains that form part of the Carpathian range, which lies in large part in Slovakia, with a smaller section in Poland.

TB: See Tuberculosis.

Temple: Term for the reform synagogue since the 19th century.

Teresópolis: City in Brazil, founded by English settlers in 1820, 95 kilometers north of Rio de Janeiro.

Theresienstadt (Terezín): Former fortress city in the modern Czech Republic; after the occupation of Bohemia and Moravia, the Nazis built a concentration camp in Theresienstadt, in which 140,000 were imprisoned until they were liberated by the Red Army in May 1945; approximately 33,500 people died there, over 88,000 were deported to extermination camps.

(Hermann) Tietz: Department store chain started by Oscar Tietz using the capital and name of his uncle, Hermann, that had to give up the Jewish name during the Nazi era and since then has done business under the name using a combination of the first letters of each name (Hertie).

Torun: City on the Vistula River, 180 kilometers northwest of Warsaw.

Transjordan: The official designation for the country of Jordan until 1950.

Treblinka: Built in July 1942 northeast of Warsaw, and therefore the last concentration camp erected during the Second World

War, it was the largest extermination camp involved in "Operation Reinhardt," with a mission of murdering all Jews in Poland, during which the estimated number of people from all over Europe who were killed is 1.1 million.

Tsriv: Hebrew for "container," in which the immigrants' furniture was transported to Palestine.

Tuberculosis: Leading bacterial disease among statistically deadly infectious diseases around the world.

Turiah: Pickaxe made of heavy wood and a broad piece of metal, which was used in agriculture in Palestine to loosen dried soils.

Turnerkreuz: Graphic depiction of the "four Fs" representing Frisch, Fromm, Fröhlich, Frei [fresh, pious, cheerful, free], the gymnast motto from Dr. Friedrich Ludwig Jahn, founder of community sports club movement.

Tzena: Food rations set up in Israel in 1949, which became necessary because of the mass immigration of oriental Jews after the founding of the state; the restrictions were lifted in 1953, but not completely until 1959.

U

Ulpan, Ulpanim (Pl): Intensive Hebrew language course.

UNRRA–United Nations Relief and Rehabilitation Administration: Aid organization founded on November 9, 1943 under the initiative of the United States, Russia, Great Britain and China, which supported repatriating displaced persons until December 31, 1946. USAFE—United States Air Force in Europe: Headquartered in Ramstein near Kaiserslautern.

Usha: Kibbutz founded in 1937 by Polish immigrants in western Galilee.

V

V2 rocket: "Retaliatory" weapons (rockets), built by forced laborers in the tunnels of the Mittelbau-Dora concentration camp after the V1 rocket (flying bomb) and was referred to as the "wonder weapon" in Nazi propaganda.

Vistula: The longest river in Poland at 1,047 kilometers.

W

War of Independence: In response to the proclamation of the State of Israel on May 14, 1948, Egypt, Syria, Jordan, Lebanon and Iraq attack on the following day; the conflict ended in July 1949 with a ceasefire agreement, which only Iraq did not sign, and Jerusalem was divided into two sectors controlled by Israel and Jordan.

Warsaw Uprising: On August 1, 1944, the Polish resistance Home Army turned against the German occupiers and fought for 63 days, until they had to capitulate; the Germans killed a large portion of the population and destroyed the city.

Weimar National Assembly: Constitutional parliament of the Weimar Republic.

Weizmann, Chaim (1874–1952): Born in Motal (today in Belarus); Chemist, president of the World Zionist Organization (1921–31 and 1935–48) as well as the first Israeli president (1948–52).

[When Jewish blood spurts from my knife] Wenn das Judenblut vom Messer spritzt: Line from a song sung by the SA while marching.

White buses: Shortly before and after the end of the war in 1945, these buses were used by the Swedish Red Cross to transport and therefore save predominately Danish and Norwegian concentration camp prisoners, to return them back to their homelands; the operation occurred with Nazi approval; the buses were stationed at the Friedsrichsruh Castle owned by Otto Von Bismarck, near Hamburg.

White Star: By order of the Gestapo, beginning on March 13, 1942, every "Jew house" had to be identified by a white, six-pointed, paper star.

Wieringermeer: Area on the North Sea coast of the Netherlands.

Wilhelm II (1858-1941): The last German Kaiser (1888–1918), who during his weeks-long trip to Palestine in October and November

1898 encouraged the Christian residents there and dedicated the German Church of the Redeemer in Jerusalem.

Wiesbaden memorial site: Memorial opened on January 27, 2011, at the Michelsberg, which is built on the ground on which the synagogue that was destroyed during the 1938 November pogrom and which contains the 1,507 names of Wiesbaden's Jewish victims of the German Nazis identified so far.

Wilhelma: German colony built by Templers in 1902 (a religious community which arose in Württemberg in 1850) and named after Kaiser Wilhelm II, approx. 15 kilometers east of Tel Aviv; after the Second World War broke out, the British Mandate government transformed this and other Templer colonies into internment camps, mostly for Germans who sympathized with the Nazis; in 1950, the Israeli government expelled the last Templers from the country; the moshav B'nei Atarot was developed on the remaining grounds.

WIZO—Women's International Zionist Organization: Charitable organization founded in Great Britain in 1920; it is the largest women's organization with 250,000 members in 50 countries.

Wolff, Jeanette (1888-1976): Born Jeanette Cohen in Bocholt; Social Democratic Party politician who was imprisoned in several ghettos and concentration camps as both a politician and a Jew; her husband and two of three daughters died; after her liberation, she became a member of the German lower house of parliament, co-founder and head of the Society for Christian-Jewish Cooperation as well as the deputy chairwoman of the Central Council of Jews in Germany.

Workers Welfare Union: A welfare union founded by Marie Juchacz in 1919, forbidden after Hitler took power and founded again in Hanover in 1946 as a helping organization independent of party politics and religious denomination.

World Zionist Organization—WZO: Founded in Basel in 1897 on the initiative of Theodor Herzl (1860–1904), with the main message that Zionism strives to create an officially legitimate, secure homeland for the Jewish people.

Y

Yad Vashem: Official designation for "the National Authority for the Remembrance of the Martyrs and Heroes of the Holocaust" in the state of Israel; opened in Jerusalem in 1953, the most significant memorial that commemorates and academically documents the extermination of Jews by the Nazis.

Yagur: Kibbutz founded in northern Israel in 1922, southeast of Haifa; today one of the largest kibbutzim with over 1,200 members.

Yangtze: Short for Yángzǐ Jiāng; China's most important and Asia's longest river, with a length of 6,380 kilometers; it springs from the highlands of Tibet and flows into the East Chinese Sea near Shanghai and is famous for catastrophes caused by flooding.

Yekke, Yekkes (Pl): Originally a mocking, but later respectful term for German-speaking immigrants to Palestine in the 1930s and 1940s who differentiated themselves from Jews living there in their arrogance and correctness.

Yekkish: To act like a yekke.

Yellow Star: Palm-sized, six-pointed star with black letters that read "Jude" (Jew); required identification badge introduced by the Nazis on September 1, 1941, it had to be purchased for 10 pfennigs and worn visibly on the clothes, on the left side at breast height.

Yerushalayim: Hebrew for Jerusalem.

Yiddish: Language that was, or is, maintained by Ashkenazi (central, northern and east European) Jews as well as some of their descendants.

Yom Kippur: Hebrew for Day of Atonement; day of penance on the 10th of Tishri, the seventh month of the Jewish calendar

(September/October); forms the high holidays with the New Year holiday, Rosh Hashanah, ten days before it.

Youth-Aliyah: Founded on the 30th of January, 1933, by Recha Freier (1892–1984), to get as many children and young people mainly to Palestine during the Nazi era; this saved around 21,000 children and young people.

Z

Zagreb: The capital of Serbia today, then part of Yugoslavia.

Zakopańe: Highest-elevated city in Poland, approx. 90 kilometers south of Krakow high up in the Tatra Mountains.

Zbąszyn: Polish city approx. 100 kilometers east of Frankfurt on the Oder and 75 kilometers west of Posen, to which 17,000 Polish Jews were pushed out of Germany during what was called the "Polenaktion" at the end of October 1938.

Zionist: Follower of Zionism, an international political movement with the goal of the establishment, defense and preservation of a Jewish nation at the modern-day location of Israel, with Zion, or Jerusalem, being the religious center point.

Andrea von Treuenfeld studied journalism and German literature and spent many years working as a columnist, correspondent, and editor for such print media as Welt am Sonntag and Wirtschaftswoche. As a freelance journalist, she now writes portraits and biographies.

Cathryn Siegal-Bergman received her M.A. in Translation Studies from Kent State University in 2007. She lives in Cleveland, Ohio.

www.ingramcontent.com/pod-product-compliance
Lightning Source LLC
Chambersburg PA
CBHW030432010526
44118CB00011B/609